CW01642517

FIRST FRENCH DICTIONARY

HARRAP'S FIRST FRENCH DICTIONARY

by Colin Henstock

Based on *le français fondamental*

HARRAP

London

First published in this edition
in Great Britain 1986
by HARRAP Ltd
19–23 Ludgate Hill, London EC4M 7PD

© Colin Henstock 1972, 1986

All rights reserved. No part of this
publication may be reproduced in any
form or by any means without the prior
permission of HARRAP Ltd

Reprinted 1987, 1988

ISBN 0 245 54412 7

Printed and bound in Great Britain by
Cox & Wyman Ltd, Reading

ACKNOWLEDGMENT

The author wishes to thank Mrs Irene Tuchfeld for her helpful suggestions and constructive criticism during the preparation of this dictionary for publication.

ABBREVIATIONS USED IN THIS DICTIONARY

adj.	adjective	*interj.*	interjection
adv.	adverb	*m.*	masculine
approx.	approximately	*pl.*	plural
conj.	conjunction	*prep.*	preposition
f.	feminine	*pron.*	pronoun
impers.	impersonal	*sing.*	singular

NOTES

ADJECTIVES. Feminine forms are only given in the case of adjectives which do not form their feminine in the regular way, that is, by the simple addition of -e.

ASTERISKS. An asterisk has been used—in both Parts of the Dictionary—to indicate French words beginning with an aspirate h.

ABREVIATIONS UTILISEES DANS CE DICTIONNAIRE

adj.	adjectif	*interj.*	interjection
adv.	adverbe	*m.*	masculin
approx.	approximativement	*pl.*	pluriel
conj.	conjonction	*prep.*	préposition
f.	féminin	*pron.*	pronom
impers.	impersonnel	*sing.*	singulier

NOTES

ADJECTIFS. Les formes féminines ne sont données pour les adjectifs que quand elles ne sont pas régulières, c'est-à-dire si elles ne se terminent pas par -e.

ASTÉRISQUES. Dans les deux parties du dictionnaire nous avons mis un astérisque pour les mots français qui commencent par un h aspiré.

PREFACE

This dictionary contains all the vocabulary of *Le français fondamental : Premier degré* together with a number of words from the *Deuxième degré* and others whose frequent usage justifies their inclusion.

It is the product of a prolonged and intensive study of school text-books and word research projects published in Britain, America and France.

It has been designed to take its place naturally in the logical shift from the mainly oral approach to the more formal oral and written work of later years.

Every effort has been made to make it both useful and interesting to as wide an intellectual range of young people as possible. It is hoped that it will not only help the slow learner but at the same time capture the interest of the more academic pupil, who might like to browse through the dictionary to extend his knowledge simply for the fun of doing so. For these reasons it contains not only entries which any beginner should know, but also a controlled number of entries which even a bright pupil cannot be expected to have met.

The final selection of the contents of this dictionary and the setting out of the material have been designed for use especially in upper Junior and Middle schools and the lower forms of all types of Secondary schools.

This book is the outcome of more than thirty years' experience as a teacher of French.

C. H.

PREFACE

Ce dictionnaire contient l'ensemble du vocabulaire du *Français fondamental : Premier degré* et un certain nombre de mots du *Deuxième degré* ainsi que d'autres mots dont la fréquence justifie l'inclusion.

C'est le produit d'une étude approfondie des ouvrages scolaires ainsi que des recherches sur le vocabulaire publiées en Grande-Bretagne, aux États-Unis et en France.

Il doit prendre sa place tout naturellement entre la phase orale du début et le travail oral et écrit qui prend sa suite plus tard.

Nous n'avons épargné aucun effort pour le rendre à la fois utile et intéressant pour le plus grand nombre de jeunes. Nous espérons que non seulement il aidera les élèves qui apprennent lentement mais aussi qu'il attirera l'attention des élèves plus avancés en les invitant à le feuilleter et à augmenter leurs connaissances par simple jeu. Nous avons donc ajouté à la liste principale un nombre limité d'articles que même les meilleurs élèves n'auront sans doute pas rencontrés.

Le contenu de ce dictionnaire et la façon dont il a été composé s'adressent particulièrement aux élèves des cours moyens de l'enseignement primaire, et pour ceux des premières classes des collèges.

Trente années passées à enseigner le français trouvent ainsi leur consécration.

C. H.

French–English

A

à (*prep.*), to (**aller à Paris,** to go to Paris); in (**être à Paris,** to be in Paris); at (**attendre à la gare,** to wait at the station; **à dix heures,** at 10 o'clock); with, in (**l'homme au complet gris,** the man in the grey suit; **le garçon au nez retroussé,** the boy with the snub nose); **le fermier va aux champs,** the farmer goes to the fields; **une poêle à frire,** a frying-pan; **une tasse à thé,** a teacup.
abaisser (*verb*), to lower; to pull down (a blind); to bring down (the value); **s'abaisser,** to sink; to slope downwards; to humble oneself.
abandonner (*verb*), to abandon (a hope); to forsake (friends).
abdiquer (*verb*), to abdicate; to renounce (one's rights).
abdomen *m.* (*noun*), abdomen.
abeille *f.* (*noun*), bee.
abolir (*verb*), to abolish, to do away with.
abolition *f.* (*noun*), abolition; suppression.
abondance *f.* (*noun*), plenty, abundance; wealth.
d'abord (*adv.*), first, at first, in the first place.
aboyer (**après**) (*verb*), to bark (at), to yelp (at).
abri *m.* (*noun*), shelter; covering; **abri en béton,** (*military*) pill-box.
abricot *m.* (*noun*), apricot.
absence *f.* (*noun*), absence.
absent (*adj.*), absent.
absolument (*adv.*), quite, absolutely.
absoudre (*verb*), to forgive (sins); to acquit (for lack of proof).
académie *f.* (*noun*), academy.
accélérer (*verb*), to accelerate; to speed up (movement).
accepter (*verb*), to accept; to agree to.
accident *m.* (*noun*), accident, mishap.
accompagner (*verb*), to attend, to accompany, to escort.
accomplir (*verb*), to achieve; to carry out (a project); to complete.
d'accord! (*adv.*), agreed! right!
accrocher (*verb*), to hang up (a picture); to hook (with a fish-hook); to pick up (a radio station).
accumuler (*verb*), to accumulate.
accuser (*verb*), to accuse, to blame; to bring charges against (someone).
achat *m.* (*noun*), purchase.
acheter (*verb*), to buy, to purchase (**à,** from).
acquitter (*verb*), to acquit; to discharge (a debt).
acrobate *m.* & *f.* (*noun*), acrobat.
acteur *m.*, **actrice** *f.* (*noun*), actor, actress.
action *f.* (*noun*), action, act, deed.
activer (*verb*), to hasten; to stir up; **s'activer,** to be busy.
addition *f.* (*noun*), addition; bill (in a restaurant).
additionner (*verb*), to add up, to tot up, to reckon up.
adieu (*pl.* **adieux**) *m.* (*noun*), farewell.
admettre (*verb*), to allow; to admit.
administration *f.* (*noun*), administration, management.
admirer (*verb*), to admire, to wonder at.
adresse *f.* (*noun*), address (on envelope); skill, dexterity, adroitness.
adresser (*verb*), to address, to send (a letter); to offer up (a prayer).
adroit (*adj.*), skilful, adroit, dexterous; shrewd.
aérer (*verb*), to air, to ventilate.
aéroport *m.* (*noun*), airport.
affaire *f.* (*noun*), affair, matter, business; cause, case; action (in war); (*pl.*) affairs; things, belongings; business; **être dans les affaires,** to be in business; **comment vont les affaires?** how is business?
affamé (*adj.*), starving, famished.
affecter (*verb*), to affect, to influence; to pretend.
affectueux *m.*, **-euse** *f.* (*adj.*), affectionate, loving.

afficher (*verb*), to stick up (a poster), to advertise (a house for sale).
âge *m.* (*noun*), age (of a person); age (period in history).
âgé (*adj.*), aged, old.
s'agenouiller (*verb*), to kneel, to kneel down.
agent *m.* **de police** (*noun*), policeman.
agneau (*pl.* **agneaux**) *m.* (*noun*), lamb.
agrandir (*verb*), to enlarge (a hole); to extend (premises).
agréable (*adj.*), agreeable, nice; comfortable; enjoyable.
agricole (*adj.*), agricultural.
agriculteur *m.* (*noun*), farmer, agriculturalist.
agriculture *f.* (*noun*), farming; agriculture.
agripper (*verb*), to grab; to clutch.
ah! (*interj.*), ah! aha! oh!
aide *f.* (*noun*), aid, assistance, help.
aider (*verb*), to help, to aid, to assist.
aigle *m.* (*noun*), eagle.
aiguille *f.* (*noun*), sewing needle; hand (of clock).
aile *f.* (*noun*), wing (of bird, aircraft, car); sail (of windmill).
aimable (*adj.*), friendly, amicable, lovable.
aimer (*verb*), to like, to love, to be fond of, to care for; to enjoy; to be in love with.
aîné (*adj.*), eldest; elder, senior.
ainsi (*adv.*), thus, so, like that, in this manner.
air *m.* (*noun*), air; appearance, aspect; bearing, carriage; **avoir l'air triste, heureux,** to look sad, happy; **avoir l'air de rêver,** to look as if one is dreaming.
aisance *f.* (*noun*), ease; freedom.
aise *f.* (*noun*), ease; pleasure.
aisé (*adj.*), easy; comfortable.
ajouter (*verb*), to add; to append; to put in.
allée *f.* (*noun*), alley; path, walk.
alléger (*verb*), to lighten (a load); to alleviate (a pain).
aller (*verb*), to go; (*health*) to be (**comment allez-vous?** how are you?); **allons! allez!** (*interj.*), come! well now!; **s'en aller,** to go away, to depart; to pass away.
allonger (*verb*), to aim (a blow); to lengthen; to eke out (food).
allumer (*verb*), to light; to switch the light on; to kindle (a fire).
allumette *f.* (*noun*), match; **boîte** *f.* **à allumettes,** match-box.
alors (*adv.*), then, at that time; then, after that; therefore.
alouette *f.* (*noun*), lark, skylark.
alphabet *m.* (*noun*), alphabet; spelling book.
alternatif *m.*, **-ive** *f.* (*adj.*), alternative.
amas *m.* (*noun*), heap, mass.
ambassadeur *m.* (*noun*), ambassador.
ambition *f.* (*noun*), ambition.
ambulance *f.* (*noun*), ambulance.
améliorer (*verb*), to improve; to better.
amener (*verb*), to bring *or* fetch (someone); to lead.
amer *m.*, **-ère** *f.* (*adj.*), bitter; sharp (pain); galling (experience).
ami *m.*, **amie** *f.* (*noun*), friend.
amical (*adj.*), friendly, amicable.
amonceler (*verb*), to heap up, to pile up; to accumulate.
amour *m.* (*noun*), love; liking.
amour-propre *m.* (*noun*), self-respect; conceit.
amusant (*adj.*), amusing; funny.
amusement *m.* (*noun*), amusement, entertainment.
amuser (*verb*), to amuse, to entertain; **s'amuser,** to enjoy oneself.
an *m.* (*noun*), year; **le nouvel an,** the new year; **le jour de l'an,** New Year's day.
ananas *m.* (*noun*), pineapple.
ancien *m.*, **-ienne** *f.* (*adj.*), ancient, old; former.
ancre *f.* (*noun*), anchor; **jeter l'ancre,** to drop anchor.
âne *m.* (*noun*), ass, jackass, donkey; blockhead, dunce.
ange *m.* (*noun*), angel.
anglais (*adj.*), English (language, people); British (army); **Anglais** *m.*, **Anglaise** *f.* (*noun*), Englishman, Englishwoman; **anglais** *m.* (*noun*), English (language).

Angleterre *f.* (*noun*), England.

angoisse *f.* (*noun*), agony, anguish, distress.

animal (*pl.* **animaux**) *m.* (*noun*), animal.

année *f.* (*noun*), year; **bonne année!** happy New Year!

anniversaire *m.* (*noun*), anniversary; birthday.

annoncer (*verb*), to announce; to report; to foretell.

annuler (*verb*), to cancel; to quash, to repeal.

anse *f.* (*noun*), handle (of basket, jug).

antique (*adj.*), antique; old-fashioned; **antique** *f.* (*noun*), antique (work of art).

antre *f.* (*noun*), lair, den (of brigand *or* lion).

anxiété *f.* (*noun*), anxiety.

août *m.* (*noun*), August.

apercevoir (*verb*), to see, to perceive; to notice; **s'apercevoir,** to realize; to become aware (**de,** of).

à peu près (*adv.*), almost, nearly (**à peu près tout le monde était là,** almost everybody was there; **il est à peu près neuf heures,** it is nearly nine o'clock).

apeuré (*adj.*), afraid, scared; timid (animal).

apparaître (*verb*), to appear; to become evident.

appareil *m.* (*noun*), apparatus, appliance; **appareil photographique,** camera.

appartement *m.* (*noun*), flat; suite.

appartenir (*verb*) **à,** to be connected with; to belong to (**cela lui appartient,** that belongs to him).

appel *m.* (*noun*), call; summons; appeal; **faire appel à,** to appeal to.

appeler (*verb*), to call, to hail; **s'appeler,** to be called or named (**il s'appelle Henri,** he is called Henry, his name is Henry).

appliquer (*verb*), to apply (paint, glue); to administer (a remedy); **s'appliquer à,** to apply to (**cela s'applique à tout le monde,** that applies to everyone); to apply oneself (to).

apporter (*verb*), to bring, to bear (news); to contribute, to provide (funds, cash).

appréhender (*verb*), to dread; to arrest.

apprendre (*verb*), to learn (a lesson, language, etc.); to hear, to hear of; **apprendre à,** to teach.

approcher (*verb*), to approach; to draw near, to bring up (**approchez votre chaise,** draw up your chair; **approchez votre chaise de la table,** bring your chair up to the table).

approuver (*verb*), to approve of; to agree to.

appuyer (*verb*), to support; to shore up, to prop; **appuyer sur un bouton,** to push a button.

après (*prep.*), after (**Henri arrive après minuit,** Henry arrives after midnight; **Henri arrivera après Paul,** Henry will come after Paul); (*adv.*), afterwards, later; behind (**Henri est sorti avant Paul. Paul est sorti après. Est-ce que Paul est avant Henri? Non, il est après,** Henry set out before Paul. Paul set out afterwards. Is Paul in front of Henry? No, he is behind); **et puis après?** and then?

après-midi *m.* (*noun*), afternoon.

aptitude *f.* (*noun*), aptitude; ability.

arachide *f.* (*noun*), ground-nut, peanut, monkey-nut.

araignée *f.* (*noun*), spider; **toile d'araignée,** spider's web.

arbre *m.* (*noun*), tree; **arbre de Noël,** Christmas tree.

arc *m.* (*noun*), bow (used in archery); arch.

arc-en-ciel (*pl.* **arcs-en-ciel**) *m.* (*noun*), rainbow.

arche *f.* (*noun*), arch, archway; (*biblical*) ark.

arête *f.* (*noun*), fish-bone; bridge (of the nose); (*geography*) ridge.

argent *m.* (*noun*), silver (*metal or money*); money.

argument *m.* (*noun*), argument; evidence; case (collection of facts).

arme *f.* (*noun*), weapon, arm; (*pl.*) arms, coat-of-arms.

armée *f.* (*noun*), army; military forces.

armoire *f.* (*noun*), wardrobe; **armoire à provisions,** cupboard; **armoire à pharmacie,** medicine chest.

arrangement *m.* (*noun*), arrangement; putting in order.

arranger (*verb*), to arrange, to put in order, to place, to dispose; **s'arranger,** to settle oneself, to settle down; to manage, to make do (**je m'arrangerai avec ce que j'ai,** I shall make do with what I have); **s'arranger les cheveux,** to tidy one's hair.

arrêt *m.* (*noun*), stop, stopping-place; arrest.

arrêter (*verb*), to stop, to pull up; to delay, to hold up; to arrest; to close, to settle (an account); **s'arrêter,** to stop, to halt, to come to a stop; to pause.

arrière (*adj. & adv.*) **marche arrière,** reverse motion; **faire marche arrière,** to back, to reverse; **entrer en marche arrière,** to back in; **sortir en marche arrière,** to back out; **aller en arrière,** to go backwards; **rester en arrière,** to remain behind; **arrière** *m.* (*noun*), back, rear; stern (of ship); (*football*) full-back.

arrivée *f.* (*noun*), arrival, coming; (*sports*) finish.

arriver (*verb*), to arrive, to come; to reach (**il arrivera à Paris demain,** he will reach Paris tomorrow); to succeed (**arriver à faire quelque chose,** to succeed in doing something); to happen; (*impers.*) **il arrive,** it happens (**il est arrivé un accident,** an accident happened).

arroser (*verb*), to water (flowers), to sprinkle (lawns), to irrigate; to wash down (**un excellent repas arrosé d'un très bon bourgogne,** an excellent meal washed down with a very good Burgundy).

art *m.* (*noun*), art; craft, profession; skill; knack.

article *m.* (*noun*), article, commodity; item; (newspaper) article; clause (of a contract).

artiste *m. & f.* (*noun*), artist; performer; artiste, actor, actress.

ascenseur *m.* (*noun*), lift; hoist (at a warehouse).

assaillant *m.* (*noun*), assailant, aggressor, attacker.

assemblée *f.* (*noun*), assembly, gathering, meeting.

assembler (*verb*), to assemble, to gather, to collect.

asseoir (*verb*), to seat, to sit (someone) (**asseyez l'enfant par terre,** sit the child on the ground); **s'asseoir,** to sit down.

assez (*adv.*), enough; sufficiently; rather, fairly (**assez en retard,** rather late).

assiette *f.* (*noun*), plate.

assis (*adj.*), seated; **être assis,** to be seated, to be sitting (down).

assistance *f.* (*noun*), assistance, help, aid.

assistant *m.*, **assistante** *f.* (*noun*), assistant, auxiliary, helper.

assister (*verb*), to assist, to help; to minister to (ill people); **assister à,** to attend, to be present at.

assurément (*adv.*), assuredly.

assurer (*verb*), to assure; to ensure; to fix; to guarantee.

atelier *m.* (*noun*), studio (of artist); workroom, workshop.

attacher (*verb*), to fasten, to tie, to attach.

attaque *f.* (*noun*), attack; criticism.

attaquer (*verb*), to attack; to assault; to criticize.

atteindre (*verb*), to reach, to attain; to overtake; to affect.

attendre (*verb*), to wait for, to await; **s'attendre à,** to expect; **en attendant,** meanwhile, in the meantime.

attentif *m.*, **-ive** *f.* (*adj.*), careful, attentive.

attention *f.* (*noun*), attention; heed, notice; **faire attention,** to pay attention, to be careful.

attirer (*verb*), to attract; to entice.

attraper (*verb*), to catch; to snare, to trap; to catch (an illness).

au: *always used instead of* **à** *followed by the definite article* **le;** *see* **à.**

aube *f.* (*noun*), dawn.

auberge *f.* (*noun*), inn, tavern; **auberge de la jeunesse,** youth hostel.

aubergiste *m. & f.* (*noun*), innkeeper, host, hostess, landlord, landlady.
aucun (*pron. & adj.*), any (**je me demande si aucun de nous réussira,** I wonder whether any of us will succeed; **je n'aime aucun d'eux,** I don't like any of them; **y a-t-il aucune raison pour ça?** is there any reason for that?); no one, none (**aucun n'a travaillé,** no one worked).
au-dessous (*adv.*), underneath, below (it); **au-dessous de** (*prep.*), below, under.
au-dessus (*adv.*), above (it); **au-dessus de** (*prep.*), above.
augmenter (*verb*), to amplify; to augment, to increase; to aggravate (a pain).
aujourd'hui (*adv.*), today; nowadays; **d'aujourd'hui en huit,** a week today.
auprès (*adv.*), close to, close by, near; **auprès de** (*prep.*), close to, close by, near, beside; compared with.
aussi (*adv.*), also, too, as well; so (**il a faim, moi aussi,** he is hungry, so am I).
aussitôt (*adv.*), at once, forthwith; **aussitôt que** (*conj.*), as soon as.
autant (*adv.*), so much, as much (**son frère ne mange pas autant,** his brother does not eat so much); the same (**je peux en faire autant,** I can do the same); (just) as soon (**il aimerait autant jouer au football,** he would just as soon play football).
auto *f.* (*noun*), (motor) car.
autobus *m.* (*noun*), town bus.
autocar *m.* (*noun*), country bus, coach.
automne *m.* (*noun*), autumn.
autour (*adv.*), around, about, round it; **autour de** (*prep.*), round, about.
autre (*adj.*), other; **autre part,** elsewhere, somewhere else; **l'un ou l'autre,** either; **l'autre, les autres** *m. & f. sing. & pl.* (*pron.*), the other (one), the others.
autrefois (*adv.*), formerly, in the past; in olden days.
autrement (*adv.*), more, far more (**c'est bien autrement sérieux,** that is far more serious); otherwise, in other respects.
aux: *always used instead of* **à** *followed by the definite article* **les;** *see* **à.**
avachi (*adj.*), flabby, sloppy; shapeless.
avaler (*verb*), to swallow; to stomach (an insult).
avance *f.* (*noun*), advance, progress; **en avance** (*adv.*), early, before time.
avancer (*verb*), to advance; to move forward; to lend (money); (*of clock, watch*) to be fast.
avant (*prep.*), before; **en avant** (*adv.*), forward, ahead, in advance; **avant que** (*conj.*), before; **ne . . . pas avant que,** not until.
avantage *m.* (*noun*), advantage, benefit.
avec (*prep.*), with; in spite of (**avec tous ses jouets il n'est pas heureux,** in spite of all his toys he is not happy); **d'avec,** from (**distinguer le jaune d'avec le bleu,** to distinguish the yellow from the blue).
avenir *m.* (*noun*), future; **à l'avenir,** in (the) future.
aventure *f.* (*noun*), adventure; venture.
avenue *f.* (*noun*), avenue, drive.
avertir (*verb*), to notify, to inform; to caution (**de,** against).
aveugle (*adj.*), blind; *m. & f.* (*noun*), blind person.
aveugler (*verb*), to blind.
aviateur *m.*, **aviatrice** *f.* (*noun*), aviator, flier.
avouer (*verb*), to acknowledge, to admit; to confess.
avide (*adj.*), greedy.
avion *m.* (*noun*), aeroplane, aircraft.
avis *m.* (*noun*), advice; judgment, view, opinion; **à mon avis,** in my opinion (**à mon avis, vous avez raison,** in my opinion, you are right).
avoir (*verb*), to have; (*in certain expressions*) to be (**avoir froid,** to be cold; **avoir faim,** to be hungry; **avoir vingt ans,** to be twenty years old); **avoir l'intention de,** to intend; **il y a** (*impers.*) there is, there are (**il y a un avion dans le ciel,** there is an aircraft in the sky); ago (**il y a deux mois,** two months ago).
avril *m.* (*noun*), April.
azur *m.* (*noun*), blue, azure.

B

babouin *m.* (*noun*), baboon.

bagages *m. pl.* (*noun*), luggage.

bague *f.* (*noun*), (jewelled) ring; clip (on fountain pen).

baguette *f.* (*noun*), rod, wand; long, thin loaf of French bread.

baie *f.* (*noun*), berry; (*geography*) bay; bay-window.

se baigner (*verb*), to take a bath; to bathe (in the sea).

baignoire *f.* (*noun*), bath (in which one takes a bath); bath-tub.

bâiller (*verb*), to yawn; to gape; to stand open (*e.g.* a door).

bain *m.* (*noun*), bath (act of bathing); bathe (in the sea).

baiser *m.* (*noun*), kiss.

baisser (*verb*), to lower, to pull down; **se baisser,** to bend down, to stoop.

bal *m.* (*noun*), dance, ball.

balai *m.* (*noun*), brush, broom.

balance *f.* (*noun*), balance, scales; balancing (of an account).

balancer (*verb*), to swing; to rock, to sway; to balance; **se balancer,** to swing to and fro, to sway.

balançoire *f.* (*noun*), see-saw; swing.

balayer (*verb*), to sweep, to brush.

balle *f.* (*noun*), small ball (used in games).

ballon *m.* (*noun*), ball, football; balloon.

balustrade *f.* (*noun*), railing, balustrade.

banane *f.* (*noun*), banana.

banc *m.* (*noun*), form, bench, pew; shelf, ledge.

banlieue *f.* (*noun*), suburbs.

banque *f.* (*noun*), bank.

baraque *f.* (*noun*), booth (at a fair); hut.

barbe *f.* (*noun*), beard; whiskers (of a cat).

baromètre *m.* (*noun*), barometer.

barre *f.* (*noun*), line, dash, stroke; bar (**une barre de chocolat,** a bar of chocolate); (*gymnastics*) bar.

barrer (*verb*), to cross out, to cancel; to bar, to obstruct.

barrière *f.* (*noun*), fence; gate (of a town).

bas *m.*, **basse** *f.* (*adj.*), low; degrading, contemptible.

bas *m.* (*noun*), lady's stocking; lower part (of something), base, foot; **en bas** (*adv.*), downstairs; below; downwards.

bascule *f.* (*noun*), see-saw; platform scales.

bassin *m.* (*noun*), basin; artificial lake.

bateau (*pl.* **bateaux**) *m.* (*noun*), boat; **bateau à voiles,** sailing boat.

bâtiment *m.* (*noun*), building, edifice; ship, vessel (**bâtiment de débarquement,** landing-craft; **bâtiment de guerre,** warship).

bâtir (*verb*), to build, to construct; to build up; **la maison se bâtit,** the house is being built.

bâton *m.* (*noun*), stick, baton, rod, staff; cudgel; truncheon.

battre (*verb*), to beat, to strike; to thresh (corn); to shuffle (cards); **battre des mains,** to clap, to applaud; **se battre** (**avec, contre**), to fight (with, against).

bavarder (*verb*), to chat.

beau (**bel**) (*pl.* **beaux**) *m.*, **belle** *f.* (*adj.*), fine; fair, handsome, beautiful, pretty, lovely; **il fait beau** (**temps**), it is fine (weather).

beaucoup (*adv.*), much, plenty, a great deal (of) (**il mange beaucoup,** he eats a lot, plenty; **beaucoup d'argent,** a great deal of money); many (**beaucoup de magasins,** many shops).

beauté *f.* (*noun*), beauty.

bébé *m.* (*noun*), baby, infant.

bec *m.* (*noun*), beak, bill.

bêche *f.* (*noun*), spade.

bénéfice *m.* (*noun*), profit, gain; benefit.

bénir (*verb*), to bless.

berceau (*pl.* **berceaux**) *m.* (*noun*), cot, cradle. *See* **lit.**

bercer (*verb*), to rock (a baby to sleep); to nurse (in one's arms).

besoin *m.* (*noun*), need, want, requirement; **avoir besoin de,** to need, to have need of.

bête (*adj.*), foolish, stupid; **qu'il est bête!** what a fool he is!
bête *f.* (*noun*), animal, beast.
beurre *m.* (*noun*), butter.
bible *f.* (*noun*), bible; **la Sainte Bible,** the Holy Bible.
bibliothèque *f.* (*noun*), library; bookcase, bookshelves.
bicyclette *f.* (*noun*), bicycle; **aller à bicyclette,** to cycle.
bien (*adv.*), well; quite; fine; exactly; **eh bien!** (*interj.*), well! now then!; **bien que** (*conj.*), although, though.
bientôt (*adv.*), soon, before long, shortly; **à bientôt!** so long!
bière *f.* (*noun*), beer; coffin.
bijou (*pl.* **bijoux**) *m.* (*noun*), jewel, gem; darling.
billet *m.* (*noun*), note; ticket; bank-note.
biscotte *f.* (*noun*), rusk.
biscuit *m.* (*noun*), biscuit; **biscuit de Savoie,** sponge-cake.
blanc *m.*, **blanche** *f.* (*adj.*), white; pure; **donner carte blanche à quelqu'un,** to give someone a free hand.
blé *m.* (*noun*), corn, wheat.
blesser (*verb*), to wound, to injure, to hurt; to offend; **se blesser,** to injure oneself; to hurt oneself; to take offence.
blessure *f.* (*noun*), wound, injury.
bleu (*adj.*), blue.
blond (*adj.*), fair, blond, flaxen.
bloquer (*verb*), to block, to obstruct; to block up; **se bloquer,** to jam; to get jammed.
blouse *f.* (*noun*), overall, blouse, smock.
bocal (*pl.* **bocaux**) *m.* (*noun*), glass jar; globe; fish-bowl.
bœuf *m.* (*noun*), ox, bullock; beef.
boire (*verb*), to drink; **boire à petits coups,** to sip.
bois *m.* (*noun*), wood, timber; forest; (*pl.*) antlers.
boisson *f.* (*noun*), drink.
boîte *f.* (*noun*), box (**boîte d'allumettes,** box of matches); tin (**boîte de sardines,** tin of sardines).
bol *m.* (*noun*), bowl, basin (for soup, etc.).
bon *m.*, **bonne** *f.* (*adj.*), good, nice, kind; **de bonne heure** (*adv.*), early.
bonbon *m.* (*noun*), sweet.
bonjour *m.* (*noun*), good morning, good day, good afternoon.
bonne *f.* (*noun*), maid (domestic servant).
bonnet *m.* (*noun*), (close-fitting and brimless) cap; bonnet; **bonnet de bain,** bathing cap.
bonsoir *m.* (*noun*), good evening, good night.
bord *m.* (*noun*), border, edge; kerb; brim; bank (of a river); **au bord de la mer,** at the seaside.
botte *f.* (*noun*), boot (**bottes de caoutchouc,** Wellingtons); bunch (of flowers, vegetables).
bouc *m.* (*noun*), billy-goat.
bouche *f.* (*noun*), mouth; opening, entrance.
bouchée *f.* (*noun*), mouthful; morsel; gulp.
boucher (*verb*), to fill in; to stop (up), to block (up); to cork.
boucher *m.* (*noun*), butcher.
boucherie *f.* (*noun*), butcher's shop; slaughter, butchery.
boucle *f.* (*noun*), buckle (of belt); loop (of knot); lock, curl (of hair).
boue *f.* (*noun*), mud, slime, mire.
bouffon *m.* (*noun*), jester, clown, buffoon.
bougie *f.* (*noun*), candle; sparking plug.
bouillie *f.* (*noun*), gruel, porridge.
bouillir (*verb*), to boil (**je fais bouillir de l'eau,** I boil some water); **bouillir de colère,** to seethe with anger.
bouilloire *f.* (*noun*), kettle.
boulanger *m.*, **boulangère** *f.* (*noun*), baker, baker's wife.
boulangerie *f.* (*noun*), baker's shop; bakery trade; breadmaking.
boulevard *m.* (*noun*), boulevard (a wide tree-lined street).
bourdon *m.* (*noun*), bumble-bee.
bourgeon *m.* (*noun*), bud, shoot.
bourse *f.* (*noun*), purse; funds; pouch (*e.g.* of kangaroo); **la Bourse,** Stock Exchange.
bout *m.* (*noun*), end; toe (of stocking); **au bout de** (*prep.*), at the end of, after (**au bout d'une heure,** after an hour).

bouteille *f.* (*noun*), bottle.
boutique *f.* (*noun*), small shop; booth (at a fair); market stall.
bouton *m.* (*noun*), bud; button, stud; knob (of door); pimple.
bracelet *m.* (*noun*), bracelet, watch-strap.
brancard *m.* (*noun*), stretcher.
branche *f.* (*noun*), branch, bough.
bras *m.* (*noun*), arm; jib (of crane); handle (of machinery).
brasserie *f.* (*noun*), brewery; beer garden (a kind of public house); restaurant.
brillant (*adj.*), bright, brilliant; gay.
briller (*verb*), to shine, to glitter, to gleam, to shimmer.
brioche *f.* (*noun*), small cake; (circular) light roll.
brique *f.* (*noun*), brick; cake (of soap).
briquet *m.* (*noun*), cigarette lighter.
briser (*verb*), to break, to smash, to shatter.
broche *f.* (*noun*), brooch; spit (for cooking).
brosse *f.* (*noun*), brush; **brosse à dents,** toothbrush.
brouette *f.* (*noun*), wheelbarrow.
brouillard *m.* (*noun*), fog; haze, mist.
bruine *f.* (*noun*), drizzle.
bruit *m.* (*noun*), noise, sound; turmoil, disturbance.
brûler (*verb*), to burn; **se brûler,** to burn oneself, to singe oneself.
brûlure *f.* (*noun*), burn, scald.
brun (*adj.*), brown; dark, swarthy, tanned.
brusque (*adj.*), abrupt, brusque; sudden.
brutal (*adj.*), rough, savage; **jeu brutal,** horseplay.
bruyant (*adj.*), loud, noisy.
buffet *m.* (*noun*), sideboard; buffet; **buffet de cuisine,** kitchen dresser.
bulbe *m. or f.* (*noun*), bulb, corm.
bureau (*pl.* **bureaux**) *m.* (*noun*), office desk; office, department; **bureau de poste,** post office; **bureau de tabac,** tobacconist's.

C

ça (*pron.*): *see* **cela.**
cabane *f.* (*noun*), hut, shack, shanty; cabin (of a small boat).
cabaret *m.* (*noun*), tavern, pub.
cabinet *m.* (*noun*), small room; (*government*) cabinet; (*pl.*) W.C., toilet.
cacahuète *f.* (*noun*), peanut, monkey-nut.
cache-cache *m.* (*noun*), hide-and-seek.
cacher (*verb*), to hide, to conceal, to mask, to cover.
cadavre *m.* (*noun*), corpse, dead body (of human or animal).
cadeau (*pl.* **cadeaux**) *m.* (*noun*), present, gift.
cadre *m.* (*noun*), frame (of picture; of bicycle).
café *m.* (*noun*), coffee; café, small restaurant.
cage *f.* (*noun*), cage; cage (of mine); shaft (of lift).
caillou (*pl.* **cailloux**) *m.* (*noun*), pebble.
calculer (*verb*), to calculate, to count.
calme (*adj.*), still (air); calm, unruffled (sea); composed, cool, sedate, quiet.
camarade *m.* *&* *f.* (*noun*), pal, comrade, companion.
camion *m.* (*noun*), lorry, truck; dray, wa(g)gon.
camionnette *f.* (*noun*), light lorry; delivery van.
camp *m.* (*noun*), camp; faction, party.
campagne *f.* (*noun*), countryside, country; campaign.
canal (*pl.* **canaux**) *m.* (*noun*), canal.
canapé *m.* (*noun*), sofa, settee.
canard *m.* (*noun*), duck (drake).
cane *f.* (*noun*), (female) duck.
canoë *m.* (*noun*), canoe.
caoutchouc *m.* (*noun*), rubber, india rubber; raincoat.
capable (*adj.*), competent, able, capable.
capacité *f.* (*noun*), capacity; ability.
capitale *f.* (*noun*), capital (city; letter).
car (*conj.*), for, because.
car *m.* (*noun*) = **autocar.**
caractère *m.* (*noun*), character.
carapace *f.* (*noun*), shell (of tortoise).
caravane *f.* (*noun*), caravan.
caresse *f.* (*noun*), caress, pat.
caresser (*verb*), to stroke, to fondle, to caress; to pat (an animal).
carie *f.* (*noun*), decay (of teeth).
se carier (*verb*), (*of teeth*) to decay.
carotte *f.* (*noun*), carrot.
carré (*adj.*), square; forthright, outspoken; plain, blunt.
carré *m.* (*noun*), square (shape); landing (head of stairs); patch (of garden).
carrefour *m.* (*noun*), crossroads.
cartable *m.* (*noun*), satchel (for books); art portfolio.
carte *f.* (*noun*), card; map, chart.
casquette *f.* (*noun*), peaked cap.
casser (*verb*), to break; to snap (a twig).
casserole *f.* (*noun*), saucepan, stew-pan; old banger, jalopy.
cause *f.* (*noun*), cause, reason, motive; **à cause de** (*prep.*), on account of, because of, owing to.
causer[1] (*verb*), to cause, to bring about.
causer[2] (*verb*), to talk, to chat.
cave *f.* (*noun*), cellar, vault.
caverne *f.* (*noun*), cave, cavern.
ce (*pron.*), it; he, she (**c'est Jean,** it is John; **c'est vrai,** it is true; **c'est mon ami,** he is my friend).
ce (**cet**) *m. sing.*, **cette** *f. sing.*, **ces** *m. & f. pl.* (*adj.*), this, these.
ceci (*pron.*), this.
ceinture *f.* (*noun*), belt (of leather); girdle, sash, waistband.
cela, ça (*pron.*), that; it.
célèbre (*adj.*), noted, celebrated, famous.
celui *m.* (*pl.* **ceux**), **celle** *f.* (*pl.* **celles**) (*pron.*), (*followed by* **qui** *or* **que**) the one, those, he, she (**ceux que nous ne voyons pas,** those whom we don't see; **celui qui dit la vérité,** he who tells the truth); (*followed by* **de**) **ce manteau et celui de mon ami**, this coat and my friend's.

celui-ci *m.* (*pl.* **ceux-ci**), **celle-ci** *f.* (*pl.* **celles-ci**),**celui-là** *m.* (*pl.* **ceux-là**),**celle-là** *f.* (*pl.* **celles-là**) (*demonstrative pron.*): **ci** *denotes that which is near*, **là** *denotes that which is further away* (**Voici deux hommes. Celui-ci est gras, mais celui-là est maigre,** Here are two men. This one is fat, but that one is thin; **Voici deux voitures. Celle-ci est rouge mais celle-là est jaune,** Here are two cars. This one is red but that one is yellow).

cent (*adj. & noun*), hundred; **cent un(e)**, a hundred and one.

centaine *f.* (*noun*), about a hundred (**une centaine de personnes,** about a hundred people).

centimètre *m.* (*noun*), centimetre (5 centimetres = 2 inches).

centre *m.* (*noun*), centre.

cerceau (*pl.* **cerceaux**) *m.* (*noun*), child's hoop.

cercle *m.* (*noun*), circle; hoop (of barrel); group (of people), club (**cercle français,** French circle).

cerf *m.* (*noun*), deer; stag.

cerf-volant (*pl.* **cerfs-volants**) *m.* (*noun*), kite; stag-beetle.

cerise *f.* (*noun*), cherry.

certain (*adj.*), certain, sure.

certainement (*adv.*), certainly, of course.

certifier (*verb*), to certify, to guarantee.

ces, cette: *see* **ce** (*adj.*).

c'est-à-dire, that is to say, i.e.

ceux: *see* **celui.**

chacun *m.*, **chacune** *f.* (*pron.*), each, each one.

chagrin *m.* (*noun*), grief, sorrow, trouble, affliction.

chaîne *f.* (*noun*), chain (of iron, gold, etc.; of mountains).

chair *f.* (*noun*), flesh; pulp (of fruit).

chaise *f.* (*noun*), chair.

chaleur *f.* (*noun*), heat, warmth.

chambre *f.* (*noun*), room; (*political*) chamber, house; **chambre à coucher,** bedroom.

champ *m.* (*noun*), field; ground (**champ de foire,** fairground).

champignon *m.* (*noun*), mushroom.

chance *f.* (*noun*), chance, luck; fortune (**souhaiter bonne chance à quelqu'un,** to wish someone good luck); risk (**il court la chance d'un accident,** he runs the risk of an accident).

chanceler (*verb*), to stagger, to totter, to reel; to falter.

chandail *m.* (*noun*), sweater, jersey, pullover.

changement *m.* (*noun*), change, alteration.

changer (*verb*), to change, to alter; to exchange; **changer en,** to turn into.

chanson *f.* (*noun*), song.

chant *m.* (*noun*), singing, song (**le chant des rossignols,** the song of the nightingales).

chanter (*verb*), to sing; to chirp.

chapeau (*pl.* **chapeaux**) *m.* (*noun*), hat.

chapitre *m.* (*noun*), chapter.

chaque (*adj.*), each, every.

charbon *m.* (*noun*), coal; carbon; **charbon de bois,** charcoal.

charcuterie *f.* (*noun*), pork-butcher's shop, delicatessen.

charcutier *m.* (*noun*), pork-butcher.

charge *f.* (*noun*), load, weight, burden.

charger (*verb*), to load (a vehicle); to feed, stoke (a fire).

charrue *f.* (*noun*), plough.

chasse *f.* (*noun*), hunt, chase.

chasser (*verb*), to stalk, to hunt.

chasseur *m.* (*noun*), stalker, hunter.

chat *m.*, **chatte** *f.* (*noun*), cat.

château (*pl.* **châteaux**) *m.* (*noun*), castle, stronghold; country seat, mansion, manor.

chaton *m.* (*noun*), kitten.

chaud (*adj.*), warm, hot; **avoir chaud,** to be warm; **il fait chaud,** it is warm.

chauffage *m.* (*noun*), heating; **chauffage central,** central heating.

chauffer (*verb*), to warm, to heat.

chauffeur *m.* (*noun*), driver; **chauffeur de taxi,** taxi-driver.

chaussée *f.* (*noun*), roadway, highway, paved road.

chaussette *f.* (*noun*), sock.

chaussure *f.* (*noun*), footwear; shoe; boot.
chauve (*adj.*), bald.
chauve-souris *f.* (*noun*), bat.
chef *m.* (*noun*), leader, chief, person in charge; **chef de train,** guard (on a train); **chef de cuisine,** chef.
chemin *m.* (*noun*), path, way, track; **chemin de fer,** railway.
cheminée *f.* (*noun*), chimney; fireplace.
chemise *f.* (*noun*), (man's) shirt; **chemise de nuit,** nightdress, nightshirt.
chêne *m.* (*noun*), oak.
chèque *m.* (*noun*), cheque.
cher *m.*, **chère** *f.* (*adj.*), dear, beloved; expensive; **pas cher,** cheap.
chercher (*verb*), to seek, to search, to look for.
chéri *m.*, **chérie** *f.* (*noun*), darling, dear.
cheval (*pl.* **chevaux**) *m.* (*noun*), horse.
cheveu (*pl.* **cheveux**) *m.* (*noun*), hair.
cheville *f.* (*noun*), ankle.
chèvre *f.* (*noun*), goat, nanny-goat.
chez (*prep.*), to the house, home, shop of (**je vais chez le docteur,** I am going to the doctor's); at the house, home, shop of (**chez moi,** at (my) home).
chien *m.*, **chienne** *f.* (*noun*), dog, bitch; **petit chien, jeune chien,** puppy.
chiffon *m.* (*noun*), rag; scrap (of paper).
chiffre *m.* (*noun*), figure (*used when writing a number, e.g. the figures* 5, 3, 8 *make the number* 538).
chirurgien *m.* (*noun*), surgeon.
chocolat *m.* (*noun*), chocolate.
choisir (*verb*), to choose, to single out, to select.
choix *m.* (*noun*), choice, selection.
choquant (*adj.*), shocking.
chose *f.* (*noun*), thing; affair; matter.
chou (*pl.* **choux**) *m.* (*noun*), cabbage; **choux de Bruxelles,** Brussels sprouts.
chrétien *m.*, **-ienne** *f.* (*noun & adj.*), Christian.
chuchotement *m.* (*noun*), whisper.
chuchoter (*verb*), to whisper.
ciel (*pl.* **cieux**) *m.* (*noun*), heaven; sky; **ciel!** good heavens! good gracious!
cigarette *f.* (*noun*), cigarette.
cimetière *m.* (*noun*), cemetery, burial ground, graveyard.
cinéma *m.* (*noun*), cinema.
cinq *m.* (*noun & adj.*), five; fifth (**Henri Cinq,** Henry the Fifth; **le cinq mars,** March the fifth).
cinquante *m.* (*noun & adj.*), fifty; **cinquante et un(e),** fifty-one.
cinquième (*noun & adj.*), fifth.
cirque *m.* (*noun*), circus.
ciseaux *m. pl.* (*noun*), scissors; clippers; shears.
cité *f.* (*noun*), city; large town; **cité-jardin** *f.*, garden city.
citron *m.* (*noun*), lemon.
citrouille *f.* (*noun*), pumpkin.
clair (*adj.*), clear; light, pale; light, bright; thin (soup).
claquement *m.* (*noun*), bang; crack (of branch).
claquer (*verb*), to bang; to crack; to clap.
classe *f.* (*noun*), class (in school); category; rank.
clé, clef *f.* (*noun*), key.
clerc *m.* (*noun*), clerk; clergyman.
client *m.*, **cliente** *f.* (*noun*), client, customer; patient; visitor (at hotel).
cloche *f.* (*noun*), bell; dish-cover.
clos (*adj.*), closed, shut.
clôture *f.* (*noun*), enclosure; closure (of a debate).
clou *m.* (*noun*), nail; **les clous,** pedestrian crossing.
clouer (*verb*), to nail up; to tack down.
clown *m.* (*noun*), circus clown; funny man.
cochon *m.* (*noun*), pig; pork.
cœur *m.* (*noun*), heart; **au cœur de la forêt,** in the heart of the forest; **avoir du cœur,** to have a kind heart.
coffre *m.* **à outils** (*noun*), toolbox.
coffre-fort (*pl.* **coffres-forts**) *m.* (*noun*), safe, strong-box.
cohue *f.* (*noun*), mob; throng; crush (of people).
coiffeur *m.*, **coiffeuse** *f.* (*noun*), hairdresser; **coiffeuse** *f.*, dressing-table.
coin *m.* (*noun*), corner; patch (of sky, etc.).
col *m.* (*noun*), collar; neck (of bottle).

colère *f.* (*noun*), anger; **être en colère,** to be angry.
colis *m.* (*noun*), parcel, package.
colle *f.* (*noun*), glue, gum, paste.
coller (*verb*), to paste, to stick, to glue (**le garçon a collé un timbre sur la lettre,** the boy stuck a stamp on the letter).
collier *m.* (*noun*), dog-collar; lady's necklace.
colline *f.* (*noun*), hill.
combat *m.* (*noun*), fight, contest.
combattre (*verb*), to fight; to struggle against (someone).
combien (*adv.*), how much, how many; **à combien sommes-nous de Paris?** how far are we from Paris?; **combien de temps restez-vous?** how long are you staying?
commander (*verb*), to order, to command.
comme (*adv.*), as, like; (*conj.*) (just) as.
commencement *m.* (*noun*), beginning.
commencer (*verb*), to begin, to commence, to start, to embark on (a career), to open (a conversation).
comment (*adv.*), how, what; **comment!** (*interj.*), what!
commerçant *m.* (*noun*), tradesman, shopkeeper.
commerce *m.* (*noun*), trade, business.
commode (*adj.*), convenient, suitable, handy.
commode *f.* (*noun*), chest of drawers.
commun (*adj.*), common (**des intérêts communs,** common interests); coarse, vulgar; ordinary; public.
communiquer (*verb*), to communicate, to make known (ideas, a plan).
compagnon *m.*, **compagne** *f.* (*noun*), companion, comrade.
compartiment *m.* (*noun*), compartment (of railway carriage; of a piece of furniture).
compétent (*adj.*), competent, efficient.
compétiteur *m.*, **compétitrice** *f.* (*noun*), competitor.
complet *m.*, **-ète** *f.* (*adj.*), full, full up; complete.
complet *m.* (*noun*), suit of clothes, lounge suit.
comprendre (*verb*), to understand, to grasp.
compte *m.* (*noun*), account, reckoning; **se rendre compte de quelque chose,** to realize, to understand something (**déjà trois heures! je me rends compte que je vais être en retard,** three o'clock already! I see that I am going to be late).
compter (*verb*), to count.
comptoir *m.* (*noun*), counter (in shop, bank).
concéder (*verb*), to allow, to grant, to concede.
concentrer (*verb*), to concentrate.
concerner (*verb*), to concern, to affect.
concevoir (*verb*), to conceive, to imagine.
concilier (*verb*), to conciliate, to reconcile; to settle (a difference).
concours *m.* (*noun*), competition; co-operation.
condenser (*verb*), to condense.
condition *f.* (*noun*), condition, circumstance.
conducteur *m.* (*noun*), driver (of vehicle); leader; conductor (of electricity, etc.).
conduire (*verb*), to accompany, to conduct, to guide; to drive; **se (mal) conduire,** to behave (badly).
conférer (*verb*), to bestow, to confer.
confiance *f.* (*noun*), confidence, trust, reliance.
confiseur *m.* (*noun*), confectioner.
confiture *f.* (*noun*), jam, preserves.
conflit *m.* (*noun*), conflict, dispute.
confondre (*verb*), to confuse, to confound, to bewilder.
confort *m.* (*noun*), comfort.
confortable (*adj.*), comfortable, snug, cosy (**ce fauteuil est très confortable,** this armchair is very comfortable).
congé *m.* (*noun*), leave (of absence); holiday.
connaître (*verb*), to know, to know of, to be acquainted with.
conquérir (*verb*), to conquer.

conscienсieux *m.*, **-euse** *f.* (*adj.*), conscientious; careful.
conseil *m.* (*noun*), advice, counsel.
conseiller (*verb*), to advise, to counsel.
consentir (*verb*), to agree, to consent.
conséquence *f.* (*noun*), consequence, result; importance.
conserver (*verb*), to keep (friends); to preserve (fruit, etc.).
considérer (*verb*), to consider, to take into account; to examine.
consister (**en**) (*verb*), to consist (of).
construire (*verb*), to construct, to build.
consumer (*verb*), to consume, to use up.
conte *m.* (*noun*), tale, story; tall story.
contempler (*verb*), to contemplate, to meditate upon.
contenir (*verb*), to contain, to hold.
content (*adj.*), glad, happy, content.
continuer (*verb*), to continue, to pursue, to go on with; to carry on (a tradition).
contraindre (*verb*), to compel, to force; to restrain, to curb.
contraire (*adj.*), contrary (**un vent contraire,** a contrary wind); opposite (**en sens contraire,** in the opposite direction); conflicting (**des idées contraires,** conflicting ideas); **contraire** *m.* (*noun*): **au contraire,** on the contrary.
contre (*prep.*), against, contrary to; versus.
contribuer (*verb*), to contribute.
contrôler (*verb*), to inspect, to check.
convalescence *f.* (*noun*), convalescence; **être en convalescence,** to convalesce.
conversation *f.* (*noun*), conversation.
converser (*verb*), to converse, to talk.
copain *m.*, **copine** *f.* (*noun*), pal, comrade.
copie *f.* (*noun*), copy, imitation.
copier (*verb*), to copy, to imitate; to reproduce; to crib; to mimic.
coq *m.* (*noun*), cockerel, rooster, cock.
coquillage *m.* (*noun*), sea-shell.
coquille *f.* (*noun*), shell (of egg); covering, outer casing; misprint.
corbeille *f.* (*noun*), basket.
corde *f.* (*noun*), cord, string, rope.
cordonnier *m.* (*noun*), cobbler, shoemaker.
corne *f.* (*noun*), horn (of animal).
corps *m.* (*noun*), body; (organized) group (**le corps enseignant,** the teaching profession).
corriger (*verb*), to correct; to chastise.
costume *m.* (*noun*), costume; dress; suit; wearing apparel.
côte *f.* (*noun*), coast; hill; rib.
côté *m.* (*noun*), side (of road, etc.); **à côté,** to one side, near (**Henri est en face de Paul, et Marie est à côté,** Henry is in front of Paul, and Mary is to one side (of Paul)); **à côté de,** beside, close to (**Marie est à côté de Paul,** Mary is beside Paul).
coton *m.* (*noun*), cotton thread; cotton-wool.
cou *m.* (*noun*), neck.
couard *m.* (*noun*), coward.
couche *f.* (*noun*), couch, bed; layer, coat (of paint, tar).
coucher (*verb*), to put to bed; **se coucher,** to go to bed.
coucher *m.* (*noun*): **le coucher du soleil,** sunset.
coude *m.* (*noun*), elbow; bend, turn (of road, river).
cou-de-pied *m.* (*noun*), instep.
coudre (*verb*), to sew, to sew on, to stitch; **machine** *f.* **à coudre,** sewing machine.
couler (*verb*), to flow, to run; to sink (a ship).
couleur *f.* (*noun*), colour; dye.
coup *m.* (*noun*), blow, hit, knock, stroke; **coup de pied,** kick; **coup de téléphone,** telephone call; **coup de poing,** punch; **coup de chance,** stroke of luck; **coup de grâce,** finishing stroke.
coupable *m.* *&* *f.* (*noun*), culprit; offender; (*adj.*), guilty.
couper (*verb*), to cut, to clip; to reap, to mow; **se couper,** to cut oneself.
coupure *f.* (*noun*), cut; gash.
cour *f.* (*noun*), courtyard; court; playground.
courage *m.* (*noun*), courage.
courageux *m.*, **-euse** *f.* (*adj.*), plucky, brave, courageous.
courber (*verb*), to bend, to curve.
courir (*verb*), to run.

course *f.* (*noun*), race; run; walk; drive; journey; **faire des courses,** to go shopping.
court (*adj.*), short.
cousin *m.*, **cousine** *f.* (*noun*), cousin.
coussin *m.* (*noun*), cushion.
coût *m.* (*noun*), cost.
couteau (*pl.* **couteaux**) *m.* (*noun*), knife.
coûter (*verb*), to cost; **à prix coûtant,** at cost price.
coûteux *m.*, **-euse** *f.* (*adj.*), costly, expensive.
coutume *f.* (*noun*), custom, practice.
couture *f.* (*noun*), sewing; seam.
couvercle *m.* (*noun*), cover, lid.
couverture *f.* (*noun*), coverlet, blanket, quilt; cover (of book).
couvre-lit *m.* (*noun*), counterpane, bed-spread.
couvre-pieds *m.* (*noun*), quilt.
couvrir (*verb*), to cover, to wrap up; **se couvrir,** to clothe oneself.
crabe *m.* (*noun*), crab.
crachat *m.* (*noun*), spittle.
cracher (*verb*), to spit.
craie *f.* (*noun*), chalk.
craindre (*verb*), to be afraid, to fear.
craquement *m.* (*noun*), crack, crackling (of dry leaves).
craquer (*verb*), to crack; to snap; to creak.
cravate *f.* (*noun*), tie.
crayon *m.* (*noun*), pencil; **crayon à bille,** ball-point pen *or* pencil.
créer (*verb*), to create; to set up; to form.
crème *f.* (*noun*), cream.
crêpe *f.* (*noun*), pancake.
creuser (*verb*), to dig (out); to hollow out; to plough; to burrow; to open up.
creux *m.*, **creuse** *f.* (*adj.*), hollow, sunken.
creux *m.* (*noun*), hollow, hole (in ground), cavity (in tree trunk).
cri *m.* (*noun*), cry, shout; **cri perçant,** scream.
crier (*verb*), to cry, to scream, to shriek, to shout, to bawl, to yell.
crime *m.* (*noun*), crime.
crochet *m.* (*noun*), hook.
croire (*verb*), to believe, to think.
croiser (*verb*), to cross; **croiser les bras,** to fold one's arms.
croix *f.* (*noun*), cross.
cru (*adj.*), raw, uncooked.
cruche *f.* (*noun*), jug; pitcher.
cruel *m.*, **cruelle** *f.* (*adj.*), cruel (act, person); hard (winter); bitter (experience).
cube *m.* (*noun*), cube.
cueillir (*verb*), to gather, to pick, to pluck.
cuillère, cuiller *f.* (*noun*), spoon; **cuiller à café,** teaspoon.
cuir *m.* (*noun*), hide; leather.
cuire (*verb*), to cook; to bake.
cuisine *f.* (*noun*), kitchen.
cuisinier *m.*, **cuisinière** *f.* (*noun*), cook.
culbuter (*verb*), to tumble over; to turn a somersault.
culotte *f.* (*noun*), short trousers; knickers (*N.B. French singular*).
cultivateur *m.* (*noun*), farmer; **cultivateur de roses,** rose-grower.
cultivé (*adj.*), cultivated (land); cultured (mind).
cultiver (*verb*), to cultivate; to farm, to till (the earth).
culture *f.* (*noun*), culture; cultivation; agriculture, farming.
curieux *m.*, **-euse** *f.* (*adj.*), curious, inquisitive.
cuvette *f.* (*noun*), wash-bowl, wash-basin.
cygne *m.* (*noun*), swan; **jeune cygne,** cygnet.

D

dactylo(graphe) *m.* *& f.* (*noun*), typist.
dame *f.* (*noun*), lady; queen (in chess); **jeu** *m.* **de dames,** draughts.
danger *m.* (*noun*), danger, risk, peril.
dangereux *m.*, **-euse** *f.* (*adj.*), dangerous, risky.
dans (*prep.*), in, into; in (a period of time) (**dans dix minutes,** in ten minutes' time).
danse *f.* (*noun*), dance.
danser (*verb*), to dance.
danseur *m.*, **danseuse** *f.* (*noun*), dancer; partner (at a dance).
davantage (*adv.*), more (**en demander davantage,** to ask for more).
de (*prep.*) of; from (**je viens de Londres,** I come from London); by (**être aimé de tous,** to be loved by all).
dé *m.* (*noun*), die; **jeter les dés,** to throw the dice; **dé** (**à coudre**), thimble.
débarquer (*verb*), to disembark; to unload, to land (goods, troops).
débat *m.* (*noun*), discussion; dispute; debate.
debout (*adv.*), upright, erect, standing; **être debout,** to be standing.
débris *m. pl.* (*noun*), fragments, remains, bits.
débrouiller (*verb*), to unravel, to disentangle; to sort out (papers); **se débrouiller,** to manage; (*of sky*) to clear up.
début *m.* (*noun*), beginning, start; **au début,** at the beginning, at the start.
décembre *m.* (*noun*), December.
décharger (*verb*), to unload, to tip out, to dump.
déchirer (*verb*), to tear, to rip, to tear up.
déchirure *f.* (*noun*), tear, rent; laceration.
décider (*verb*), to decide, to settle; to resolve, to determine; **se décider,** to make up one's mind.
décision *f.* (*noun*), decision; resolution.
déclarer (*verb*), to declare, to announce.
décliner (*verb*), to decline, to wane.
décorer (*verb*), to decorate; to confer an honour or order (on someone).
découper (*verb*), to cut up (a cake), to carve (meat).
découverte *f.* (*noun*), discovery.
découvrir (*verb*), to discover, to uncover, to reveal.
décrépitude *f.* (*noun*), decay (of buildings).
dedans (*adv.*), inside, in it, within.
défaite *f.* (*noun*), defeat.
défendre (*verb*), to defend; to screen; to vindicate; to support, to stand by; to forbid, to prohibit.
défense *f.* (*noun*), defence, protection; tusk.
défiance *f.* (*noun*), distrust.
défier (*verb*), to defy; to challenge.
défilé *m.* (*noun*), pass, gorge (in mountains); procession, parade.
dégager (*verb*), to extricate; to withdraw; to disengage.
dehors (*adv.*), outside, out; **en dehors de** (*prep.*), outside (**en dehors de la ville,** outside the town).
déjà (*adv.*), already; previously, before.
déjeuner *m.* (*noun*), lunch (at midday); **petit déjeuner,** breakfast.
déjeuner (*verb*), to breakfast, to have breakfast; to lunch, to have lunch.
delà: au delà de (*prep.*), beyond, past, on the other side of; **de delà** (*adv.*), from beyond; **en delà** (*adv.*), farther on.
délabré (*adj.*), dilapidated.
délai *m.* (*noun*), delay; postponement; a period of time (**à bref délai,** at short notice).
délicat (*adj.*), delicate; refined.
délicieux *m.*, **-euse** *f.* (*adj.*), delicious; charming, delightful.
délivrer (*verb*), to deliver; to free, to rescue.
demain (*adv.*), tomorrow; **à demain!** goodbye till tomorrow!
demander (*verb*), to ask (for), to apply for, to request, to entreat; **se demander,** to ask oneself, to wonder.

déménager (*verb*), to move house, to move.

démentir (*verb*), to contradict; to deny, to refute.

demeurer (*verb*), to dwell, to live, to reside.

demi *m.*, **demie** *f.* (*adj.*), half; **une livre et demie,** one and a half pounds; **une demi-livre,** half a pound; **un litre et demi,** one and a half litres; **un demi-litre,** half a litre.

démolir (*verb*), to demolish, to pull down; to do away with; to break up, to smash; to overthrow.

dénoter (*verb*), to denote; to mark.

dénouer (*verb*), to untie, to undo; to solve, to unravel.

denrée *f.* (*noun*), commodity; (*pl.*) food-stuffs, produce.

dense (*adj.*), dense, thick.

dent *f.* (*noun*), tooth; prong (of fork).

dentelle *f.* (*noun*), lace.

dentiste *m.* (*noun*), dentist.

départ *m.* (*noun*), departure; start, take-off (of aircraft).

dépasser (*verb*), to move beyond, to go past, to overtake; to exceed.

se dépêcher (*verb*), to hasten, to hurry; **dépêchez-vous!** hurry up!

dépenser (*verb*), to spend.

dépensier *m.*, **-ière** *f.* (*noun & adj.*), spendthrift.

déployer (*verb*), to unfold, to spread out, to extend.

déposer (*verb*), to deposit; to depose (a king).

déprimé (*adj.*), depressed, dejected.

depuis (*prep.*), (*of time*) for, since (**je suis ici depuis six mois,** I have been here for six months); **depuis que** (*conj.*), since (**je suis ici depuis que la nuit est tombée,** I have been here since nightfall).

dérangé (*adj.*), deranged, (mentally) unbalanced.

déranger (*verb*), to disarrange; to inconvenience, to upset; to disturb, to trouble.

dernier *m.*, **-ière** *f.* (*noun & adj.*), last.

derrière (*adv. & prep.*), behind.

derrière *m.* (*noun*), back, rear (of a house); behind, backside.

des *m. & f. pl.*, of the (**les livres des enfants,** the books of the children); (*pl. of* **un** *and* **une**) some, any (**Avez-vous des cerises?** Have you any cherries? **Non, mais j'ai des fraises et des abricots,** No, but I have (some) strawberries and (some) apricots).

désagréable (*adj.*), unpleasant, offensive, disagreeable.

désappointer (*verb*), to disappoint.

désapprouver (*verb*), to disapprove of; to disagree with.

désastre *m.* (*noun*), disaster, catastrophe, tragedy.

désavantage *m.* (*noun*), disadvantage; handicap; drawback.

descendre (*verb*), to descend; to come down; to dismount; to alight; to sink.

désert *m.* (*noun*), desert.

désespérer (*verb*), to despair.

désespoir *m.* (*noun*), despair; desperation.

déshabiller (*verb*), to undress (someone); **se déshabiller,** to undress (oneself); to take off one's clothes.

désir *m.* (*noun*), desire, wish.

désirer (*verb*), to desire, to wish; **désirer intensément,** to crave; to long for.

désobéir (**à**) (*verb*), to disobey.

dessein *m.* (*noun*), project, plan; purpose.

dessert *m.* (*noun*), dessert (fruit or cake taken at the end of a meal).

dessin *m.* (*noun*), drawing, sketch; pattern, design; outline.

dessiner (*verb*), to draw, to sketch; to design.

dessous (*adv.*), below, underneath. *See also* **au-dessous.**

dessus (*adv.*), above, on top, on it. *See also* **au-dessus.**

destination *f.* (*noun*), destination.

détacher (*verb*), to unfasten, to untie, to detach.

détester (*verb*), to detest, to hate.

détruire (*verb*), to destroy, to ruin; to demolish (building, etc.).

deux *m.* (*noun & adj.*), two; second (**Philippe Deux,** Philip the Second; **le deux juin,** June the second); **les deux,** both; **deux par deux,** in twos.
deuxième (*noun & adj.*), second.
devant (*adv. & prep.*), in front (of), before.
devant *m.* (*noun*), front (of a building).
développer (*verb*), to develop, to improve.
devenir (*verb*), to become, to grow into, to change into.
deviner (*verb*), to guess, to sense, to foretell.
devoir *m.* (*noun*), duty; exercise, task; (*pl.*) homework, prep.
devoir (*verb*), to have to, to be obliged to, must; to owe.
dévoué (*adj.*), devoted, attached (to).
diable *m.* (*noun*), devil; two-wheeled luggage trolley.
diagramme *m.* (*noun*), diagram.
diamant *m.* (*noun*), diamond.
dictionnaire *m.* (*noun*), dictionary.
Dieu *m.* (*noun*), God; **les dieux,** the gods.
différence *f.* (*noun*), difference, disparity, discrepancy.
différent (*adj.*), different, unlike, dissimilar.
différer (*verb*), to disagree; to differ; to postpone, to delay.
difficile (*adj.*), difficult, hard; trying; finicky.
difficulté *f.* (*noun*), difficulty; trouble.
dignité *f.* (*noun*), dignity; **plein de dignité,** dignified.
dimanche *m.* (*noun*), Sunday.
diminuer (*verb*), to decrease, to shorten, to diminish.
dinde *f.* (*noun*), turkey hen, turkey (*as food*).
dindon *m.* (*noun*), turkey-cock.
dîner *m.* (*noun*), dinner.
dîner (*verb*), to dine, to have dinner.
dire (*verb*), to say; to tell; to recite; to mean (**cela ne me dit rien,** that means nothing to me).
directeur *m.*, **directrice** *f.* (*noun*), director; manager, manageress; head teacher.
direction *f.* (*noun*), direction, course, way; guidance; management.
diriger (*verb*), to direct, to steer, to guide; to conduct (an orchestra).
discerner (*verb*), to detect, to discern, to make out.
discrétion *f.* (*noun*), discretion.
discuter (*verb*), to discuss, to debate, to argue; to question, to dispute.
disparaître (*verb*), to disappear, to vanish.
dispensaire *m.* (*noun*), dispensary; welfare centre.
dispenser (*verb*), to dispense; to distribute; to excuse.
disposer (*verb*), to dispose, to arrange; **se disposer à faire quelque chose,** to make ready to do something, to compose oneself to do something.
disputer (*verb*), to dispute, to contest; **disputer quelque chose à quelqu'un,** to fight *or* contend with someone for something; **se disputer,** to quarrel, to row, to wrangle.
disque *m.* (*noun*), (*music*) record, disc; disc (of moon); (*sports*) discus.
distance *f.* (*noun*), distance.
distribution *f.* (*noun*), distribution; delivery (of letters).
divertir (*verb*), to entertain; to distract.
division *f.* (*noun*), division, partition, splitting up; branch, department.
dix *m.* (*noun & adj.*), ten; tenth (**Charles Dix,** Charles the Tenth; **le dix mars,** the tenth of March).
dix-huit *m.* (*noun & adj.*), eighteen; eighteenth (**le dix-huit décembre,** the eighteenth of December).
dixième (*noun & adj.*), tenth.
dix-neuf *m.* (*noun & adj.*), nineteen; nineteenth (**le dix-neuf janvier,** January the nineteenth).
dix-sept *m.* (*noun & adj.*), seventeen; seventeenth (**le dix-sept janvier,** the seventeenth of January).
dizaine *f.* (*noun*), (about) ten; **compter par dizaines,** to count in tens.
docteur *m.* (*noun*), doctor.
document *m.* (*noun*), document; record; evidence.

doigt *m.* (*noun*), finger; finger's breadth (**un doigt de vin,** a drop of wine); **doigt de pied,** toe.

dommage *m.* (*noun*), damage; pity (**quel dommage!** what a pity!).

don *m.* (*noun*), gift, present; gift, talent.

donc (*conj.*), therefore, so (**j'ai mal à l'estomac, donc je suis malade,** I have stomach-ache, therefore I am ill); (*adv.*), then, now (**dis donc, est-ce que c'est un chat?** tell me then (now), is it a cat?); well, now (**alors donc, comme je disais . . .,** well (now), as I was saying . . .).

donner (*verb*), to give, to bestow, to present; to yield, to bear (fruit).

dont (*pron.*), whose, of whom (**la dame dont je connais le fils,** the lady whose son I know); of which, about which (**le livre dont je parle,** the book about which I am speaking).

dorloter (*verb*), to fondle; to pamper, to coddle.

dormir (*verb*), to sleep, to be asleep; to lie idle.

dos *m.* (*noun*), back (of body); back (of book, house, clothing, etc.).

douane *f.* (*noun*), customs (house); customs duty.

double (*adj.*), double, twofold.

double *m.* (*noun*), duplicate.

douche *f.* (*noun*), shower; **prendre une douche,** to take a shower.

douillet *m.*, **-ette** *f.* (*adj.*), soft; cosy, snug.

douleur *f.* (*noun*), pain, ache; grief, sorrow.

douloureux *m.*, **-euse** *f.* (*adj.*), aching, painful, sore; sad, distressing, mournful.

doute *m.* (*noun*), doubt; **sans doute,** I dare say, no doubt.

doux *m.*, **douce** *f.* (*adj.*), gentle, mild; sweet; soft, smooth; quiet; calm; fresh (**eau douce,** fresh (as opposed to salt) water).

douze *m.* (*noun & adj.*), twelve; twelfth (**Louis Douze,** Louis the Twelfth; **le douze avril,** the twelfth of April).

douzième (*noun & adj.*), twelfth.

drap *m.* (*noun*), cloth; sheet, bed-sheet.

drapeau (*pl.* **drapeaux**) *m.* (*noun*), flag.

droit (*adj.*), straight; right (**levez le bras droit,** raise your right arm).

droit *m.* (*noun*), the right (to do something); law (**un étudiant en droit,** a law student).

droite *f.* (*noun*), right hand; right-hand side; **tourner à droite,** to turn to the right; **Paul marche à droite de son père,** Paul walks on the right of his father.

drôle (*adj.*), funny, amusing.

du, from the (**du matin au soir,** from morning till night); some (**donnez-moi du fromage s'il vous plaît,** please give me some cheese); of the, the . . .'s (**le stylo du garçon,** the boy's pen).

dur (*adj.*), hard (**le plancher est dur,** the floor is hard); (*adv.*), hard (**il travaille dur,** he works hard).

durer (*verb*), to last, to wear well, to endure.

E

eau (*pl.* **eaux**) *f.* (*noun*), water; **porter de l'eau à la rivière,** to carry coals to Newcastle.

écaille *f.* (*noun*), scale (of fish); shell (of oyster, etc.).

échanger (*verb*), to exchange, to barter, to interchange.

échapper (*verb*), to escape; to slip (**la tasse m'est échappée de la main,** the cup slipped out of my hand).

échelle *f.* (*noun*), ladder; scale, range.

échelon *m.* (*noun*), rung (of ladder).

éclair *m.* (*noun*), flash of lightning.

éclairer (*verb*), to light up (a room), to illuminate.

éclatement *m.* (*noun*), burst, explosion.

éclater (*verb*), to burst, to explode, to split.

écluse *f.* (*noun*), lock (on canal).

école *f.* (*noun*), school; college; academy.

écolier *m.*, **écolière** *f.* (*noun*), schoolboy, schoolgirl.

économie *f.* (*noun*), economy, saving, thrift.

économique (*adj.*), economic; economical.

écorce *f.* (*noun*), bark (of tree).

écouter (*verb*), to listen to, to heed.

écraser (*verb*), to crush, to grind, to press; to run over (in a car).

écrire (*verb*), to write, to write down; **s'écrire,** to be spelt (**comment cela s'écrit-il?** how is it spelt?).

écriteau (*pl.* **écriteaux**) *m.* (*noun*), notice-board, bulletin-board.

écriture *f.* (*noun*), handwriting; writing, script.

écrivain *m.* (*noun*), writer, author.

écrou *m.* (*noun*), nut (to go with bolt).

s'écrouler (*verb*), to collapse, to fall down.

écureuil *m.* (*noun*), squirrel.

écurie *f.* (*noun*), stable (for horses only).

éduquer (*verb*), to educate (a child), to bring up, to nurture; to train.

effacer (*verb*), to blot out, to rub out, to erase, to efface; to sponge out, to wipe out.

effort *m.* (*noun*), effort, exertion, attempt, endeavour.

effrayer (*verb*), to frighten, to scare.

égal (*adj.*), equal.

église *f.* (*noun*), church.

eh bien! (*interj.*): *see* **bien.**

éjecter (*verb*), to eject.

électricien *m.* (*noun*), electrician.

électricité *f.* (*noun*), electricity.

électrique (*adj.*), electric (current, shock); electrical (gadget, machine).

électrophone *m.* (*noun*), record-player.

éléphant *m.* (*noun*), elephant.

élévateur *m.* (*noun*), elevator, lift, hoist.

élève *m.* & *f.* (*noun*), pupil (of a school); student (at college).

élever (*verb*), to erect, to raise (*e.g.* a wall or building); to elevate; to bring up (children); **s'élever,** to soar, to ascend, to rise; to tower.

elle *f.* (*pron.*), she; it (**elle a dix ans,** she is ten years old; **regardez la fenêtre, est-elle fermée?** look at the window, is it shut?); her; it (**avec elle,** with her *or* it); **elle-même,** herself; **elles-mêmes,** themselves.

éluder (*verb*), to dodge (a difficulty); to evade (a question).

embardée *f.* (*noun*), lurch; skid; swerve; **faire une embardée,** to lurch; to skid; to swerve.

embarquer (*verb*), to embark; to ship (goods); to load.

emboutir (*verb*), to crash into; to stamp, to emboss.

embrassement *m.* (*noun*), hug, embrace.

embrasser (*verb*), to embrace, to hug, to kiss.

embrouiller (*verb*), to entangle; to embroil; to mix up (papers).

émerger (*verb*), to emerge.

émettre (*verb*), to emit, to eject; to issue (stamps); to give off (fumes, etc.).

emmener (*verb*), to take away, to take out (a person); **emmener quelqu'un au cinéma,** to take someone to the cinema.
empaqueter (*verb*), to pack, to wrap up.
empêcher (*verb*), to prevent, to hinder.
empereur *m.* (*noun*), emperor.
emplette *f.* (*noun*), purchase; **faire des emplettes,** to go shopping.
employé *m.*, **employée** *f.* (*noun*), employee, clerk, sales assistant.
employer (*verb*), to employ, to make use of, to use.
employeur *m.* (*noun*), employer.
emporter (*verb*), to take away, to carry off, to bear away.
empreinte *f.* (*noun*), imprint, impression (*e.g.* footprints).
emprunter (*verb*), to borrow (**à,** from).
en (*prep.*), (*place*) in (**en France,** in France); (*time*) during (a season) (**en été,** in (the) summer); of (**en bois,** (made) of wood); (*adv.*), from there (**Vous avez été à Paris? Oui, j'en arrive,** You have been to Paris? Yes, I've just come from there); (*pron.*), of it, of them (**les rues en sont pleines,** the streets are full of it *or* them); some, any (**j'en ai,** I have some; **je n'en ai pas,** I haven't any).
enclos *m.* (*noun*), enclosure, pen, paddock.
encore (*adv.*), more; again; still (**encore là,** still there).
encourager (*verb*), to encourage, to stimulate.
encre *f.* (*noun*), ink.
encrier *m.* (*noun*), inkwell.
endormi (*adj.*), asleep.
endormir (*verb*), to send to sleep, to lull to sleep; to numb; **s'endormir,** to fall asleep, to go to sleep.
endroit *m.* (*noun*), place, spot.
énergique (*adj.*), energetic, spirited.
enfant *m.* & *f.* (*noun*), child, infant.
enfermer (*verb*), to enclose; to shut in.
enfin (*adv.*), at last, finally; in a word, in short.
enflammé (*adj.*), ablaze; inflamed, angry.
enfoncer (*verb*), to drive in (a nail), to hammer in, to stick in; **s'enfoncer,** to sink in.
enlever (*verb*), to raise, to lift up; to remove; to take away, to carry off, to kidnap.
ennemi *m.* (*noun*), enemy, foe.
ennuyer (*verb*), to annoy, to pester; to bore stiff; **s'ennuyer,** to be bored.
enquête *f.* (*noun*), inquiry, investigation; inquest.
enregistrer (*verb*), to record; to register, to book.
enrichir (*verb*), to enrich; **s'enrichir,** to grow rich.
enrouler (*verb*), to wind round, to roll up, to wrap up.
enseigner (*verb*), to teach, to instruct.
ensemble (*adv.*), together; **ensemble** *m.* (*noun*), whole, entirety (**dans l'ensemble,** on the whole).
ensuite (*adv.*), next, then.
entendre (*verb*), to hear; to understand; **s'entendre à,** to know all about (**il s'entend aux autos,** he knows all about cars).
enterrer (*verb*), to bury; to forget, to shelve (some matter); to scrap (a project).
entier *m.*, **-ière** *f.* (*adj.*), whole, entire, complete.
entonnoir *m.* (*noun*), funnel.
entourer (*verb*), to surround; to edge; to fence in, to hem in.
entre (*prep.*), between; among.
entrée *f.* (*noun*), entrance; entry.
entrer (*verb*), to enter, to go in, to come in.
entretien *m.* (*noun*), conversation; interview.
énumérer (*verb*), to enumerate.
envahir (*verb*), to invade, to overrun, to occupy.
enveloppe *f.* (*noun*), envelope; wrapper; jacket, casing, cover.
envelopper (*verb*), to envelop, to wrap up.
envers (*prep.*), towards.
envie *f.* (*noun*), desire, longing (**avoir envie de,** to have a fancy for, to long for); envy.

envier (*verb*), to envy.
envieux *m.*, **-euse** *f.* (**de**) (*adj.*), envious (of).
envoyer (*verb*), to send (a letter); to throw (a ball); to deliver (a blow).
épais *m.*, **épaisse** *f.* (*adj.*), thick; dense (fog).
épaule *f.* (*noun*), shoulder.
épi *m.* (*noun*), ear (of corn); cluster (of diamonds).
épicerie *f.* (*noun*), grocer's shop, grocery.
épicier *m.*, **épicière** *f.* (*noun*), grocer, grocer's wife.
épingle *f.* (*noun*), pin; **épingle de sûreté,** safety-pin.
épisode *m.* (*noun*), episode.
éplucher (*verb*), to clean (vegetables) (*general sense*), *e.g.* to peel potatoes, shell peas, clean lettuce.
éponge *f.* (*noun*), sponge.
équiper (*verb*), to equip, to fit out.
équivalent *m.* (*noun*), equivalent.
erreur *f.* (*noun*), mistake, error.
escalier *m.* (*noun*), stairs, stairway; **escalier roulant,** escalator.
escargot *m.* (*noun*), snail.
espace *m.* (*noun*), space.
espérance *f.* (*noun*), hope; expectation.
espérer (*verb*), to hope.
espièglerie *f.* (*noun*), mischievousness; prank, trick.
esprit *m.* (*noun*), spirit (**le Saint-Esprit,** the Holy Spirit), ghost; mind, disposition; wit (**il a de l'esprit,** he is witty).
esquiver (*verb*), to elude, to dodge (a blow); **s'esquiver,** to slip away, to steal off, to make oneself scarce.
essayer (*verb*), to try, to test; to try on; to attempt, to endeavour.
essence *f.* (*noun*), petrol; essence, pith (of a matter).
essentiel *m.*, **-ielle** *f.* (*adj.*), essential.
essuie-mains *m.* (*noun*), hand-towel, face-towel.
essuyer (*verb*), to wipe, to dust, to mop.
est *m.* (*noun*), east.
est: *part of* **être.**
est-ce que . . . ?: *used to form questions* (**est-ce qu'il fait froid?** is it cold?).
estomac *m.* (*noun*), stomach.
et (*conj.*), and.
étable *f.* (*noun*), cowshed.
établir (*verb*), to establish, to set up; to prove.
établissement *m.* (*noun*), establishment; installation.
étage *m.* (*noun*), storey, floor.
étagère *f.* (*noun*), set of shelves.
étalage *m.* (*noun*), display, window-dressing; stand, stall.
étaler (*verb*), to display, to show off, to parade.
étang *m.* (*noun*), pond.
état *m.* (*noun*), state, country (**homme d'état,** statesman); state, condition (**état d'âme,** mood).
et caetera (*phrase*), et cetera, and so on.
été *m.* (*noun*), summer.
éteindre (*verb*), to extinguish, to put out, to switch off (the light).
éternuement *m.* (*noun*), sneeze.
éternuer (*verb*), to sneeze.
étiqueter (*verb*), to label; to put a price tag on.
étiquette *f.* (*noun*), label; etiquette (code of conduct).
étoffe *f.* (*noun*), material, fabric.
étoile *f.* (*noun*), star; asterisk.
étonnant (*adj.*), astonishing.
étonner (*verb*), to surprise, to amaze, to astonish.
étrange (*adj.*), strange, queer, odd.
étranger *m.*, **-ère** *f.* (*adj.*), foreign (person); strange (house).
étranger[1] *m.* (*noun*), foreign parts; **un voyage à l'étranger,** a trip abroad.
étranger[2] *m.*, **-ère** *f.* (*noun*), foreigner, alien.
être (*verb*), to be, to exist.
étreindre (*verb*), to squeeze, to embrace; to hug; to grasp, to clutch.
étreinte *f.* (*noun*), embrace, hug; clasp, grip.
étroit (*adj.*), narrow; tight (clothes); strict (rules).
étude *f.* (*noun*), study, investigation; (*school*) prep.

étudiant *m.*, **étudiante** *f.* (*noun*), student, undergraduate.
étudier (*verb*), to study, to prepare (lessons), to learn; to investigate.
étuve *f.* (*noun*), drying-room; drying-cupboard.
eux *m. pl.* (*pron.*), they, them (**c'est eux,** it is they, it is them; **avec eux,** with them); **eux-mêmes** *m.pl.* (*pron.*), themselves.
évaluation *f.* (*noun*), valuation; estimate.
éveiller (*verb*), to awake, to wake up (someone); **s'éveiller,** to awaken.
éventail *m.* (*noun*), fan.
évidence *f.* (*noun*), evidence; conspicuousness.
évier *m.* (*noun*), (kitchen) sink.
éviter (*verb*), to avoid; to elude, to dodge (someone).
exact (*adj.*), exact; punctual; right.
exagérer (*verb*), to exaggerate, to overstate.
examiner (*verb*), to examine; to investigate.
excaver (*verb*), to excavate, to dig.
excellent (*adj.*), excellent, first-class.
excepté (*prep.*), except for.
exciter (*verb*), to excite; to spur on; to rouse.
excuse *f.* (*noun*), excuse, pretext.
excuser (*verb*), to excuse (a fault), to pardon; **s'excuser,** to apologize; to decline an invitation.
exécuter (*verb*), to execute; to carry out, to perform.
exemple *m.* (*noun*), example; warning; precedent; **par exemple,** for instance, for example.
exercice *m.* (*noun*), exercise; training.
exiger (*verb*), to demand; to claim.
exonérer (**de**) (*verb*), to exonerate (from); to acquit.
explication *f.* (*noun*), explanation, reason.
expliquer (*verb*), to explain; to account for.
explorer (*verb*), to explore; to examine (documents).
exploser (*verb*), to explode, to burst, to blow up.
explosion *f.* (*noun*), explosion, blowing up.
exporter (*verb*), to export.
exposer (*verb*), to expose; to display, to show, to exhibit (animals, works of art, etc.).
exposition *f.* (*noun*), exhibition, display, show; exposition.
exprimer (*verb*), to express (an idea); to squeeze out, to crush out.
extérieur *m.* (*noun & adj.*), exterior, outside; **à l'extérieur,** on the outside; **à l'extérieur de la gare,** outside the station.
extraordinaire (*adj.*), extraordinary; odd, surprising.

F

fable *f.* (*noun*), fable.
fabrication *f.* (*noun*), manufacture (**de fabrication française,** of French manufacture, made in France); forgery.
fabriquer (*verb*), to manufacture, to make, to produce; to forge (money, etc.).
en face (*adv.*), opposite; **face à** (*prep.*), facing; **en face de** (*prep.*), facing; opposite.
fâché (*adj.*), angry, annoyed; **être fâché avec quelqu'un,** to have fallen out with someone.
facile (*adj.*), easy.
facilement (*adv.*), easily.
façon *f.* (*noun*), fashion; way; a means (of doing something) (**je pourrai vous voir d'une façon ou d'une autre,** I shall be able to see you by some means or other); **de toute façon,** anyhow, in any case; **à sa façon,** in his own way, after his own manner; **de cette façon,** in this way, in this manner (**l'homme va prendre un taxi. De cette façon il arrivera chez lui plus vite,** the man is going to take a taxi. In this way he will arrive home more quickly); **de façon que,** so as to, so that (**parlez lentement de façon qu'on vous comprenne,** speak slowly so as to be understood).
facteur *m.* (*noun*), postman.
faible (*adj.*), weak, feeble, slight.
faillir (*verb*), to fail.
faim *f.* (*noun*), hunger; **avoir faim,** to be hungry.
faire (*verb*), to make (**le boulanger fait le pain,** the baker is making bread); to do (**Henri fait ses devoirs,** Henry is doing his homework); to cause (**Pierre a fait tomber la bouteille,** Peter has caused the bottle to fall); to be (**il fait beau,** it is fine; **il fait chaud,** it is warm).
fait *m.* (*noun*), act, deed; fact; occurrence.
falaise *f.* (*noun*), cliff.
falloir (*verb*), to have to, to be obliged to (**il faut que cette dent soit arrachée,** that tooth will have to come out; **il m'a fallu obéir,** I was obliged to obey); to need, to require (**j'ai tout ce qu'il me faut,** I have all that I need).
famuex *m.*, **-euse** *f.* (*adj.*), famous; first-rate (idea).
familier *m.*, **-ière** *f.* (*adj.*), familiar, well-known, intimate.
famille *f.* (*noun.*), family; relatives, kindred; household.
fantastique (*adj.*), fantastic.
fardeau (*pl.* **fardeaux**) *m.* (*noun*), load, burden.
farine *f.* (*noun*), flour, meal.
fatigue *f.* (*noun*), fatigue, tiredness, strain, weariness.
fatigué (*adj.*), tired, fatigued, weary.
fausseté *f.* (*noun*), falseness; untruth.
faut: *see* **falloir.**
faute *f.* (*noun*), fault, misdeed, error; lack, want.
fauteuil *m.* (*noun*), armchair, easy-chair.
faux *m.*, **fausse** *f.* (*adj.*), false, untrue, wrong, mistaken.
faveur *f.* (*noun*), favour.
fée *f.* (*noun*), fairy.
feindre (*verb*), to pretend, to feign, to simulate, to sham.
fêler (*verb*), to crack (a cup, etc.).
féliciter (*verb*), to congratulate.
femme *f.* (*noun*), woman; wife; **femme de ménage,** charwoman, daily help.
fenêtre *f.* (*noun*), window.
fer *m.* (*noun*), iron; **fer à repasser,** (laundry) iron.
ferme *f.* (*noun*), farm.
fermer (*verb*), to close.
fermier *m.* (*noun*), farmer.
féroce (*adj.*), fierce, ferocious.
fête *f.* (*noun*), feast, festival, fête.
feu (*pl.* **feux**) *m.* (*noun*), fire (in grate); fire (of guns); **en feu,** ablaze.

feuille *f.* (*noun*), leaf (of plant); leaf, sheet (of paper).
février *m.* (*noun*), February.
ficelle *f.* (*noun*), string, twine, thread.
fiche *f.* (*noun*), index-card, filing-card.
fidèle (*adj.*), faithful, loyal.
fièvre *f.* (*noun*), fever; excitement, restlessness.
figure *f.* (*noun*), face (of person); look, appearance.
fil *m.* (*noun*), thread; grain (of wood); edge (of blade); **fil de fer,** wire.
filet *m.* (*noun*), net (**filet de pêche,** fishing-net); string bag; luggage rack.
fille *f.* (*noun*), daughter; girl.
film *m.* (*noun*), film.
fils *m.* (*noun*), son.
fin *f.* (*noun*), end; aim, object.
finir (*verb*), to finish, to end, to stop.
flamme *f.* (*noun*), flame; **en flammes,** ablaze, in flames.
flanelle *f.* (*noun*), flannel.
flâner (*verb*), to stroll about; to loiter.
flèche *f.* (*noun*), arrow; spire (of church); side (of bacon).
fléchette *f.* (*noun*), dart; **jouer aux fléchettes,** to play darts.
fleur *f.* (*noun*), flower; blossom.
fleuriste *m.* & *f.* (*noun*), florist.
fleuve *m.* (*noun*), river (which flows into the sea).
flottant (*adj.*), floating; flowing.
flotter (*verb*), to float.
foi *f.* (*noun*), faith; trust; word (of honour).
foin *m.* (*noun*), hay.
foire *f.* (*noun*), fair.
fois *f.* (*noun*), time, occasion; **une fois,** once.
foncé (*adj.*), dark (colour).
fond *m.* (*noun*), end, bottom (of an object) (**le fond du verre,** the bottom of the glass).
fondamental (*adj.*), basic, fundamental.
fondre (*verb*), to melt (metal); to thaw (ice); to blend (colours).
fontaine *f.* (*noun*), fountain.
force *f.* (*noun*), force, power, strength.
forcer (*verb*), to force, to break open, to break into; to strain; to compel.
forêt *f.* (*noun*), forest.
forge *f.* (*noun*), forge; smithy; (*pl.*) ironworks.
forger (*verb*), to forge (iron); to forge (document); to invent (*e.g.* a new word).
forgeron *m.* (*noun*), (black)smith.
forme *f.* (*noun*), form, shape, figure; appearance, aspect.
formidable (*adj.*), formidable; stupendous; smashing.
fort (*adj.*), strong; considerable; loud; (*adv.*), very, extremely.
fortifier (*verb*), to fortify; to strengthen.
fortune *f.* (*noun*), fortune, wealth; chance.
fortuné (*adj.*), fortunate; wealthy.
fosse *f.* (*noun*), pit; den.
fossé *m.* (*noun*), ditch, trench, drain; breach, gulf.
fou (**fol**), (*pl.* **fous**) *m.*, **folle** *f.* (*adj.*), mad; (*noun*), madman, madwoman, lunatic.
foudre *f.* (*noun*), lightning; thunderbolt.
foule *f.* (*noun*), crowd, mob, throng.
four *m.* (*noun*), oven.
fourchette *f.* (*noun*), fork.
fourneau (*pl.* **fourneaux**) *m.* (*noun*), cooker; kitchen-range; **fourneau à gaz,** gas-cooker; **fourneau à charbon,** solid-fuel cooker.
fournir (*verb*), to furnish, to provide, to supply.
fourrure *f.* (*noun*), fur; lining.
foyer *m.* (*noun*), hearth; fireplace; foyer.
fracas *m.* (*noun*), din; (sound of a) crash.
fracture *f.* (*noun*), fracture; breaking.
fragile (*adj.*), fragile; weak, frail.
fragment *m.* (*noun*), fr agment.
frais *m.*, **fraîche** *f.* (*adj.*), fresh; cool; freshly gathered (fruit, vegetables).
fraise *f.* (*noun*), strawberry.
franc *m.* (*noun*), franc (*French money*).
franc *m.*, **franche** *f.* (*adj.*), frank, sincere, straightforward.
français (*adj.*), French; **Français** *m.*, **Française** *f.* (*noun*), Frenchman, Frenchwoman; **les Français,** the French; **le français** (*noun*), the French language; **traduire en français,** to translate into French.

France *f.* (*noun*), France.
frapper (*verb*), to hit, to strike; to type (a letter).
frayeur *f.* (*noun*), fright, fear.
fréquemment (*adv.*), frequently.
fréquent (*adj.*), frequent; rapid (pulse).
frère *m.* (*noun*), brother.
friandise *f.* (*noun*), delicacy, dainty, tit-bit.
frire (*verb*), to fry; **pommes frites,** chips.
friser (*verb*), to curl.
frivole (*adj.*), frivolous; flighty.
froid (*adj.*), cold; cool; frigid; **avoir froid,** to be cold; **prendre froid,** to catch cold; **il fait froid,** it is cold.
froid *m.* (*noun*), cold.
fromage *m.* (*noun*), cheese.
froment *m.* (*noun*), wheat.
front *m.* (*noun*), forehead; front.
frontière *f.* (*noun*), frontier, border.
frotter (*verb*), to rub, to polish.
fruit *m.* (*noun*), fruit.
fruitier *m.* (*noun*), fruiterer, greengrocer.
fuir (*verb*), to flee; to escape.
fuite *f.* (*noun*), flight; escape.
fumée *f.* (*noun*), smoke; steam (from cooking).
fumer (*verb*), to smoke; to steam.
fureur *f.* (*noun*), rage, fury, passion; **être en fureur,** to be in a rage.
furieux *m.*, **-euse** *f.* (*adj.*), furious; wild (storm), raging (torrent).
fusée *f.* (*noun*), rocket.
fusil *m.* (*noun*), gun.
futile (*adj.*), futile, frivolous (person); trifling (incident); idle (wish).
futur (*adj.*), future; (*noun*), future (tense).

G

gage *m.* (*noun*), pawn, security; pledge; (*pl.*) wages.

gagner (*verb*), to earn; to make money; to reach (a destination); to gain (weight); to save (time); to win (a race).

gai (*adj.*), cheerful, merry, gay; bright (colour).

galet *m.* (*noun*), pebble (on beach); (*pl.*) shingle.

galette *f.* (*noun*), pancake, girdle-cake, griddle-cake; ship's biscuit; **plat comme une galette,** flat as a pancake.

gamin *m.* (*noun*), urchin, street-boy, kid.

gant *m.* (*noun*), glove.

garage *m.* (*noun*), garage; **garage en bord de route,** lay-by.

garagiste *m.* (*noun*), garage proprietor, garage man.

garçon *m.* (*noun*), boy, lad, young fellow; **garçon (de café),** waiter.

garde *m.* (*noun*), guard; watchman, keeper.

garde-feu *m.* (*noun*), firescreen; fender.

garder (*verb*), to guard, to protect, to watch over, to care for; to preserve, to keep.

gare *f.* (*noun*), station.

gare! (*interj.*), beware!

garer (*verb*), to park, to garage (a car).

gaspiller (*verb*), to waste (food), to squander (money), to fritter away (time).

gâteau (*pl.* **gâteaux**) *m.* (*noun*), cake; sweet pudding; **gâteau de miel,** honey-comb.

gauche (*adj.*), left (hand, etc.); clumsy, awkward; **gauche** *f.* (*noun*), left hand; left-hand side; **à gauche,** on the left; **Henri marche à gauche de son père,** Henry walks on the left of his father.

gaz *m.* (*noun*), gas; **ouvrir les gaz,** to open the throttle, to step on the gas.

géant *m.* (*noun*), giant.

gel *m.* (*noun*), frost; freezing.

gelée *f.* (*noun*), frost; jelly; **gelée blanche,** hoar-frost.

geler (*verb*), to freeze, to change into ice; to solidify.

gendarme *m.* (*noun*), soldier of the police militia; constable.

gendre *m.* (*noun*), son-in-law.

gêner (*verb*), to hinder, to impede, to be in the way.

généreux *m.*, **-euse** *f.* (*adj.*), generous, bountiful.

genou (*pl.* **genoux**) *m.* (*noun*), knee.

genre *m.* (*noun*), sort, kind; race, family; fashion, taste.

gens *m.* & *f. pl.* (*noun*), people, folk, men and women.

gentil *m.*, **-ille** *f.* (*adj.*), kind, nice, pleasing, amiable.

germer (*verb*), to germinate; to sprout; to spring up.

glace *f.* (*noun*), ice; looking-glass, mirror; ice-cream.

glacer (*verb*), to chill, to freeze; to ice (a cake).

gland *m.* (*noun*), acorn.

glissade *f.* (*noun*), slide (on ice); slip.

glisser (*verb*), to slide, to glide.

glissoire *f.* (*noun*), slide (on ice).

gloire *f.* (*noun*), glory, honour, fame.

gloussement *m.* (*noun*), chuckle (of person); cluck (of hen); gobble (of turkey).

glousser (*verb*), to chuckle; to cluck; to gobble.

gomme *f.* (*noun*), gum; eraser; india-rubber.

goulot *m.* (*noun*), neck (of bottle); gullet.

goût *m.* (*noun*), taste, flavour.

goûter (*verb*), to taste, to sample, to catch the flavour of; to take a snack.

goûter *m.* (*noun*), snack, light meal.

goutte *f.* (*noun*), drop; blob.

gouvernement *m.* (*noun*), government; administration; cabinet (in politics).

grain *m.* (*noun*), grain (of wheat, coffee, etc.); bead (of necklace).

graine *f.* (*noun*), seed.
graisse *f.* (*noun*), fat (of meat); fatness (of person); oil, grease.
graisser (*verb*), to oil, to grease, to lubricate.
grand (*adj.*), large, big; tall; great (highly regarded).
grandir (*verb*), to grow up, to grow (in wisdom); to grow tall; to increase.
grand-mère *f.* (*noun*), grandmother.
grand-père *m.* (*noun*), grandfather.
grands-parents *m. pl.* (*noun*), grandparents.
grange *f.* (*noun*), barn.
gras *m.*, **grasse** *f.* (*adj.*), fat, fleshy, stout.
gratis (*adv.*), free of charge.
gratter (*verb*), to scratch, to rake, to scrape.
gratuitement (*adv.*), gratuitously, free of charge, for nothing.
grave (*adj.*), serious, grave, solemn.
grenier *m.* (*noun*), loft, lumber-room, attic.
grenouille *f.* (*noun*), frog.
griffe *f.* (*noun*), claw, talon.
griffer (*verb*), to claw, to scratch, to seize in one's claws.
grignoter (*verb*), to nibble; to pick at.
grimper (*verb*), to climb, to scramble up, to clamber.
gris (*adj.*), grey; dull.
gros *m.*, **grosse** *f.* (*adj.*), big, large; fat, stout; strong; thick; heavy.
grossir (*verb*), to magnify, to enlarge, to make bigger; to swell.
groupe *m.* (*noun*), group (of people); clump (of trees).
grue *f.* (*noun*), crane (bird *or* machine).
guéri (*adj.*), well, cured, better.
guérir (*verb*), to heal (a wound), to cure (someone of something); to recover, to be cured.
guerre *f.* (*noun*), war, warfare.
guide[1] *m.* (*noun*), guide; guide-book.
guide[2] *f.* (*noun*), girl-guide.
guider (*verb*), to lead or guide (a person); to drive (a vehicle); to steer (a boat).
guitare *f.* (*noun*), guitar.

H

NOTE: *Words beginning with an aspirate* h *are marked with an asterisk.*

habillement *m.* (*noun*), clothing, clothes.
habiller (*verb*), to dress, to clothe; **s'habiller,** to dress oneself, to get dressed; to buy one's clothes (**chez,** at).
habit *m.* (*noun*), outfit, dress, costume; coat; (*pl.*) clothes.
habitation *f.* (*noun*), dwelling, habitation.
habiter (*verb*), to reside, to dwell, to live; to inhabit.
habitude *f.* (*noun*), habit, custom, practice; **d'habitude,** generally, usually, as a rule.
***hache** *f.* (*noun*), axe.
***hachette** *f.* (*noun*), hatchet.
***haie** *f.* (*noun*), hedge.
***haine** *f.* (*noun*), hatred, detestation.
***haïr** (*verb*), to hate, to detest, to loathe.
***halte** *f.* (*noun*), stop, stopping-place; halt.
hameçon *m.* (*noun*), fish-hook.
***haricot** *m.* (*noun*), bean.
***hasard** *m.* (*noun*), chance, luck; risk, danger, hazard.
***hâte** *f.* (*noun*), haste; quickness.
***hâter** (*verb*), to hurry on, to speed up; **se hâter,** to hasten, to make haste, to hurry.
***hâtif** *m.*, **-ive** *f.* (*adj.*), hasty, hurried; cursory.
***haut** (*adj.*), high, tall, lofty, towering; loud (sound); **en haut** (*adv.*), upstairs, above.
***hauteur** *f.* (*noun*), height; elevation.
***hein!** (*interj.*), what? (*expressing surprise*); *sometimes* = **n'est-ce pas?**
herbe *f.* (*noun*), grass; herb; **mauvaises herbes,** weeds.
hésiter (*verb*), to hesitate, to waver, to falter (when speaking).
heure *f.* (*noun*), hour; time; period; **de bonne heure,** early; **à la bonne heure!** well done! splendid!
heureusement (*adv.*), happily; successfully; **heureusement que . . . ,** it is a good thing that . . .
heureux *m.*, **-euse** *f.* (*adj.*), happy; glad, delighted; lucky.
***hibou** (*pl.* **hiboux**) *m.* (*noun*), owl.
hier (*adv.*), yesterday.
hindou (*adj.* & *noun*), Hindu.
hirondelle *f.* (*noun*), swallow (*bird*).
histoire *f.* (*noun*), history; story.
hiver *m.* (*noun*), winter.
homme *m.* (*noun*), man; mankind.
honnête (*adj.*), honest; decent; reasonable.
honneur *m.* (*noun*), honour.
hôpital (*pl.* **hôpitaux**) *m.* (*noun*), hospital.
horloge *f.* (*noun*), public clock; clock (with pendulum).
horrible (*adj.*), horrible, horrid; gruesome.
hôtel *m.* (*noun*), hotel; **Hôtel de Ville,** Town Hall.
***houx** *m.* (*noun*), holly.
huile *f.* (*noun*), oil.
***huit** *m.* (*noun* & *adj.*), eight; eighth (**le huit juin,** the eighth of June).
***huitième** (*noun* & *adj.*), eighth.
humide (*adj.*), damp, humid, dank, wet, moist.

I

ici (*adv.*), here.
idée *f.* (*noun*), idea, notion.
identifier (*verb*), to identify; **s'identifier,** to identify oneself (**à, avec,** with).
identité *f.* (*noun*), identity; **carte** *f.* **d'identité,** identity card.
il *m.* (*pron.*), he; it.
île *f.* (*noun*), island, isle.
illuminer (*verb*), to illuminate, to light up; to enlighten.
illustrer (*verb*), to illustrate (a book); to make famous.
ils *m. pl.* (*pron.*), they.
image *f.* (*noun*), picture, image; likeness; (mental) impression.
imaginer (*verb*), to imagine, to fancy; to invent (a plan).
imiter (*verb*), to imitate, to copy; to mimic.
immense (*adj.*), immense, huge, vast.
imparfait (*adj.*), faulty, defective, imperfect; unfinished.
impassable (*adj.*), impassable (river).
impliquer (*verb*), to implicate; to imply.
important (*adj.*), important, considerable, outstanding.
importer (*verb*), to matter, to be of importance; **n'importe,** never mind; **n'importe quel,** any (**il peut venir à n'importe quelle date,** he can come at any time); **n'importe qui,** anybody (**n'importe qui peut faire ce travail,** anybody can do this work); **n'importe quoi,** anything (**il ferait n'importe quoi pour moi,** he would do anything for me).
impossible (*adj.*), impossible.
imprimer (*verb*), to print; to impress; to stamp; to mark.
inactif *m.*, **-ive** *f.* (*adj.*), inactive; idle.
incapable (*adj.*), incapable, incompetent, inefficient.
incendie *m.* (*noun*), fire, conflagration.
inciter (*verb*), to incite; to spur on.
incliner (*verb*), to tilt, to tip, to slope; to bend (the body).
incommode (*adj.*), inconvenient, untimely; uncomfortable.
indicateur *m.* (*noun*), indicator; signpost; (railway) time-table.
indien *m.*, **-ienne** *f.* (*adj. & noun*), Indian (of India, of America).
indubitablement (*adj.*), doubtless, indubitably.
industrie *f.* (*noun*), industry; manufacture.
industriel *m.* (*noun*), manufacturer, industrialist.
industriel *m.*, **-ielle** *f.* (*adj.*), industrial, manufacturing.
inégal (*adj.*), uneven, rough (ground); unequal, irregular (movement).
inexact (*adj.*), inaccurate, inexact.
infirmier *m.*, **-ière** *f.* (*noun*), nurse; medical orderly.
infortune *f.* (*noun*), misfortune, trouble.
ingénieur *m.* (*noun*), engineer.
inhaler (*verb*), to inhale, to breathe in.
inquiétude *f.* (*noun*), anxiety; restlessness.
insecte *m.* (*noun*), insect.
insister (*verb*), to insist; to press (a point).
installer (*verb*), to install; to equip, to fit out (a workshop); to furnish (a house); to put in (electricity); **s'installer,** to install oneself; to settle oneself.
instant *m.* (*noun*), instant, moment.
instruire (*verb*), to educate; to instruct, to teach; to inform; **s'instruire,** to educate oneself.
intact (*adj.*), whole, undamaged, intact.
intelligence *f.* (*noun*), understanding; intelligence; intellect.
intelligent (*adj.*), intelligent, clever.
interdire (*verb*), to forbid; to prohibit; to veto.
intéressant (*adj.*), interesting, attractive.
intéresser (*verb*), to interest, to concern, to appeal to; **s'intéresser à,** to be interested in; to concern oneself with.

intérieur *m.* (*noun*), inside; interior (of house); **à l'intérieur,** inside, on the inside, within.
interpréter (*verb*), to interpret, to explain, to make clear; to translate.
interrompre (*verb*), to interrupt, to break (a journey).
intervalle *m.* (*noun*), interval; period (of time); gap, space; **dans l'intervalle,** meanwhile.
inutile (*adj.*), useless; unnecessary, needless.
inventer (*verb*), to invent; to make up.
investigation *f.* (*noun*), investigation; inquiry.
irriter (*verb*), to irritate; to make angry; to inflame (the skin).

J

jaloux *m.*, **-ouse** *f.* (*adj.*), jealous; envious (**de,** of).
jamais (*adv.*), ever; never, not ever (**elle ne lit jamais,** she never reads; **jamais!** never!); **pour jamais,** for ever; **jamais plus,** never again.
jambe *f.* (*noun*), leg.
jambon *m.* (*noun*), ham.
janvier *m.* (*noun*), January.
jardin *m.* (*noun*), garden; **jardin d'agrément,** flower garden; **jardin potager,** vegetable garden.
jarre *f.* (*noun*), earthenware jar.
jaune (*adj.*), yellow; **jaune** *m.* (*noun*), yellow; **jaune d'œuf,** yolk of egg.
javelot *m.* (*noun*), javelin.
je (*pron.*), I.
jetée *f.* (*noun*), jetty, pier; breakwater.
jeter (*verb*), to throw, to toss, to cast.
jeu (*pl.* **jeux**) *m.* (*noun*), game, play, sport; acting (of an actor).
jeudi *m.* (*noun*), Thursday.
jeune (*adj.*), young, youthful; **jeune homme,** young man; **jeune fille,** young lady, girl; **jeunes gens** (*always pl.*), young people, young men, youths.
joie *f.* (*noun*), joy, gladness, delight.
joindre (*verb*), to join; to unite; to weld.
joli (*adj.*), pretty, good-looking.
jongleur *m.* (*noun*), juggler.
joue *f.* (*noun*), cheek (of face).
jouer (*verb*), to play (**jouer aux cartes,** to play cards; **jouer du piano,** to play the piano); to gamble (for money).
jouet *m.* (*noun*), toy, plaything.
jouir de (*verb*), to enjoy (health, holiday).
jour *m.* (*noun*), day; daytime, daylight (**il fait jour,** it is daylight).
journal (*pl.* **journaux**) *m.* (*noun*), newspaper.
journaliste *m.* & *f.* (*noun*), journalist; reporter.
journée *f.* (*noun*), day, daytime (**pendant la journée,** in the daytime).
joyeux *m.*, **-euse** *f.* (*adj.*), cheerful, merry, gay, joyful.
juge *m.* (*noun*), judge, justice, magistrate; umpire.
juger (*verb*), to judge, to decide; to try (a case in court).
juillet *m.* (*noun*), July.
juin *m.* (*noun*), June.
jumeau (*pl.* **jumeaux**) *m.*, **jumelle** *f.* (*noun* & *adj.*), twin; **maisons jumelles,** semi-detached houses.
jupe *f.* (*noun*), skirt.
jupon *m.* (*noun*), petticoat; slip.
jus *m.* (*noun*), juice; gravy.
jusque (*prep.*), up to, as far as (**compter jusqu'à dix,** to count up to ten; **jusque-là,** up to that point); until (**jusqu'à neuf heures,** until nine o'clock).
juste (*adj.*), fair, just; right; exact.
justement (*adv.*), justly, rightly; precisely, exactly.
justice *f.* (*noun*), justice.

K

kangourou *m.* (*noun*), kangaroo.

kilo (**kilogramme**) *m.* (*noun*), kilogramme (= *approx.* 2 lbs. 3 ozs.).

kilomètre *m.* (*noun*), kilometre (= *approx.* $\frac{5}{8}$ mile).

L

l' *m.* *& f.*, **la** *f.* (*definite article & pron.*) : *see* **le.**

là (*adv.*), there; **là-bas** (*adv.*), over there, yonder; **là-dedans** (*adv.*), in there, within; **là-dessous** (*adv.*), under there, underneath; **là-dessus** (*adv.*), on that; thereupon (**là-dessus, il est parti,** thereupon, he left); **là-haut** (*adv.*), up there; upstairs.

labourer (*verb*), to plough.

laboureur *m.* (*noun*), ploughman.

lac *m.* (*noun*), lake.

lacer (*verb*), to lace up (shoes).

lacet *m.* (*noun*), boot-lace, shoe-lace.

lâche *m.* (*noun*), coward; (*adj.*), cowardly.

lâcher (*verb*), to let out; to slacken; to release.

laid (*adj.*), ugly.

laine *f.* (*noun*), wool.

laisser (*verb*), to leave (behind) (**j'ai laissé mon chapeau dans la voiture,** I left my hat in the car); to leave out, to omit; to give away; to let, to allow; **laisser entrer,** to let in, to admit.

lait *m.* (*noun*), milk.

laitier *m.* (*noun*), milkman, dairyman.

lame *f.* (*noun*), blade (of razor, knife).

lampe *f.* (*noun*), lamp.

lancer (*verb*), to throw, to hurl, to cast; to drop (a bomb); to launch (a ship); **lancer un appel,** to appeal.

langage *m.* (*noun*), language, speech (in general).

langue *f.* (*noun*), tongue; language (of a particular country).

lapin *m.* (*noun*), rabbit.

lard *m.* (*noun*), fat (of pork); bacon.

large (*adj.*), wide, broad, sweeping.

larme *f.* (*noun*), tear (from the eye).

lavabo *m.* (*noun*), wash-basin; (school) lavatory.

laver (*verb*), to wash, to clean; **se laver,** to wash (oneself).

le (**l'**) *m.*, **la** (**l'**) *f.*, **les** *pl.* (*definite article*), the (**le garçon,** the boy; **la chaise,** the chair; **l'île,** the island; **les oiseaux,** the birds); (*pron.*), him; her; it; them (**je le vois,** I see him, it; **le loup la mange,** the wolf eats her, it, up; **regardez-les,** look at them).

lécher (*verb*), to lick.

leçon *f.* (*noun*), lesson.

léger *m.*, **-ère** *f.* (*adj.*), light(weight); mild (drink); weak (tea); light, frivolous (person).

légume *m.* (*noun*), vegetable.

lent (*adj.*), slow.

lentement (*adv.*), slowly, deliberately.

lequel (*pl.* **lesquels**) *m.*, **laquelle** (*pl.* **lesquelles**) *f.* (*relative pron.*), which (**le banc sur lequel je suis assis,** the bench on which I am sitting); who, whom (**la dame avec laquelle elle était sortie,** the lady with whom she had gone out); (*interrogative pron.*), which (one) (**lequel de ces deux garçons est le plus grand?** which of these two boys is the taller?).

les: *see* **le.**

lessive *f.* (*noun*), washing (**faire la lessive,** to do the washing); detergent.

lettre *f.* (*noun*), letter.

leur (*possessive adj.*), their (**leur fille,** their daughter; **leurs livres,** their books).

leur (*personal pron.*), (to) them (**montrez-leur le jardin,** show them the garden); (*possessive pron.*), **le leur, la leur, les leurs,** theirs (**notre maison a plus de chambres que la leur,** our house has more rooms than theirs).

levé (*adj.*), up (standing); raised.

lever (*verb*), to raise, to lift; to heave; **se lever,** to arise, to get up, to stand up; *m.* (*noun*), **le lever du soleil,** sunrise.

lèvre *f.* (*noun*), lip.

libération *f.* (*noun*), liberation; release (of a prisoner).

libérer (*verb*), to set free, to liberate.

liberté *f.* (*noun*), freedom, liberty.

librairie *f.* (*noun*), bookshop.

libre (*adj.*), free; unoccupied.
lieu (*pl.* **lieux**) *m.* (*noun*), place, locality, spot, site.
ligne *f.* (*noun*), line, row; fishing-line.
limonade *f.* (*noun*), lemonade.
linge *m.* (*noun*), linen; underwear.
lion *m.*, **lionne** *f.* (*noun*), lion, lioness.
liquide *m.* (*noun*), liquid, fluid.
lire (*verb*), to read.
lit *m.* (*noun*), bed; **petit lit,** cot, child's bed. *See* **berceau.**
litre *m.* (*noun*), litre (= *approx.* 1¾ pints).
livre[1] *m.* (*noun*), book.
livre[2] *f.* (*noun*), (*weight*) pound (= *approx.* 1 lb. 1½ ozs.); (*money*) **une livre (sterling),** one pound (sterling).
livrer (*verb*), to deliver; to give up, to surrender.
localité *f.* (*noun*), locality, place, spot.
locomotive *f.* (*noun*), railway engine; locomotive.
loge *f.* (*noun*), lodge (of caretaker); hut, cabin.
loger (*verb*), to live, to lodge.
loi *f.* (*noun*), law.
loin (*adv.*), far; **loin de,** far from (**Pierre est loin de chez lui,** Peter is far from home; **loin d'être en colère, il aime le projet,** far from being angry, he likes the plan); far away, far off (**Henri n'est pas ici; il est loin,** Henry is not here; he is far away); **plus loin,** further; *m.* (*noun*), **au loin,** in the distance.
loisir *m.* (*noun*), leisure, spare time.
long *m.*, **longue** *f.* (*adj.*), long.
long *m.* (*noun*), length (**un bâton deux pieds de long,** a stick two feet in length); **de long en large,** up and down, to and fro.
longtemps (*adv.*), long, for a long time.
longueur *f.* (*noun*), length.
louche *f.* (*noun*), ladle (for soup).
louer (*verb*), to hire out, to rent; to reserve, to book.
loup *m.* (*noun*), wolf.
lourd (*adj.*), heavy; sultry (weather).
loyal (*adj.*), honest, fair; faithful; sincere; loyal.
lubrifiant *m.* (*noun*), lubricant.
lubrifier (*verb*), to lubricate.
lui (*m.* & *f. pron.*), (to) him, (to) her (**dites-lui tout,** tell him, her, everything; **écrivez-lui,** write to him, her); *m.*, he (**c'est lui,** it is he); **lui-même,** himself; itself.
luire (*verb*), to shine, to gleam, to glimmer.
lumière *f.* (*noun*), light.
lundi *m.* (*noun*), Monday.
lune *f.* (*noun*), moon.
lunette *f.* (*noun*), telescope, spy-glass; (*pl.*) spectacles.
lutte *f.* (*noun*), struggle; contest.
luxueux *m.*, **-euse** *f.* (*adj.*), luxurious, sumptuous.
lycée *m.* (*noun*), = grammar school.

M

ma *f.* (*adj.*): *see* **mon.**

machine *f.* (*noun*), machine; **machine à coudre,** sewing machine; **machine à écrire,** typewriter.

maçon *m.* (*noun*), mason, bricklayer.

madame (*pl.* **mesdames**) *f.* (*noun*), Mrs.; madam.

mademoiselle (*pl.* **mesdemoiselles**) *f.* (*noun*), Miss; madam.

magasin *m.* (*noun*), large shop, store; warehouse, storeroom.

magistrat *m.* (*noun*), magistrate, judge.

mai *m.* (*noun*), May.

maigre (*adj.*), meagre, scanty; thin, skinny, lean; poor.

maigrir (*verb*), to get thin, to lose flesh, to get lean.

maillet *m.* (*noun*), mallet, wooden hammer.

main *f.* (*noun*), hand; deal (at cards).

maintenant (*adv.*), now.

maire *m.*, **mairesse** *f.* (*noun*), mayor, mayoress.

mairie *f.* (*noun*), town hall.

mais (*conj.*), but.

maïs *m.* (*noun*), maize.

maison *f.* (*noun*), house; home, household.

maître *m.*, **maîtresse** *f.* (*noun*), master, mistress; **maître, maîtresse d'école,** schoolmaster, schoolmistress; **maître d'hôtel,** head waiter.

mal (*pl.* **maux**) *m.* (*noun*), evil; illness, ailment, disease; pain, hurt; **avoir mal,** to have a pain; **faire du mal,** to do harm; **faire mal,** to hurt (**les dents du garçon lui font mal,** the boy's teeth hurt him).

mal (*adv.*), badly; **mal à l'aise,** ill at ease.

malade (*adj.*), ill, poorly, sick, unwell; **malade** *m.* & *f.* (*noun*), patient.

maladie *f.* (*noun*), sickness, disease, illness.

malaise *m.* (*noun*), ailment, indisposition.

malgré (*prep.*), in spite of.

malheur *m.* (*noun*), misfortune, bad luck; calamity.

malheureux *m.*, **-euse** *f.* (*adj.*), unlucky, ill-fated, unfortunate, wretched.

malhonnête (*adj.*), dishonest; impolite.

malle *f.* (*noun*), trunk, box; cabin trunk.

maman *f.* (*noun*), mummy, mamma.

manche[1] *m.* (*noun*), handle; **manche à balai,** broomstick.

manche[2] *f.* (*noun*), sleeve; **la Manche,** the English Channel.

mandat *m.* (*noun*), money order; mandate, warrant.

manger (*verb*), to eat.

manière *f.* (*noun*), way, manner, method; (*pl.*) manners.

manipuler (*verb*), to manipulate; to operate (piece of machinery); to wangle.

manoir *m.* (*noun*), manor, manor house.

manquer (*verb*), to miss (target, train, opportunity, etc.) (**le soldat a manqué son coup,** the soldier has missed his aim); to lack, to be short of (**je manque d'argent,** I am short of money); (*impers.*) **il me manque un franc,** I am one franc short.

manteau (*pl.* **manteaux**) *m.* (*noun*), overcoat, top coat, (*army*) great-coat; cloak; **manteau de cheminée,** mantelpiece.

marchand *m.*, **marchande** *f.* (*noun*), dealer, tradesman, tradeswoman; **marchand de légumes,** greengrocer.

marche *f.* (*noun*), march; walking; progress.

marché *m.* (*noun*), market; **bon marché,** cheap.

marcher (*verb*), to walk, to go; to march.

mardi *m.* (*noun*), Tuesday; **mardi gras,** Shrove Tuesday.

mari *m.* (*noun*), husband.

marier (*verb*), to marry; to join; to mix (colours); **se marier,** to get married.

marin *m.* (*noun*), sailor, mariner.

marmite *f.* (*noun*), large pot, pan (with lid).

mars *m.* (*noun*), March.
marteau (*pl.* **marteaux**) *m.* (*noun*), hammer.
mât *m.* (*noun*), mast; gymnastic pole.
matelas *m.* (*noun*), mattress; **matelas d'air,** air-cushion.
matière *f.* (*noun*), material; subject, topic; **table des matières,** table of contents.
matin *m.* (*noun*), morning.
maussade (*adj.*), sullen, surly, glum, moody.
mauvais (*adj.*), bad, evil; unkind; wrong (**prendre le mauvais chemin,** to take the wrong road).
me (*pron.*), me (**il me gronde,** he scolds me); to me (**elle me parle,** she speaks to me); myself (**je m'habille,** I am dressing myself).
mécanicien *m.* (*noun*), mechanic.
méchant (*adj.*), mischievous, naughty; wicked; spiteful.
médecin *m.* (*noun*), doctor, physician.
médicament *m.* (*noun*), medicine, medicament.
médiocre (*adj.*), average; middling; poor (quality).
méduse *f.* (*noun*), jelly-fish.
meilleur (*adj.*), better; **le meilleur,** the better (of two); the best.
mélanger (*verb*), to mix, to blend (with care and in definite proportions).
mêler (*verb*), to mix, to blend (generally, and without special care).
mélodie *f.* (*noun*), melody, tune.
même (*adv.*), even; (*adj.*), same; self; *see also* **moi-même, toi-même, lui-même, elle-même, nous-mêmes, vous-même(s), eux-mêmes, elles-mêmes.**
mémoire *f.* (*noun*), memory; recollection; remembrance.
ménage *m.* (*noun*), household; **faire le ménage,** to do the housework; **femme de ménage,** charwoman, daily help; **jeune ménage,** young married couple.
ménager (*verb*), to manage; to save; to arrange (**ménager une rencontre,** to arrange a meeting); to treat considerately.
mendier (*verb*), to beg.
mener (*verb*), to lead (**le garçon mène son chien en laisse,** the boy is leading his dog on a leash); to take (**elle mène ses enfants au parc,** she is taking her children to the park).
mensonge *m.* (*noun*), lie, falsehood, untruth.
mentir (*verb*), to lie, to tell lies, to fib.
menton *m.* (*noun*), chin.
menu *m.* (*noun*), menu, bill of fare.
menuisier *m.* (*noun*), joiner, carpenter.
mer *f.* (*noun*), sea; **en pleine mer,** in the open sea, out at sea.
merci (**de** *or* **pour**) (*adv.*), thank you, thanks (for).
mercredi *m.* (*noun*), Wednesday.
messieurs: *see* **monsieur.**
mère *f.* (*noun*), mother.
mes *m.* & *f. pl.* (*adj.*): *see* **mon.**
mesure *f.* (*noun*), measurement, measure.
mesurer (*verb*), to measure, to calculate.
métal (*pl.* **métaux**) *m.* (*noun*), metal.
méthode *f.* (*noun*), method, way, system.
métier *m.* (*noun*), trade, profession, craft.
mètre *m.* (*noun*), metre (= 3.281 ft.).
métro *m.* (*noun*), underground railway, tube.
mettre (*verb*), to put, to set, to place; **mettre tout son soin à,** to take great care to; **mettre en réserve,** to store; **mettre en danger,** to endanger; **se mettre à,** to begin to, to start.
meuble *m.* (*noun*), piece of furniture; (*pl.*) (pieces of) furniture.
midi *m.* (*noun*), midday, 12 o'clock.
miel *m.* (*noun*), honey.
le mien *m.*, **la mienne** *f.* (*pron.*), mine (**voilà le parapluie volé, voici le mien,** there is the stolen umbrella, here is mine).
mieux (*adv.*), better; **le mieux,** (the) best.
milieu (*pl.* **milieux**) *m.* (*noun*), middle (**au milieu de l'été,** at the height of summer; **au milieu de l'hiver,** in midwinter); surroundings, environment; social sphere.
mille[1] *m.* (*noun* & *adj.*), thousand; **mille un,** a thousand and one.
mille[2] *m.* (*noun*), mile (*approx.* 1.6 kilometres).

milliard *m.* (*noun*), one thousand million(s).
millier *m.* (*noun*), (about a) thousand; **des milliers de gens,** thousands of people.
million *m.* (*noun*), million; **six millions d'hommes,** six million men.
mince (*adj.*), thin, slim.
minet *m.* (*noun*), pussy.
minime (*adj.*), minute, tiny.
minuit *m.* (*noun*), midnight, 12 o'clock; **vers minuit,** about midnight; **messe de minuit,** midnight mass.
minute *f.* (*noun*), minute (*measure of time*).
miroir *m.* (*noun*), mirror.
miroiter (*verb*), to glisten, to gleam, to sparkle.
mitaine *f.* (*noun*), mitten.
mode *f.* (*noun*), fashion; manner; **à la dernière mode,** in the latest fashion.
moderne (*adj.*), modern, up-to-date.
modeste (*adj.*), modest, retiring, unassuming.
modifier (*verb*), to modify; to qualify; to alter, to change.
moelleux *m.*, **-euse** *f.* (*adj.*), soft, downy.
moi (*pron.*), I (**c'est moi,** it is I); (to) me (**donnez-le-moi,** give it (to) me); me (**invitez-moi,** invite me); **moi-même,** myself.
moins (*adv.*), less; **de moins en moins,** less and less; **à moins que ... ne,** unless (**à moins qu'il ne vienne,** unless he comes).
mois *m.* (*noun*), month.
moisson *f.* (*noun*), harvest, crop; **faire la moisson,** to harvest.
moitié *f.* (*noun*), half; **partager par moitié,** to go halves.
moment *m.* (*noun*), moment.
mon *m.*, **ma** *f.*, **mes** *m.* & *f. pl.* (*adj.*), my (**mon chien,** my dog; **ma femme,** my wife; **mes enfants,** my children).
monde *m.* (*noun*), world, earth; **tout le monde,** everybody, everyone.
monnaie *f.* (*noun*), money, currency; change.
monsieur (*pl.* **messieurs**) *m.* (*noun*), Mr., master; sir; gentleman.
montagne *f.* (*noun*), mountain.
monter (*verb*), to climb up, to ascend.
montre *f.* (*noun*), show, display.
montre(-bracelet) *f.* (*noun*), (wrist-) watch.
montrer (*verb*), to show, to exhibit, to display.
se moquer de (*verb*), to mock at, to laugh at, to make fun of.
morceau (*pl.* **morceaux**) *m.* (*noun*), morsel, bit, piece, patch.
mordre (*verb*), to bite.
morose (*adj.*), gloomy; sullen, surly.
mort[1] (*adj.*), dead.
mort[2] *f.* (*noun*), death.
mort[3] *m.*, **morte** *f.* (*noun*), deceased, dead person; **les morts** *m. pl.*, the dead, the departed.
mot *m.* (*noun*), word; **bon mot,** witty remark.
moteur *m.* (*noun*), motor, engine.
moto(cyclette) *f.* (*noun*), motorcycle.
mou (mol) (*pl.* **mous**) *m.*, **molle** *f.* (*adj.*), soft.
mouche *f.* (*noun*), fly (*insect*).
moucher (*verb*), to wipe (someone's nose); **se moucher,** to blow, wipe one's nose.
mouchoir *m.* (*noun*), handkerchief.
mouillé (*adj.*), wet, sodden, soggy.
mouiller (*verb*), to damp, to wet; **mouiller l'ancre,** to drop anchor; **se mouiller,** to get wet; **mes yeux commencèrent à se mouiller,** my eyes began to fill with tears.
moulin *m.* (*noun*), mill; **moulin à vent,** windmill.
mourir (*verb*), to die.
moustique *m.* (*noun*), mosquito; gnat.
mouton *m.* (*noun*), sheep.
mouvement *m.* (*noun*), motion, movement.
moyen *m.* (*noun*), way, means; **au moyen de,** by means of.
muet *m.*, **-ette** *f.* (*adj.*), dumb, mute, silent, speechless; (*noun*), dumb person.
mur *m.* (*noun*), wall.
mûr (*adj.*), ripe, mellow; mature.
musique *f.* (*noun*), music.
mystérieux *m.*, **-euse** *f.* (*adj.*), mysterious.

N

nager (*verb*), to swim; to float.
nageur *m.*, **nageuse** *f.* (*noun*), swimmer.
naissance *f.* (*noun*), birth; beginning.
naître (*verb*), to be born; **elle est née à Paris,** she was born in Paris.
nappe *f.* (*noun*), tablecloth, cloth.
nationalité *f.* (*noun*), nationality.
natte *f.* (*noun*), mat (of straw); plait (of hair).
nature *f.* (*noun*), nature; temperament.
naturel *m.*, **-elle** *f.* (*adj.*), natural; unaffected; genuine.
naturellement (*adv.*), naturally; of course.
navire *m.* (*noun*), ship, vessel.
ne: *see* **pas; jamais; plus; que.**
né (*past participle*)**:** *see* **naître.**
nécessaire (*adj.*), necessary.
négliger (*verb*), to neglect; to ignore; to fail (**de,** to).
neige *f.* (*noun*), snow; **bonhomme de neige,** snowman.
neiger (*verb*), to snow.
n'est-ce pas? isn't that so? isn't it true?; **vous restez, n'est-ce pas?** you are staying, aren't you?; **il est très fatigué, n'est-ce pas?** he is very tired, isn't he?
nettoyer (*verb*), to clean; to cleanse.
neuf[1] *m.* (*noun & adj.*), nine; ninth (**Charles Neuf,** Charles the Ninth; **le neuf avril,** April the ninth).
neuf[2] *m.*, **neuve** *f.* (*adj.*), new (unused), fresh.
neuvième (*noun & adj.*), ninth.
neveu (*pl.* **neveux**) *m.* (*noun*), nephew.
nez *m.* (*noun*), nose.
ni . . . ni (*conj.*), neither . . . nor (**ni vous ni moi,** neither you nor I).
nickel *m.* (*noun*), nickel.
nid *m.* (*noun*), nest.
nièce *f.* (*noun*), niece.
nier (*verb*), to deny.
Noël *m.* (*noun*), Christmas; **le père Noël,** Father Christmas; **l'arbre de Noël,** Christmas tree; **la veille de Noël,** Christmas Eve; **à la** (**fête de**) **Noël, à Noël,** at Christmas.
nœud *m.* (*noun*), knot.
noir (*adj.*), black; **tableau noir,** blackboard.
noix *f.* (*noun*), nut; walnut.
nom *m.* (*noun*), name; noun.
nombre *m.* (*noun*), number.
nommer (*verb*), to name, to give a name to; to appoint.
non (*adv.*), no; **que non!** not a bit; **non pas!** not at all!; **non plus,** neither, (not) either (**ni moi non plus,** nor me either).
nord *m.* (*noun*), north; **la mer du Nord,** the North Sea.
note *f.* (*noun*), note (observation); mark; note (music).
notre (*pl.* **nos**) (*adj.*), our.
nôtre: le, la nôtre, les nôtres (*pron.*), ours.
nouer (*verb*), to tie (up), to knot; **se nouer les cheveux,** to tie up, put up, one's hair.
nourrir (*verb*), to nourish, to feed, to nurture.
nourriture *f.* (*noun*), nourishment, food.
nous (*pron.*), we; us; to us; **nous-mêmes,** ourselves.
nouveau (**nouvel**) *m.* (*pl.* **nouveaux**), **-elle** *f.* (*adj.*), new, fresh.
nouvelle *f.* (*noun*), item of news; report; (*pl.*) news.
novembre *m.* (*noun*), November.
nuage *m.* (*noun*), cloud.
nuit *f.* (*noun*), night; **il se fait nuit,** it is growing dark, night is falling.
nulle part (*adv.*), nowhere; anywhere (**nous ne l'avons vu nulle part,** we haven't seen him anywhere).
numéro *m.* (*noun*), number (**le numéro quatorze,** number 14); **vieux numéro,** back number (of newspaper).
nylon *m.* (*noun*), nylon; **bas en nylon,** nylon stockings.

O

obéir (**à**) (*verb*), to obey; to submit to.
obéissant (*adj.*), obedient; submissive; dutiful.
objecter (**à**) (*verb*), to object (to).
objet *m.* (*noun*), object, thing.
obliger (*verb*), to oblige, to compel; to bind (in law).
observer (*verb*), to observe, to watch; to remark.
obtenir (*verb*), to get, to obtain; to gain; to achieve.
occuper (*verb*), to occupy; to hold; **s'occuper,** to keep oneself busy, to occupy oneself.
océan *m.* (*noun*), ocean.
octobre *m.* (*noun*), October.
odeur *f.* (*noun*), smell, scent, odour.
œil (*pl.* **yeux**) *m.* (*noun*), eye.
œuf *m.* (*noun*), egg.
office *m.* (*noun*), duty; service; bureau.
offre *f.* (*noun*), offer, proposal.
offrir (*verb*), to offer; to present; to give, to bid.
oh! (*interj.*), oh!
ohé! (*interj.*), (*calling to someone*) hello!
oie *f.* (*noun*), goose.
oignon *m.* (*noun*), onion.
oiseau (*pl.* **oiseaux**) *m.* (*noun*), bird.
ombre *f.* (*noun*), shadow, shade.
omettre (*verb*), to omit, to miss out; to leave out.
on (*pron.*), one, you (**on dit bonjour quand on rencontre un ami,** one says (you say) hello when one meets (you meet) a friend); somebody (**on frappe à la porte,** somebody is knocking at the door); they (**on dit qu'il va pleuvoir,** they say it is going to rain).
oncle *m.* (*noun*), uncle.
ondulation *f.* (*noun*), waving (of corn); wave (in hair).
ongle *m.* (*noun*), (finger-)nail; claw (of animal); talon (of bird of prey).
onguent *m.* (*noun*), ointment, liniment.
onze *m.* (*noun & adj.*), eleven; eleventh (**Louis Onze,** Louis the Eleventh; **le onze mars,** March the eleventh).
opération *f.* (*noun*), medical *or* military operation; mathematical operation *or* exercise.
opérer (*verb*), to operate; to perform an operation.
opposer (*verb*), to oppose.
or *m.* (*noun*), gold.
orage *m.* (*noun*), storm, thunderstorm, tempest.
orange *f.* (*noun*), orange (*fruit*); (*invariable adj.*) orange (coloured) (**un chapeau orange et des gants orange,** an orange hat and orange gloves).
orchestre *m.* (*noun*), orchestra.
ordonner (*verb*), to order; to organize; to arrange.
ordre *m.* (*noun*), command, order; method; sequence; **en ordre,** well arranged; ship-shape.
ordures *f. pl.* (*noun*), refuse, filth, dirt; **ordures ménagères,** household refuse.
oreille *f.* (*noun*), ear.
oreiller *m.* (*noun*), pillow.
organiser (*verb*), to organize; to arrange; to get up (something).
orge *f.* (*noun*), barley.
orgue *m.* (*noun*), organ.
orteil *m.* (*noun*), toe.
os *m.* (*noun*), bone.
oser (*verb*), to dare, to dare to.
ou (*conj.*), or; **ou . . . ou,** either . . . or.
où (*adv.*), where (**où êtes-vous?** where are you?; **le village où je suis né,** the village where I was born); when (**je ne sais le jour où il arrivera,** I do not know the day when he will arrive).
oublier (*verb*), to forget.
ouest *m.* (*noun*), west.
oui (*adv.*), yes; **je crois que oui,** I think so.
ours *m.* (*noun*), bear.
outil *m.* (*noun*), tool, implement.

outre (*adv.*), beyond, further; **en outre,** moreover, besides.

ouvert (*adj.*), open.

ouverture *f.* (*noun*), opening; mouth (of cave, etc.); (*music*) overture.

ouvrier *m.*, **-ière** *f.* (*noun*), workman, worker.

ouvrir (*verb*), to open, to unlock (a door); to open (a bank account); to break (an electrical circuit).

P

page *f.* (*noun*)**,** page.
paillasson *m.* (*noun*)**,** mat, doormat; matting.
paille *f.* (*noun*)**,** straw.
pain *m.* (*noun*)**,** bread; loaf.
paire *f.* (*noun*)**,** pair.
paix *f.* (*noun*)**,** peace, quiet.
palais *m.* (*noun*)**,** palace; palate.
pâle (*adj.*)**,** pale, faint (light), colourless.
palissade *f.* (*noun*)**,** fence, paling.
palper (*verb*)**,** to feel (an object).
panier *m.* (*noun*)**,** basket.
pansement *m.* (*noun*)**,** bandage, dressing.
pantalon *m.* (*noun*)**,** (pair of) trousers, pants, slacks (NOTE: *French sing., English pl.*).
pantoufle *f.* (*noun*)**,** slipper.
papa *m.* (*noun*)**,** daddy, dad, pa, papa.
papeterie *f.* (*noun*)**,** stationer's shop; stationery.
papier *m.* (*noun*)**,** paper (NOT newspaper); **papier à lettres,** writing paper, note-paper.
papillon *m.* (*noun*)**,** butterfly.
paquebot *m.* (*noun*)**,** packet-boat, steamer, liner.
Pâques *m.* (*noun*)**,** Easter.
paquet *m.* (*noun*)**,** packet, bundle, parcel.
par (*prep.*)**,** by; through; out of (**jeter par la fenêtre,** to throw out of the window).
parachute *m.* (*noun*)**,** parachute.
parachuter (*verb*)**,** to parachute, to drop by parachute.
paradis *m.* (*noun*)**,** paradise; heaven.
paraître (*verb*)**,** to look, to appear (**il paraît triste,** he looks sad); (*impers.*) it seems (**il paraît qu'il a beaucoup d'argent,** it seems he has plenty of money).
parapluie *m.* (*noun*)**,** umbrella.
parasol *m.* (*noun*)**,** sunshade, parasol, beach-umbrella.
parc *m.* (*noun*)**,** park; pen (**parc pour enfants,** play-pen); fleet (of lorries, etc.).
parce que (*conj.*)**,** because.
par-dessous (*prep.*)**,** under, beneath.
par-dessus (*prep.*)**,** over, above.
pardessus *m.* (*noun*)**,** overcoat (*see* **manteau**).
pardon *m.* (*noun*)**,** forgiveness, pardon; **pardon!** (*exclamation*)**,** I beg your pardon! excuse me!
pardonner (*verb*)**,** to forgive, to pardon.
pare-chocs *m.* (*noun*)**,** car bumper.
pareil *m.*, **-eille** *f.* (*adj.*)**,** similar, like, of that kind.
parents *m. pl.* (*noun*)**,** parents, father and mother; relatives, (blood) relations.
paresseux *m.*, **-euse** *f.* (*adj.*)**,** idle, lazy; sluggish.
parfait (*adj.*)**,** perfect; exquisite; **c'est parfait!** splendid!
parler (*verb*)**,** to speak, to talk.
parmi (*prep.*)**,** among, amongst.
part *f.* (*noun*)**,** share, part, slice; **autre part,** elsewhere, somewhere else.
partager (*verb*)**,** to share, to share out, to divide.
partie *f.* (*noun*)**,** part (of something); game (of cards, football).
partir (*verb*)**,** to start (**de,** from), to set off, to depart, to leave (**le train part de Paris à trois heures,** the train leaves Paris at three o'clock).
partout (*adv.*)**,** everywhere.
pas *m.* (*noun*)**,** step, pace; walk, gait.
pas (*adv.*)**,** not; **ce n'est pas,** it is not; **je ne fume pas,** I do not smoke; **pourquoi pas?** why not?; **pas du tout,** not at all; **pas encore,** not yet.
passage *m.* (*noun*)**,** passage; right of way; **passage clouté,** pedestrian crossing.
passé *m.* (*noun*)**,** the past.
passeport *m.* (*noun*)**,** passport.
passer (*verb*)**,** to sit for (an examination); to hand (to someone); to pass (in front of someone or something).
passerelle *f.* (*noun*)**,** small bridge, foot-bridge.

pâte *f.* (*noun*), pastry, dough.
pâté *m.* (*noun*), pâté, potted meat; blot (of ink).
patience *f.* (*noun*), patience, composure.
patin *m.* (*noun*), skate; (sledge) runner.
patiner (*verb*), to skate.
patineur *m.*, **patineuse** *f.* (*noun*), skater.
patron *m.*, **patronne** *f.* (*noun*), employer, boss, proprietor, proprietress.
patte *f.* (*noun*), paw (of dog or cat); leg (of insect).
paupière *f.* (*noun*), eyelid.
pauvre (*adj.*), poor, hard up (**homme pauvre,** poor man); unfortunate (**pauvre homme,** unlucky man).
pavé *m.* (*noun*), paving-stone; pavement.
paye *f.* (*noun*), wages (of workmen).
payer (*verb*), to pay, to pay for; **je le lui ai payé cent francs,** I paid him a hundred francs for it.
pays *m.* (*noun*), land, country.
paysan *m.*, **paysanne** *f.* (*noun*), peasant, countryman, countrywoman.
peau (*pl.* **peaux**) *f.* (*noun*), skin; peel.
pêche *f.* (*noun*), peach; fishing.
pêcher (*verb*), to fish; to fish for; to catch (a fish).
pêcheur *m.* (*noun*), fisherman, angler.
peigne *m.* (*noun*), comb.
peigner (*verb*), to comb; **se peigner,** to comb one's hair, to do one's hair.
peindre (*verb*), to paint (a picture); to cover with paint.
peine *f.* (*noun*), pain, suffering, anguish; difficulty.
peiner (*verb*), to toil, to labour; to afflict, to distress.
peinture *f.* (*noun*), painting; paint (**prenez garde à la peinture!** wet paint!).
pelage *m.* (*noun*), fur, pelt (of animal).
pelle *f.* (*noun*), shovel; scoop; dustpan; (*seaside*) spade.
pelleter (*verb*), to shovel.
pellicule *f.* (*noun*), film (for photographs).
pelote *f.* (*noun*), ball (of string, wool).
pelouse *f.* (*noun*), lawn, grass plot, green.
pelure *f.* (*noun*), skin or peel (of fruit).
pencher (*verb*), to lean, to bend; to slope; **se pencher,** to stoop; to lean (**se pencher par la fenêtre,** to lean out of the window).
pendant (*prep.*), during; **pendant que** (*conj.*), while, whilst.
pendre (*verb*), to hang (someone); to hang up (something); to hang, to be hanging.
pendule *m.* (*noun*), pendulum; *f.* clock.
pensée *f.* (*noun*), thought.
penser (*verb*), to think, to have an opinion.
percevoir (*verb*), to perceive; to sense.
perdre (*verb*), to lose; **se perdre,** to lose one's way, to be lost.
père *m.* (*noun*), father; (*priest*) Father; **père Noël,** Father Christmas.
perle *f.* (*noun*), pearl; glass bead.
permettre (*verb*), to permit, to allow; to enable (**cet argent me permet de vivre dans le luxe,** this money enables me to live in luxury).
permis *m.* (*noun*), permit; leave; pass; certificate; licence (**permis de conduire,** driving licence).
permission *f.* (*noun*), permission, leave.
perroquet *m.* (*noun*), parrot.
persévérer (*verb*), to persevere; to carry on.
persister (*verb*), to persist; to stick to it.
personnage *m.* (*noun*), (important) person; character (in play, novel).
personne *f.* (*noun*), person, individual; (*pron.*), anyone, anybody (**elle chante mieux que personne,** she sings better than anyone); no one (**il ne reste personne,** there is no one left; **personne ne pourra arriver ce soir,** no one can get here this evening).
perspicace (*adj.*), shrewd, perspicacious, discerning.
persuader (*verb*), to persuade.
peser (*verb*), to weigh; to ponder.
petit (*adj.*), small, little; **tout petit,** tiny, teeny-weeny; **petit chien,** puppy; **petit déjeuner,** breakfast; **petit** *m.*, **petite** *f.* (*noun*), child, little one; **la petite,** our little girl; **pauvre petit,** poor little thing.
petite-fille *f.* (*noun*), grand-daughter.

petit-fils *m.* (*noun*), grandson.
petits-enfants *m.pl.* (*noun*), grandchildren.
pétrole *m.* (*noun*), petroleum; **lampe** *f.* **à pétrole,** paraffin lamp.
peu (*adv.*), little (**il mange peu,** he eats little); **peu de,** little, not much (**il mange peu de viande,** he doesn't eat much meat); few (**peu d'enfants,** few children); **un peu,** a little (**veux-tu du gâteau? Oui, un peu s'il te plaît,** do you want some cake? Yes, a little please).
peuple *m.* (*noun*), people, nation; the masses.
peur *f.* (*noun*), fear, dread, fright; **avoir peur,** to be frightened, to feel frightened (**le petit garçon a peur du tigre,** the small boy is frightened of the tiger); **faire peur à,** to frighten (someone); to give (someone) a fright (**le tigre lui fait peur,** the tiger frightens him).
peut-être (*adv.*), perhaps, maybe.
pharmacie *f.* (*noun*), chemist's shop.
pharmacien *m.*, **-ienne** *f.* (*noun*), chemist.
phono(**graphe**) *m.* (*noun*), gramophone, record-player.
phoque *m.* (*noun*), seal (*animal*).
photographe *m.* (*noun*), photographer.
photo(**graphie**) *f.* (*noun*), photo(graph).
photographier (*verb*), to photograph, to take someone's picture.
phrase *f.* (*noun*), sentence; phrase; **phrase à décrocher la mâchoire,** tongue-twister.
piano *m.* (*noun*), piano.
pic *m.* (*noun*), pick, pickaxe (*see* **pioche**); woodpecker.
pièce *f.* (*noun*), piece, bit; coin; room, apartment.
pied *m.* (*noun*), foot (of man or animal); foot (of tree); (*measure*) foot; **à pied,** on foot.
pierre *f.* (*noun*), stone.
pigeon *m.* (*noun*), pigeon.
pile *f.* (*noun*), pile, stack (of wood); electric battery.
pilule *f.* (*noun*), pill.
pioche *f.* (*noun*), pickaxe, pick (*see* **pic**).
piocher (*verb*), to dig (with a pick).
pipe *f.* (*noun*), pipe (for smoking tobacco).
pique-nique *m.* (*noun*), picnic.
piquer (*verb*), to prick (with needle); (*of wasp, etc.*) to sting; to offend (someone); to goad.
piquet *m.* (*noun*), post, stake; strike picket (for workmen).
piqûre *f.* (*noun*), prick (with pin, etc.); sting; injection.
pire (*adj.*), worse; **le pire,** the worst.
pitié *f.* (*noun*), pity.
placard *m.* (*noun*), hanging cupboard.
place *f.* (*noun*), place, position, seat; room, space; public square, market-square.
placement *m.* (*noun*), placing (**bureau de placement,** employment bureau); investment (**faire des placements,** to invest money, to make investments).
placer (*verb*), to place; to locate.
plafond *m.* (*noun*), ceiling.
plage *f.* (*noun*), beach, sea-shore.
plaider (*verb*), to plead, to argue.
plaie *f.* (*noun*), sore, wound.
plaindre (*verb*), to pity, to feel sorry for; **se plaindre,** to complain, to grumble.
plaine *f.* (*noun*), plain, flat country.
plaire (*verb*), to be pleasing, to please; **cette maison me plaît beaucoup,** I like this house very much; **je me plais ici,** I am happy here; **se plaire,** to be happy (in a place), to like, to enjoy, to take pleasure in (**il se plaît à contempler le paysage,** he enjoys gazing at the landscape).
plaisanterie *f.* (*noun*), joke, prank.
plaisir *m.* (*noun*), pleasure, delight; amusement; **prendre plaisir à,** to enjoy; to relish.
plan *m.* (*noun*), plan, project.
plan (*adj.*), flat, even, level.
planche *f.* (*noun*), plank, board.
plancher *m.* (*noun*), floor.
planeur *m.* (*noun*), glider (*aircraft*).
plante *f.* (*noun*), plant.
planter (*verb*), to plant, to set, to lay out (a garden).
plat (*adj.*), flat, level, smooth, even.
plat *m.* (*noun*), dish (*container or contents*).

plateau (*pl.* **plateaux**) *m.* (*noun*), tray; scale (of a balance); plateau.
plein (*adj.*), full, crammed, replete; covered (**ses doigts sont pleins d'encre,** his fingers are covered with ink).
pleurer (*verb*), to weep, to cry; to lament, to mourn for.
pleuvoir (*verb*), to rain, to shower.
pli *m.* (*noun*), fold (of cloth); crease; pleat.
plier (*verb*), to fold, to bend, to roll up.
plonger (*verb*), to plunge; to dive; to dip.
plongeur *m.* (*noun*), diver; dish-washer (*person*).
pluie *f.* (*noun*), rain.
plume *f.* (*noun*), feather; (quill-)pen.
plus (*adv.*), more; **il est plus grand que moi,** he is taller than I; **Paul a plus d'argent que moi,** Paul has more money than I have; **ne . . . plus,** no more, not any longer, no longer (**je ne vais plus à l'école,** I no longer go to school).
plusieurs (*adj.*), several.
plutôt (*adv.*), rather, sooner; **plutôt . . . que,** rather . . . than.
pneu *m.* (*noun*), tyre.
poche *f.* (*noun*), pocket; pouch.
poêle *m.* (*noun*), stove; **poêle à gaz,** gas-stove; **poêle de cuisine,** cooker.
poème *m.* (*noun*), poem.
poésie *f.* (*noun*), poetry; poem.
poète *m.* (*noun*), poet.
poids *m.* (*noun*), weight, heaviness; load; burden.
poignée *f.* (*noun*), door handle; handful.
poil *m.* (*noun*), hair, fur (of animal); pile (of velvet); nap (of cloth); bristle (of brush).
poing *m.* (*noun*), fist.
point *m.* (*noun*), point, dot; full-stop; punctuation mark (**point d'interrogation,** question mark).
pointe *f.* (*noun*), point (of pin or needle); head (of something).
pointer (*verb*), to point; to tally, to tick off (figures); to prick up (ears).
pointu (*adj.*), (sharp-)pointed.
poire *f.* (*noun*), pear.
pois *m.* (*noun*), pea; spot, polka-dot; **petits pois,** garden peas.
poisson *m.* (*noun*), fish; **poisson rouge,** gold-fish.
poitrine *f.* (*noun*), chest, breast, bosom.
poivre *m.* (*noun*), pepper.
poivré (*adj.*), peppery; **menthe poivrée,** peppermint.
poli (*adj.*), polished; polite, courteous.
police *f.* (*noun*), police; constabulary; policy (*e.g.* insurance).
pomme *f.* (*noun*), apple; **pomme de terre,** potato.
pondre (*verb*), to lay (an egg).
poney *m.* (*noun*), pony.
pont *m.* (*noun*), bridge; deck (of ship).
porc *m.* (*noun*), pig; pork.
porcelaine *f.* (*noun*), porcelain, china-ware.
port *m.* (*noun*), harbour, port; **arriver à bon port,** to arrive safely.
porte *f.* (*noun*), door, doorway; gate (of a town).
porte-fenêtre *f.* (*noun*), French window.
portefeuille *m.* (*noun*), wallet, note-case; portfolio.
porte-monnaie *m.* (*noun*), purse.
porter (*verb*), to carry, to bear; to wear.
portion *f.* (*noun*), share, portion, part; helping (at a meal).
poser (*verb*), to lay, to put, to place, to set; to hang (a curtain); **poser une question,** to ask a question.
position *f.* (*noun*), position; attitude; situation.
posséder (*verb*), to possess, to own, to have.
possible (*adj.*), possible.
poste[1] *m.* (*noun*), post (position); **poste de T.S.F.,** radio set; **poste d'essence,** petrol pump, filling station.
poste[2] *f.* (*noun*), post, mail.
pot *m.* (*noun*), pot; jug; jar; **pot à fleurs,** flower pot; **pot de confiture,** jar of jam; **pot au lait,** milk-jug.
poteau (*pl.* **poteaux**) *m.* (*noun*), post, pole.
potiron *m.* (*noun*), pumpkin.
pouce *m.* (*noun*), thumb; inch; **pouce!** pax! truce!

poule *f.* (*noun*), hen.
poulet *m.* (*noun*), chicken.
poulette *f.* (*noun*), pullet, young hen.
poupée *f.* (*noun*), doll.
pour (*prep.*), for; **pour que** (*conj.*), in order that, so that.
pourquoi (*adv.*), why; **pourquoi faire?** what for?
poursuivre (*verb*), to pursue, to chase, to dog, to hound.
pourtant (*adv.*), yet, however, nevertheless.
pourvoir (*verb*), to provide (**à**, for) (**elle pourvoit aux besoins de ses enfants,** she provides for the needs of her children); to supply, to provide (**de,** with) (**l'agent immobilier a pourvu l'homme d'une maison,** the estate agent supplied the man with a house).
pousser (*verb*), to push, to shove; to press hard (an attack); (*of plants*) to grow.
poussière *f.* (*noun*), dust.
poussin *m.* (*noun*), chick; spring chicken.
pouvoir (*verb*), to be able, can (**je ne peux plus travailler parce que je suis fatigué,** I cannot work any more because I am tired); may (**vous pouvez partir,** you may go).
pouvoir *m.* (*noun*), power; means, ability; authority.
prairie *f.* (*noun*), grassland; meadow.
pré *m.* (*noun*), meadow.
précaution *f.* (*noun*), precaution, prudence.
précieux *m.*, **-euse** *f.* (*adj.*), precious, invaluable.
précipiter (*verb*), to hurl, to throw (something, someone); to accelerate, to hasten; **se précipiter,** to throw oneself; to dash headlong.
précis (*adj.*), exact, precise.
prédire (*verb*), to foretell, to predict.
préférer (*verb*), to prefer, to like better.
premier *m.*, **-ière** *f.* (*adj.*), first.
prendre (*verb*), to take, to grasp, to lay hold of, to pick up; to catch (a bus, a train); to occupy (a house); **prendre garde,** to beware.
prénom *m.* (*noun*), Christian name, first name.
préparer (*verb*), to prepare, to get ready; to train.
près (*adv.*), near, close, hard by, at hand; **près de** (*prep.*), near, close to.
présenter (*verb*), to present, to introduce, to show; to set forth (an idea); **se présenter,** to occur; to present oneself.
préserver (*verb*), to preserve; to protect (**de,** from).
presque (*adv.*), almost, nearly; **presque jamais,** almost never, hardly ever.
pressant (*adj.*), pressing, urgent.
presse *f.* (*noun*), the press, newspapers; crowd, throng.
pressé (*adj.*), crowded; pressed for time; hard-pressed.
presser (*verb*), to press, to squeeze (something); to hurry; to urge; **se presser,** to crowd, to throng, to press; to hurry, to make haste.
prêt (*adj.*), ready; prepared.
prêter (*verb*), to lend.
prétexte *m.* (*noun*), excuse, pretext.
prévenir (*verb*), to forestall, to anticipate (desires); to warn.
prévenu (*adj.*), prejudiced (**contre,** against); forewarned (**de,** of); (*noun*), accused person.
prier (*verb*), to pray; to beg, to request, to entreat.
prière *f.* (*noun*), prayer; request.
prince *m.*, **princesse** *f.* (*noun*), prince, princess.
principal (*pl.* **principaux**) *m.* (*noun*), principal, headmaster; principal, capital sum; chief thing, main point; (*adj.*), principal, chief, leading (thing, person).
principe *m.* (*noun*), principle.
printemps *m.* (*noun*), spring(time).
prise *f.* (*noun*), grasp, hold, grip (when seizing someone); catch (**une bonne prise,** a good catch; **une prise de poisson,** a catch of fish); pinch (**une prise de tabac,** a pinch of snuff).
prison *f.* (*noun*), prison, gaol.
priver (*verb*), to deprive.
prix *m.* (*noun*), price, cost; prize, reward.

prochain (*adj.*), nearest; next (**la prochaine fois,** next time); neighbouring.
proche (*adj.*), near, close, approximate.
procurer (*verb*), to get, to procure, to obtain (for someone else); **se procurer,** to get (for oneself).
produire (*verb*), to produce, to yield, to bring forth.
produit *m.* (*noun*), produce, product; proceeds.
profession *f.* (*noun*), profession, calling, trade, occupation.
profit *m.* (*noun*), profit, benefit; advantage.
profiter (*verb*), to benefit, to profit.
profond (*adj.*), deep; profound; heartfelt.
profondeur *f.* (*noun*), depth.
progrès *m.* (*noun*), progress, advancement, improvement.
progresser (*verb*), to progress, to advance; to improve.
promenade *f.* (*noun*), walk, outing; **promenade en auto,** drive; **promenade à bicyclette,** (bicycle) ride; **promenade en bateau,** sail, row.
promener (*verb*), to take out for a walk, a sail, a drive, a ride; **se promener,** to go for a walk, a sail, a drive, a ride.
promesse *f.* (*noun*), promise, pledge.
promettre (*verb*), to promise.
prompt (*adj.*), prompt, quick, agile.
proposer (*verb*), to propose; to offer; to recommend.
proposition *f.* (*noun*), proposal, offer.
propre (*adj.*), fit, proper; clean, neat; own (**dans votre propre maison,** in your own house).
propriétaire *m.* (*noun*), proprietor, owner; landlord (of house).
protéger (*verb*), to protect (**de,** from); to shield, to guard (**de, contre,** against).
prouver (*verb*), to prove, to give evidence of.
provisions *f. pl.* (*noun*), supplies, provisions.
prudent (*adj.*), prudent; discreet.
prune *f.* (*noun*), plum.
prunier *m.* (*noun*), plum-tree.
public *m.* (*noun*), the public; **en public,** in public.
public *m.*, **-ique** *f.* (*adj.*), public.
puis (*adv.*), then; afterwards; next.
puissance *f.* (*noun*), power, force, strength.
puissant (*adj.*), forceful, powerful, strong.
puits *m.* (*noun*), well; mineshaft.
pull(**-over**) *m.* (*noun*), pullover.
punir (*verb*), to punish.
pupitre *m.* (*noun*), (school) desk.
pur (*adj.*), pure, clean, fresh, unsullied, spotless.
pyjama *m.* (*noun*), (pair of) pyjamas (*N.B. French singular, English plural*).

Q

quai *m.* (*noun*), embankment; quay, wharf; (railway) platform.

qualifier (*verb*), to qualify; to call, to term (**qualifier quelqu'un d'escroc,** to call someone a crook).

qualité *f.* (*noun*), quality; qualification.

quand (*adv. & conj.*), when; **quand même,** all the same, for all that, just the same.

quant à, as for, as regards; **quant à moi,** as for me; **quant à votre oncle,** as regards your uncle.

quantité *f.* (*noun*), quantity, amount; extent.

quarante *m.* (*noun & adj.*), forty; **quarante et un(e),** forty-one.

quart *m.* (*noun*), quarter.

quartier *m.* (*noun*), district, quarter (of a town); fourth part, quarter.

quatorze *m.* (*noun & adj.*), fourteen; fourteenth (**Louis Quatorze,** Louis the Fourteenth; **le quatorze juillet,** the fourteenth of July).

quatre *m.* (*noun & adj.*), four; fourth (**Henri Quatre,** Henry the Fourth; **le quatre mai,** May the fourth); **à quatre pattes,** on all fours.

quatre-vingt-dix *m.* (*noun & adj.*), ninety.

quatre-vingt-onze *m.* (*noun & adj.*), ninety-one.

quatre-vingts *m.* (*noun & adj.*), eighty.

quatrième (*noun & adj.*), fourth.

que (*pron.*), which, that (**la table que j'ai achetée,** the table which I have bought); (*interrogative*), what? (**que faites-vous?** what are you doing?); (*conj.*), than (**plus âgé que,** older than); that (**je crois que . . .** I believe that . . .; **je veux que tu m'attendes,** I want you to wait for me); (*adv.*), **ne . . . que,** only, no more than (**Marie a six francs, mais Paul n'a que trois francs,** Mary has six francs, but Paul has only three francs); (*exclamatory*), **qu'il est beau!** how handsome he is! **que de gens!** what a lot of people!

quel *m.*, **quelle** *f.* (*adj.*), what, which (**quel livre avez-vous pris?** which book have you taken? **quelle heure est-il?** what is the time?).

quelque (*adj.*), some, any; **pendant quelque temps,** for some time; **il y a quelques jours,** a few days ago; **quelque chose** (*pron.*), something, anything.

quelquefois (*adv.*), sometimes, now and then.

quelques-uns *m.*, **quelques-unes** *f.*, some (**quelques-uns des magasins,** some of the shops); a few (**quelques-un(e)s d'entre nous,** a few of us).

quelqu'un *m.*, **quelqu'une** *f.* (*pron.*), someone, anyone (**quelqu'un peut-il répondre?** can anyone answer?).

querelle *f.* (*noun*), quarrel, dispute.

qu'est-ce que (*pron.*), what? (*used as object*) (**qu'est-ce que vous voulez?** what do you want?).

qu'est-ce qui (*pron.*), what? (*used as subject*) (**qu'est-ce qui est arrivé?** what has happened?).

question *f.* (*noun*), question; point, matter.

queue *f.* (*noun*), tail (of animal); handle (of pan); queue (of people) (**faire la queue,** to queue up).

qui (*pron.*), who (**l'homme qui parle,** the man who is speaking); which, that (**les fleurs qui sont sur la table,** the flowers that are on the table); **à qui,** to whom; **qui?** (*pron.*), who? whom? (**qui vient?** who is coming?; **qui voyez-vous?** whom do you see?; **à qui parlez-vous?** to whom are you speaking?); **qui est-ce qui vous l'a dit?** who told you so?; **qui est-ce que vous désirez voir?** whom to do you wish to see?

quinze *m.* (*noun & adj.*), fifteen; fifteenth (**Louis Quinze,** Louis the Fifteenth; **le quinze août,** August the fifteenth).

quinzième (*noun & adj.*), fifteenth.
quitter (*verb*), to quit; to leave; to lay aside; **se quitter,** to part; to separate.
quoi (*pron.*), what; **quoi que,** whatever (**quoi qu'il fasse, il a toujours tort,** whatever he does, he is always wrong).
quoique (*conj.*), (al)though (**quoiqu'il fût bon élève, il était très distrait,** although he was a very good pupil, he was very inattentive).
quotidien *m.*, **-ienne** *f.* (*adj.*), daily; *m.* (*noun*), daily paper.

R

race *f.* (*noun*), race; ancestry; breed.
racine *f.* (*noun*), root (of plant, tooth, hair).
raconter (*verb*), to tell (a story), to recount, to relate, to narrate.
radio *f.* (*noun*), radio, wireless.
radiographie *f.* (*noun*), X-ray photograph.
rafraîchir (*verb*), to cool, to freshen; to refresh.
rafraîchissement *m.* (*noun*), cooling (of liquid); (*pl.*) refreshments.
raie *f.* (*noun*), parting (in hair); stripe (on material).
rail *m.* (*noun*), rail (on railway); rail transport.
raisin *m.* (*noun*), grape.
raison *f.* (*noun*), reason, intellect; justification; **avoir raison,** to be correct, to be right.
ramasser (*verb*), to collect, to gather; to pick up.
rame *f.* (*noun*), oar, scull.
ramoner (*verb*), to sweep (the chimney); to clear, to rake out.
ramper (*verb*), to crawl; to creep.
rang *m.* (*noun*), row, line; rank; **en rang,** in line.
rangée *f.* (*noun*), row (of trees, knitting, etc.).
ranger (*verb*), to tidy up, to arrange neatly, to put in place.
rapide (*adj.*), rapid, swift; brisk (walk); sharp (trot); *m.* (*noun*), express train.
rapidité *f.* (*noun*), speed, swiftness, rapidity, quickness (of a movement).
rapiécer (*verb*), to patch, to patch up.
rappeler (*verb*), to remind; to call back to mind; to recover (one's courage); **se rappeler,** to recollect, to remember, to recall.
rapporter (*verb*), to bring back; to report, to relate; to bring in, to yield.
rare (*adj.*), rare, unusual; (*of hair, etc.*) sparse, thin, scanty.
rarement (*adv.*), seldom, rarely.
raser (*verb*), to shave (someone); to graze, to pass close to; **se raser,** to shave (oneself).
rasoir *m.* (*noun*), razor.
rassembler (*verb*), to collect, to gather together; to reassemble, to bring together again.
rat *m.* (*noun*), rat.
rayon *m.* (*noun*), ray, beam (of light); radius (of circle); shelf (of bookcase); department (of large store).
rayonne *f.* (*noun*), rayon, artificial silk.
récent (*adj.*), recent, new, fresh.
recevoir (*verb*), to receive, to get; to entertain (friends); **être reçu à un examen,** to pass an examination.
réciter (*verb*), to recite; to say (a lesson).
récolte *f.* (*noun*), harvesting; harvest, crop(s).
récolter (*verb*), to harvest, to gather in; to collect.
recommencer (*verb*), to begin again, to start afresh.
récompense *f.* (*noun*), reward, recompense, prize.
récompenser (*verb*), to reward, to recompense.
reconnaissant (*adj.*), grateful (**envers quelqu'un,** to someone); thankful (**de,** for).
reconnaître (*verb*), to recognize, to know again; to identify.
recouvrer (*verb*), to recover, to retrieve; to regain (health).
recouvrir (*verb*), to cover again, to recover; to cover up.
reçu (*past participle*): *see* **recevoir.**
reculer (*verb*), to back, to reverse; to push back (a chair); to put off, to postpone; **se reculer,** to step back, to draw back.
réduire (*verb*), to reduce; to scale down.
réfléchir (*verb*), to ponder; to reflect, to think; **se réfléchir,** (*of light*) to be reflected; (*of sound*) to reverberate.

réfrigérateur *m.* (*noun*), refrigerator.
refuser (*verb*), to refuse, to decline.
regard *m.* (*noun*), look, gaze, glance, expression; **regard fixe,** stare.
regarder (*verb*), to look, to look at, to watch; to regard, to view; to consider; to concern; **regarder fixement,** to stare at.
région *f.* (*noun*), area, region, district.
règle *f.* (*noun*), rule, ruler (for measuring); rule (of a game).
reine *f.* (*noun*), queen.
rejeter (*verb*), to reject; to cast off; to throw out.
rejoindre (*verb*), to rejoin (someone); to reunite.
relâcher (*verb*), to relax; to release; to loosen.
relation *f.* (*noun*), relationship; (*pl.*) terms (**être en relations d'amitié avec quelqu'un,** to be on friendly terms with someone); connection (**relation de cause à effet,** connection between cause and effect); account, narrative, tale (**relations de voyage,** travellers' tales); **relations entre Calais et Paris,** train service between Calais and Paris. (*N.B.* **relation** *never means* 'relation' *in the sense of* 'relative'; *see* **parents**).
religieux *m.*, **-euse** *f.* (*adj.*), religious.
religion *f.* (*noun*), religion.
remarquer (*verb*), to notice, to observe; to distinguish, to make out.
rembourser (*verb*), to repay, to reimburse; to settle (a debt).
remède *m.* (*noun*), remedy, cure.
remercier (*verb*), to thank (someone) (**de,** for); to refuse with thanks (**Encore du gâteau?—Je vous remercie.**—Some more cake?—No, thank you).
remettre (*verb*), to replace, to put back; to postpone; to put on again (clothes).
remonter (*verb*), to climb up again, to go up again; (*of barometer*) to go up.
remplacer (*verb*), to replace (**par,** by); to deputize for; to supersede.
remplir (*verb*), to fill (**de,** with); to refill, to fill up; to fill up (a space), to complete (a form).
remuer (*verb*), to move, to stir, to shift; to stir up (liquid).
rémunération *f.* (*noun*), remuneration, payment, reward.
renard *m.* (*noun*), fox.
rencontrer (*verb*), to meet with (something); to meet (someone); to come up against; **se rencontrer,** to meet; to join; to collide.
rendre (*verb*), to give back, to return, to restore; to make (**rendre malade,** to make ill; **rendre élégant,** to make elegant).
renne *m.* (*noun*), reindeer.
renoncer (**à**) (*verb*), to renounce, to give up (one's rights); to disown; to deny; to renounce (one's faith).
rentrer (*verb*), to re-enter, to return, to come *or* go back; to go in; to return to school (after holidays) (**les enfants rentrent** (**en classe**) **le 20 septembre,** the children go back to school on September 20th).
renverser (*verb*), to knock over, to upset, to spill, to tip over.
réparation *f.* (*noun*), repair; amends, redress (of a wrong).
réparer (*verb*), to mend, to repair; to refit (a boat).
repartir (*verb*), to set off *or* out again.
repas *m.* (*noun*), meal.
repasser (*verb*), to repass; to call again; to pass by again; to iron (clothes); to strop (a razor).
répéter (*verb*), to repeat, to say again; to rehearse (a play).
répliquer (*verb*), to retort, to answer back.
répondre (*verb*), to reply; **répondre à une question,** to answer a question.
réponse *f.* (*noun*), reply, answer.
repos *m.* (*noun*), rest, repose; peace and quiet.
reposer (*verb*), to put *or* set down again, to put back in its place; to rest (in death); **se reposer,** to rest, to have a rest; to settle again (**l'oiseau se reposa sur la branche,** the bird settled on the bough again).

reprendre (*verb*), to take back (**Marie reprend la poupée qu'elle avait prêtée à Pauline,** Mary takes back the doll she lent to Pauline); to recapture (**les soldats ont repris la ville à l'ennemi,** the soldiers have recaptured the town from the enemy); to pick up (someone) (**je viendrai vous reprendre chez vous,** I will pick you up at your house); to restart, to resume, to take up again (**reprendre les travaux, une conversation,** to resume work, a conversation).

représenter (*verb*), to represent, to stand *or* act for; to exhibit, to show.

reproduire (*verb*), to reproduce; to copy.

république *f.* (*noun*), republic.

réservé (*adj.*), reserved, shy.

résigner (*verb*), to resign (one's office); **se résigner à,** to reconcile oneself to.

respirer (*verb*), to breathe.

ressembler (**à**) (*verb*), to resemble, to look like.

ressort *m.* (*noun*), spring (of car); springiness, elasticity.

restaurant *m.* (*noun*), restaurant.

reste *m.* (*noun*), rest, remainder; (*pl.*) remains (of meal); scraps.

rester (*verb*), to remain, to be left (over); to remain, to stay; to dwell, to stay.

résultat *m.* (*noun*), result, outcome, consequence.

retard *m.* (*noun*), delay, lateness, slowness; **en retard,** in arrears; slow (watch); late (person); backward (pupil).

retarder (*verb*), to postpone, to delay, to put off; to hinder, to impede; (*of watch*) to lose time.

retirer (*verb*), to pull out, to draw out, to take out; to withdraw (a court action); **se retirer,** to withdraw; to retire (to bed, from business); to retreat.

retour *m.* (*noun*), return; (*cinema*) flashback.

retourner (*verb*), to turn over, to turn again, to turn round; to return; **retourner une situation,** to turn the tables; **se retourner,** to turn over (in bed); to turn oneself round.

retraite *f.* (*noun*), retreat (in battle); retirement (from work).

retrouver (*verb*), to rediscover; to find again; to recover; to get back; **se retrouver,** to meet again; **se retrouver dans la même position,** to find oneself again in the same position.

réussir (*verb*), to succeed, to be successful (**il a réussi à monter l'échelle,** he has succeeded (been successful) in climbing the ladder); to result, to turn out (**il ne sait comment le projet réussira,** he does not know how the plan will turn out); to thrive (**la plante a réussi dans le jardin,** the plant has thrived in the garden).

rêve *m.* (*noun*), dream; day-dream.

réveil *m.* (*noun*), waking, awakening (**c'est l'heure du réveil,** it is time to wake up; **à mon réveil,** on waking).

réveille-matin *m.* (*noun*), alarm-clock.

réveiller (*verb*), to wake up, to rouse; to arouse (attention); **se réveiller,** to awaken, to wake up; (*of feelings*) to be aroused.

revenir (*verb*), to return, to come back; to cost, to come to; to please (**sa figure ne me revient pas,** I don't like the look of him).

rêver (*verb*), to dream; to day-dream; to think, to reflect; to meditate.

réverbère *m.* (*noun*), lamp-post, street lamp.

revoir (*verb*), to see again, to meet again; (*noun*), **au revoir!** so long! cheerio! goodbye!

rez-de-chaussée *m.* (*noun*), ground floor, ground level.

rhume *m.* (*noun*), cold (*illness*).

riche (*adj.*), rich, well off, wealthy; abundant; fertile (soil).

rideau (*pl.* **rideaux**) *m.* (*noun*), curtain.

rien (*pron.*), anything (**il est entré dans la salle et n'a rien remarqué,** he entered the room and didn't notice anything); nothing (**il n'y avait rien dans la boîte,** there was nothing in the

box); hardly anything (**obtenir pour rien,** to get for next to nothing).
rire (*verb*), to laugh; to jest; **rire** *m.* (*noun*), laughter, laugh.
risque *m.* (*noun*), risk, hazard.
risquer (*verb*), to risk; to endanger; to chance; to jeopardize.
rivage *m.* (*noun*), beach, sea-shore; bank *or* side (of river).
rivière *f.* (*noun*), river, stream (which flows into larger river) (*see* **fleuve**).
riz *m.* (*noun*), rice.
robe *f.* (*noun*), dress, frock, gown, robe; coat (of animal).
robinet *m.* (*noun*), tap.
roche *f.* (*noun*), boulder; (small) rock.
rocher *m.* (*noun*), (large) rock; **rocher escarpé,** crag.
roi *m.* (*noun*), king.
rompre (*verb*), to break; to snap (a twig).
rond (*adj.*), round (table); full (face); full (voice); straightforward (person).
rond *m.* (*noun*), circle, ring; round; **en rond,** in a circle.
ronger (*verb*), to gnaw, to nibble; **se ronger les ongles,** to bite one's nails.
rose *f.* (*noun*), rose; rose-window; (*adj.*), pink, rosy.
roue *f.* (*noun*), wheel; cartwheel.
rouge (*adj.*), red; **rouge de colère,** flushed with anger.
rouge-gorge *m.* (*noun*), robin (redbreast).
rouleau (*pl.* **rouleaux**) *m.* (*noun*), roller; roll (of cloth, paper); **rouleau à pâtisserie,** rolling-pin.
rouler (*verb*), to roll (a cigarette, field, pastry); to travel along; to furl (an umbrella); to lurch about.
roulette *f.* (*noun*), small wheel; caster; dentist's drill; roulette (*game*).
route *f.* (*noun*), way, road, path, route; **grande route,** highway, main road.
ruban *m.* (*noun*), ribbon, band; tape.
rude (*adj.*), rough; uneven; hard (climate, winter, master).
rue *f.* (*noun*), street.
rugir (*verb*), (*of animal*) to roar; (*of sea*) to boom; (*of wind*) to howl.
rugissement *m.* (*noun*), roaring (of lion); howling (of storm).
rusé (*adj.*), crafty.

S

sa *f.* (*adj.*): *see* **son.**
sable *m.* (*noun*), sand; sable (fur).
sabot *m.* (*noun*), clog, sabot; hoof (of horse).
sac *m.* (*noun*), sack; bag (**sac à main,** handbag); pouch; pack, haversack.
sagace (*adj.*), shrewd; sagacious, acute.
sage (*adj.*), wise, prudent; quiet, well-behaved.
saigner (*verb*), to bleed.
saint (*adj.*), holy; consecrated; **la Sainte Bible,** the Holy Bible; (*noun*), saint.
saisir (*verb*), to seize; to grasp; to grab.
saison *f.* (*noun*), season.
salade *f.* (*noun*), salad.
salaire *m.* (*noun*), salary, wages; reward, recompense, retribution.
sale (*adj.*), dirty, unclean, soiled; dull, dingy.
salir (*verb*), to dirty, to make dirty, to soil; to stain, to tarnish, to sully.
salle *f.* (*noun*), room; hall; **salle à manger,** dining room; **salle de bain(s),** bathroom; **salle de bal,** ballroom; **salle de classe,** classroom.
salon *m.* (*noun*), drawing room, lounge.
saluer (*verb*), to salute, to greet; to wave; to hail (someone).
salut *m.* (*noun*), salute; greeting; safety (**Comité** *m.* **de salut public,** Committee of Public Safety); salvation (**Armée** *f.* **du Salut,** Salvation Army).
samedi *m.* (*noun*), Saturday.
sandwich *m.* (*noun*), sandwich; **sandwich au jambon,** ham sandwich.
sang *m.* (*noun*), blood.
sans (*prep.*), without; but for (**sans cela,** but for that); **sans doute,** no doubt, doubtless; **sans aucun doute,** without any doubt.
santé *f.* (*noun*), health; **à votre santé!** good health!
sapin *m.* (*noun*), fir-tree.
sauf (*prep.*), except, unless; barring (accidents).
sauter (*verb*), to jump, to leap; (*of a button*) to come off, to fly off.
sauteur *m.*, **sauteuse** *f.* (*noun*), jumper (*athlete*).
sauvage (*adj.*), wild, savage, untamed.
sauver (*verb*), to save, to preserve, to rescue; **se sauver,** to run away, to make one's escape; to make off.
savoir (*verb*), to know; to be aware of; to know how.
savon *m.* (*noun*), soap.
scandaleux *m.*, **-euse** *f.* (*adj.*), scandalous, shocking, shameful.
scie *f.* (*noun*), saw.
scier (*verb*), to saw, to cut with a saw, to saw off (a branch).
scintiller (*verb*), to glitter; (*of star*) to twinkle; to glisten.
sculpter (*verb*), to sculpt, to carve (**dans,** in).
sculpteur *m.* (*noun*), sculptor; **sculpteur sur bois,** wood carver.
sculpture *f.* (*noun*), sculpture.
se (*pers. pron.*), himself, herself, itself (**il se lave,** he washes himself); themselves; each other, one another.
seau (*pl.* **seaux**) *m.* (*noun*), bucket, pail; **seau à charbon,** coal-scuttle.
sec *m.*, **sèche** *f.* (*adj.*), dry, parched, arid.
sécher (*verb*), to dry; to become dry, to dry up.
second (*adj.*), second.
seconde *f.* (*noun*), (*time*) second.
seconder (*verb*), to second, to back up, to support.
secouer (*verb*), to shake (a branch, the head); to plump up (a pillow); to shake off (dust).
secours *m.* (*noun*), help, aid, assistance; **au secours!** help!
seize *m.* (*noun & adj.*), sixteen; sixteenth (**Louis Seize,** Louis the Sixteenth; **le seize janvier,** January the sixteenth).
seizième (*noun & adj.*), sixteenth.
sel *m.* (*noun*), salt.

semaine *f.* (*noun*), week.
semblable (*adj.*), alike, similar.
sembler (*verb*), to seem, to appear.
semer (*verb*), to sow (seed); to scatter, to strew.
sens *m.* (*noun*), sense; opinion, point of view, feeling; direction, way.
senteur *f.* (*noun*), smell, scent, odour, perfume.
sentier *m.* (*noun*), footpath, path.
sentir (*verb*), to feel, to be conscious of; to experience; to smell (a flower); **je me sens fatigué,** I feel tired.
sept *m.* (*noun & adj.*), seven; seventh (**Édouard Sept,** Edward the Seventh; **le sept février,** February the seventh).
septembre *m.* (*noun*), September.
septième (*noun & adj.*), seventh.
sérieux *m.*, **-euse** *f.* (*adj.*), serious, grave; dangerous; earnest.
serpent *m.* (*noun*), snake, serpent.
serre *f.* (*noun*), claw, talon (of bird of prey); greenhouse; **serre chaude,** hothouse.
serrer (*verb*), to shake, to squeeze, to clasp, to clutch (**serrer la main à quelqu'un,** to shake hands with someone); to tighten.
serrure *f.* (*noun*), lock.
service *m.* (*noun*), assistance, service; **rendre (un) service à quelqu'un,** to do someone a good turn.
serviette *f.* (*noun*), table napkin, serviette; child's bib; towel; briefcase.
servir (*verb*), to help, to assist; to serve (food), to wait at table; to be used (**de,** as); **se servir,** to help oneself, to serve oneself; to use (something) (**il se sert d'un crayon pour écrire,** he uses a pencil to write with).
ses *m. & f. pl.* (*adj.*): *see* **son.**
seul (*adj.*), alone, single, sole, single-handed; only.
seulement (*adv.*), only, alone, solely.
si (*conj.*), if; whether; (*adv.*), so (**si joli,** so pretty); yes (*in reply to a question put negatively*).
siège *m.* (*noun*), siege; seat, chair; bench (of magistrate).
le sien, la sienne (*poss. pron.*), his, hers, its, one's (**mon frère est plus grand que le sien,** my brother is taller than his *or* than hers).
sifflement *m.* (*noun*), whistling; whistle (of the wind).
siffler (*verb*), to whistle; to hiss; to wheeze.
sifflet *m.* (*noun*), whistle (*instrument*).
signature *f.* (*noun*), signature; signing.
signe *m.* (*noun*), sign; mark, token; birthmark.
signer (*verb*), to sign, to put one's name to.
signifier (*verb*), to signify, to mean; to make known, to declare.
silence *m.* (*noun*), silence, quiet; **silence!** hush!
sillage *m.* (*noun*), wake (of ship).
sillon *m.* (*noun*), furrow.
simple (*adj.*), simple, ordinary; plain (food, people), unpretentious; simple (-minded), naïve.
simuler (*verb*), to pretend; to simulate, to sham.
singe *m.* (*noun*), monkey; **grand singe,** ape.
six *m.* (*noun & adj.*), six; sixth (**Henri Six,** Henry the Sixth; **le six septembre,** September the sixth).
sixième (*noun & adj.*), sixth.
sœur *f.* (*noun*), sister; nun.
soie *f.* (*noun*), silk.
soif *f.* (*noun*), thirst; craving; **avoir soif,** to be thirsty.
soigné (*adj.*), trim, well-groomed; well-kept (garden).
soigner (*verb*), to care for, to look after, to see to; to nurse, to tend; **se soigner,** to take care of oneself, to look after oneself.
soin *m.* (*noun*), care, attention, trouble.
soir *m.* (*noun*), evening; **ce soir,** this evening, tonight.
soixante *m.* (*noun & adj.*), sixty; **soixante et onze,** seventy-one.
soixante-dix *m.* (*noun & adj.*), seventy.
soixante-douze *m.* (*noun & adj.*), seventy-two.
sol *m.* (*noun*), ground, earth; soil.
soldat *m.* (*noun*), soldier.

soleil *m.* (*noun*), sun; **coup** *m.* **de soleil,** sun-stroke.
solide (*adj.*), solid, strong, well built; firm, staunch, sound; **solide** *m.* (*noun*), solid (body).
sombre (*adj.*), dark, sombre, dull, dim, gloomy.
somme *f.* (*noun*), sum, amount, quantity; **somme toute,** altogether; **en somme,** in short.
sommeil *m.* (*noun*), sleep; drowsiness; **avoir sommeil,** to be sleepy, to feel sleepy.
sommet *m.* (*noun*), summit, peak, top; apex (of triangle).
sommier *m.* (*noun*), mattress.
son *m.*, **sa** *f.*, **ses** *pl.* (*adj.*), his, her (**son frère,** his *or* her brother; **sa sœur,** his *or* her sister; **ses enfants,** his *or* her children); its; one's.
sonner (*verb*), to ring, to peal, to strike.
sonnette *f.* (*noun*), small bell, hand bell, house bell.
sorcier *m.*, **sorcière** *f.* (*noun*), sorcerer, sorceress, witch.
sorte *f.* (*noun*), sort, kind, species; manner, fashion, way.
sortie *f.* (*noun*), exit, way out; going out, coming out (*action*).
sortir (*verb*), to go out, to come out, to leave; to take out, to bring out, to pull out.
sot *m.*, **sotte** *f.* (*adj.*), stupid, foolish, silly; (*noun*), fool, simpleton.
soucoupe *f.* (*noun*), saucer; **soucoupe volante,** flying saucer.
soudain (*adj.*), sudden, unexpected; (*adv.*), suddenly, all at once.
souffle *m.* (*noun*), breath; blow, blast.
soufflé *m.* (*noun*), soufflé (omelette).
souffler (*verb*), to blow; to puff.
souhait *m.* (*noun*), wish.
souhaiter (*verb*), to wish, to wish for.
soulever (*verb*), to lift up, to raise, to heave; to provoke (indignation); to stir up (people).
soulier *m.* (*noun*), shoe.
soumettre (*verb*), to subdue, to bring into subjection; to submit, to present; **se soumettre,** to submit, to give in.
soupe *f.* (*noun*), soup.
souper *m.* (*noun*), supper.
source *f.* (*noun*), source, spring; head (of river); origin.
sourd (*adj.*), deaf; muffled (sound); (*noun*), deaf person.
sourire (*verb*), to smile; **sourire à,** to smile on, to favour, to appeal to (**ce projet ne me sourit pas,** this plan does not appeal to me); **sourire** *m.* (*noun*), smile.
souris *f.* (*noun*), mouse.
sous (*prep.*), under, beneath; **sous le nom de,** by the name of; **sous la main,** at hand.
sous-vêtements *m. pl.* (*noun*), underclothes.
soutenir (*verb*), to support, to hold up; to maintain (an opinion).
soutien-gorge (*pl.* **soutiens-gorge**) *m.* (*noun*), bra(ssière).
se souvenir de (*verb*), to remember, to recall.
souvenir *m.* (*noun*), memory, recollection; souvenir, memento.
souvent (*adv.*), frequently, often.
spécifier (*verb*), to state definitely, to specify.
sport *m.* (*noun*), sport; **sports athlétiques,** athletics.
stationnaire (*adj.*), stationary; steady (barometer); fixed (machine).
store *m.* (*noun*), (window-)blind.
structure *f.* (*noun*), structure.
stupéfier (*verb*), to amaze, to astound; to stupefy.
stupide (*adj.*), stupid, dull; idiotic, silly.
stylo *m.* (*noun*), fountain pen; **stylo à bille,** ball-point pen.
sucer (*verb*), to suck.
sucre *m.* (*noun*), sugar.
sucré (*adj.*), sugared, sweetened; honeyed (words).
sucrier *m.* (*noun*), sugar-basin, sugar-bowl.
sud *m.* (*noun*), south.
suffisant (*adj.*), sufficient, enough, adequate.

suggérer (*verb*), to suggest, to propose.
suivant (*adj.*), following, next; (*prep.*), according to.
suivre (*verb*), to follow.
sujet *m.* (*noun*), subject; cause, reason; **au sujet de,** about, concerning.
superbe (*adj.*), fine; superb, magnificent; imposing,
supposer (*verb*), to suppose; to surmise.
sur (*prep.*), on, upon (**sur l'eau,** on the water); above (**sur toute(s) chose(s),** above all (things)); about (**un débat sur le cinéma,** a discussion about the cinema); over (**le roi avait autorité sur ses sujets,** the king had authority over his subjects).
sûr (*adj.*), sure, certain (**bien sûr!** of course!); unfailing; reliable, trustworthy.
sûrement (*adv.*), surely, certainly, for sure; safely.
surprise *f.* (*noun*), surprise, astonishment.
surtout (*adv.*), above all, especially.
surveiller (*verb*), to watch over, to look after, to supervise.
survivre (*verb*): **survivre à quelqu'un,** to survive someone, to outlive someone.
suspendre (*verb*), to hang up, to suspend (clear of the ground); to leave abeyance.
syllabe *f.* (*noun*), syllable.

T

ta *f.* (*adj.*): *see* **ton.**

tabac *m.* (*noun*), tobacco.

table *f.* (*noun*), table; **table de multiplication,** multiplication table.

tableau (*pl.* **tableaux**) *m.* (*noun*), picture, painting; board; notice-board; **tableau noir,** blackboard.

tablier *m.* (*noun*), apron, pinafore.

tablier-blouse *f.* (*noun*), overall.

tache *f.* (*noun*), splash, stain, blob; blemish.

taché (*adj.*), stained, spotted (with dirt).

tâche *f.* (*noun*), task, job.

tacheté (*adj.*), speckled, mottled.

taille *f.* (*noun*), cutting; pruning, trimming; waist; size (of clothes); height (of person); **tour** *m.* **de taille,** waist measurement.

tailler (*verb*), to cut; to trim (a hedge); to prune (a tree); to sharpen (a pencil).

tailleur *m.* (*noun*), tailor; cutter (of precious stones); (tailor-made) suit.

taire (*verb*), to suppress, to hush up, to silence; **se taire,** to be silent, to hold one's tongue; **taisez-vous!** be quiet!

tambour *m.* (*noun*), drum; drummer.

tandis que (*conj.*), whilst, while (**tandis qu'il parlait quelqu'un entra,** whilst he was speaking someone entered); whereas (**son frère a peiné jusqu'à sa mort, tandis que lui n'a jamais rien fait,** his brother toiled to the end of his life, whereas he has never done anything).

tant (*adv.*), so much (**il boit tant,** he drinks so much); so many (**il a tant d'amis,** he has so many friends).

tante *f.* (*noun*), aunt.

tape *f.* (*noun*), tap, pat, rap.

taper (*verb*), to tap, to pat, to rap.

tapis *m.* (*noun*), carpet; cover, cloth.

tapis-brosse *m.* (*noun*), doormat.

taquiner (*verb*), to tease, to torment.

tard (*adv.*), late; **plus tard,** later, later on.

tarte *f.* (*noun*), open tart; flan.

tartine *f.* (*noun*), slice of bread and butter.

tas *m.* (*noun*), heap, pile; lot, crowd.

tasse *f.* (*noun*), cup.

tâter (*verb*), to touch, to feel; to handle, to finger.

taureau (*pl.* **taureaux**) *m.* (*noun*), bull.

taxi *m.* (*noun*), taxi(-cab).

te (*pron.*), you (**je te vois,** I see you); to you (**je te donne ce livre,** I give this book to you); yourself (**tu ne te soignes pas,** you don't look after yourself).

tel *m.*, **telle** *f.* (*adj.*), such a (**un tel homme, une telle femme,** such a man, such a woman); like, as (**tel père, tel fils,** like father, like son); this, that (**en tel ou tel cas,** in this or that case); **tel quel** *m.*, **telle quelle** *f.* (*adj.*), just as he (she, it) is (**Prenez-vous du lait avec votre café? Non, merci, je le bois tel quel,** Are you having some milk with your coffee? No, thank you, I'll drink it as it is); **tel que,** such that (**ce bruit est tel que l'on . . .** this noise is such that one (we) . . .).

télégramme *m.* (*noun*), telegram.

télégraphier (*verb*), to telegraph, to wire.

téléphone *m.* (*noun*), telephone.

téléphoner (*verb*), to telephone.

télescope *m.* (*noun*), telescope.

télévision *f.* (*noun*), television.

tellement (*adv.*), in such a manner; to such a degree; so (**il est tellement sourd qu'il faut crier,** he is so deaf that one has to shout; **il fait tellement froid qu'il porte des gants,** it is so cold that he wears gloves).

tempête *f.* (*noun*), tempest, storm, gale.

temps *m.* (*noun*), time (**le temps passe,** time passes); period, duration, while (**pendant quelque temps,** for a short while); leisure (**je n'ai pas le temps de lire,** I haven't the leisure to read); **tout le temps,** the whole time, all the time, incessantly; **quel temps fait-il?** what is the weather like?

tendre (*adj.*), tender; affectionate.
tendre (*verb*), to stretch, to tighten (a rope); to hold out (one's hand), to offer (a present).
tenez! (*interj.*), look! look here! here you are!
tenir (*verb*), to hold, to grip; to keep, to retain; **tenir à faire quelque chose,** to be bent on doing something; **se tenir,** to stand (**il se tient droit,** he stands straight); to be connected, to hold together (**ces arguments se tiennent,** these arguments hold together); to be held, to take place (**la réunion se tient à l'Hôtel Atlantique,** the reunion is being held at the Atlantic Hotel).
tente *f.* (*noun*), tent.
terminer (*verb*), to finish, to terminate, to end.
terrain *m.* (*noun*), piece of ground, stretch of land; terrain.
terre *f.* (*noun*), land (as opposed to sea); earth, world; ground, soil.
terrible (*adj.*), terrible, dreadful.
terrifiant (*adj.*), terrifying.
terrifier (*verb*), to appal, to horrify, to terrify.
tes *m. & f. pl.* (*adj.*): *see* **ton.**
têtard *m.* (*noun*), tadpole.
tête *f.* (*noun*), head; sense, reason; top (of tree); **se laver la tête,** to wash one's hair; **en tête,** foremost, leading, at the front.
texture *f.* (*noun*), texture (of fabric).
thé *m.* (*noun*), tea.
théâtre *m.* (*noun*), theatre; the stage (*the profession*).
le tien, la tienne (*poss. pron.*), yours (*familiar*) (**ma chaise et la tienne,** my chair and yours).
tiens! (*interj.*), hullo! hold it! just a minute!
tiers *m.* (*noun*), third, third part.
timbre *m.* (*noun*), small bell (of cycle, etc.).
timbre(-poste) *m.* (*noun*), postage-stamp.
tirelire *f.* (*noun*), money-box, piggy-bank.
tirer (*verb*), to pull, to draw; to shoot; to draw (a plan); to print (a negative).
tissu *m.* (*noun*), fabric, cloth, material; texture; **tissu de mensonges,** tissue of lies.
toboggan *m.* (*noun*), toboggan; chute (in swimming bath).
toi (*pron.*), you (*familiar*) (**c'est toi,** it's you); **toi-même,** yourself (*familiar*).
toile *f.* (*noun*), cloth (*generally speaking*); linen; **toile d'araignée** *f.*, spider's web.
toilette *f.* (*noun*), dressing-table; lavatory, toilet; **faire sa toilette,** to wash and dress.
toit *m.* (*noun*), roof.
tôle *f.* (*noun*), sheet-metal; **tôle ondulée,** corrugated iron.
tomate *f.* (*noun*), tomato.
tomber (*verb*), to fall, to fall down, to drop.
ton *m.*, **ta** *f.*, *pl.* **tes** (*adj.*), your (*familiar*) (**ton père,** your father; **ta maison,** your house; **tes fleurs,** your flowers).
tonneau (*pl.* **tonneaux**) *m.* (*noun*), barrel, cask, tun.
tonnerre *m.* (*noun*), thunder.
torchon *m.* (*noun*), duster; dishcloth.
tordre (*verb*), to twist; **se tordre,** to writhe about, to wriggle.
tort *m.* (*noun*), harm, injury, hurt; wrong; fault; **avoir tort,** to be wrong.
tortue *f.* (*noun*), tortoise; **tortue de mer,** turtle; **soupe à la tortue,** turtle soup.
tôt (*adv.*), soon, early.
total *m.* (*noun*), sum, total, whole.
toucher (*verb*), to touch; to graze; to damage; to affect.
toujours (*adv.*), always, forever; still; nevertheless.
toupie *f.* (*noun*), top, spinning-top.
tour[1] *f.* (*noun*), tower (**la Tour Eiffel,** the Eiffel Tower).
tour[2] *m.* (*noun*), turn (of a wheel); circuit; distance round; **faire un tour,** to go for a walk, a ride.
tournant *m.* (*noun*), turn, bend (in road or river), corner, turning.
tourne-disques *m.* (*noun*), record player.
tourner (*verb*), to turn, to rotate, to wind, to twist, to revolve.

tourte *f.* (*noun*), covered tart, pie.
tousser (*verb*), to cough.
tout (*pl.* **tous**) *m.*, **toute** *f.* (*adj.*), all, every (**Paul a mangé tout le gâteau,** Paul has eaten all the cake; **tous les jours,** every day; **toute la journée,** the whole day); **tout le monde,** everyone, everybody; (*adv.*), **à tout jamais,** forever; **tout à fait,** quite, entirely, wholly, thoroughly, absolutely; **tout à coup,** suddenly, all at once; **tout à l'heure,** presently, directly, by and by (*future sense*); **tout de suite,** at once, right away; **tout confus,** quite *or* completely confused; (*pron.*), all (**ils sont tous arrivés,** they have all arrived).
toux *f.* (*noun*), cough.
trace *f.* (*noun*), track, trace, spoor (of animal).
tracteur *m.* (*noun*), tractor, traction-engine.
traduire (*verb*), to translate; to explain, to interpret.
train *m.* (*noun*), (railway) train; drove (of cattle); procession (of vehicles); **en train de,** in the process of.
traîne *f.* (*noun*), train (of dress).
traîneau (*pl.* **traîneaux**) *m.* (*noun*), sledge, sleigh; **aller en traîneau,** to sledge.
traire (*verb*), to milk (a cow).
trait *m.* (*noun*), stroke (of pen); flash (of light); deed, act; feature, characteristic.
traitement *m.* (*noun*), treatment; processing; salary.
tranchant (*adj.*), sharp, keen, cutting; self-assertive.
tranche *f.* (*noun*), slice (of bread); rasher (of bacon); edge (of a book); ridge (of a furrow).
trancher (*verb*), to slice; to cut; to chop off.
tranquille (*adj.*), still, quiet, placid, calm (water); **soyez tranquille!** don't worry!; **se tenir tranquille,** to keep still, to keep quiet.
transporter (*verb*), to convey, to transport.
travail (*pl.* **travaux**) *m.* (*noun*), work, labour, occupation, job.
travailler (*verb*), to work; to fashion; **travailler dur,** to toil, to work hard.
travailleur *m.*, **-euse** *f.* (*noun*), worker.
travers *m.* (*noun*), breadth; **en travers de** (*prep.*), across; **à travers, au travers de** (*prep.*), through.
traverser (*verb*), to cross, to go across; to go through, to make one's way through.
trébucher (*verb*), to stumble, to trip, to totter.
treize *m.* (*noun & adj.*), thirteen; thirteenth (**Louis Treize,** Louis the Thirteenth; **le treize juin,** June the thirteenth).
treizième (*noun & adj.*), thirteenth.
tremper (*verb*), to dip; to soak.
trente *m.* (*noun & adj.*), thirty; **trente et un,** thirty-one.
très (*adv.*), very; very much, greatly.
tribunal (*pl.* **tribunaux**) *m.* (*noun*), tribunal, law-court.
tricot *m.* (*noun*), knitting; knitted wear; jumper, jersey, sweater.
tricoter (*verb*), to knit.
trier (*verb*), to pick out, to select; to sort (letters); to marshal (railway waggons).
triste (*adj.*), sad, melancholy, sorrowful.
trois *m.* (*noun & adj.*), three; third (**Henri Trois,** Henry the Third; **le trois septembre,** September the third).
troisième (*noun & adj.*), third.
tromper (*verb*), to deceive; to cheat; to betray; **se tromper**, to deceive oneself, to delude oneself; to make a mistake, to be mistaken.
trompette *f.* (*noun*), trumpet.
tronc *m.* (*noun*), trunk; bole (of tree); poor-box, collecting-box (in church).
trône *m.* (*noun*), throne.
trop (*adv.*), too (**trop froid,** too cold); too much (**il boit trop,** he drinks too much); **trop de,** too much, too many (**trop de beurre,** too much butter; **trop d'enfants,** too many children).
trot *m.* (*noun*), trot.
trotter (*verb*), to trot.
trottoir *m.* (*noun*), pavement, footpath.
trou *m.* (*noun*), hole.

trouver (*verb*), to find; to observe, to notice; **se trouver,** to find oneself (in a situation); to be present; to be (**l'église se trouve au centre de la ville,** the church is in the centre of the town).

tu (*pron.*), you (*familiar*).

tube *m.* (*noun*), tube (of tooth-paste, etc.).

tuer (*verb*), to kill, to slay, to slaughter.

tulipe *f.* (*noun*), tulip.

tuyau (*pl.* **tuyaux**) *m.* (*noun*), tube, pipe.

U

un, *m.*, **une** *f.* (*numeral adj.*), one; (*indefinite article*), a, an; (*pron.*), one (**l'un de nous,** one of us).
univers *m.* (*noun*), universe.
université *f.* (*noun*), university.
usé (*adj.*), worn, used; exhausted (land); **usé jusqu' à la corde,** threadbare.
user (*verb*), to use up; to wear (out); **user de,** to use, to make use of.
usine *f.* (*noun*), factory, works, mill.
ustensile *m.* (*noun*), utensil, implement.
utile (*adj.*), useful, of use, of advantage, serviceable.

V

vacances *f. pl.* (*noun*), holidays, vacation; recess (of court of law).

vacant (*adj.*), vacant; unoccupied; unfilled (position).

vacciner (*verb*), to vaccinate, to inoculate.

vache *f.* (*noun*), cow.

vague *f.* (*noun*), wave, breaker; **vague de chaleur,** heat-wave.

valable (*adj.*), valid (ticket, etc.), good (excuse, etc.).

valise *f.* (*noun*), suitcase.

vallée *f.* (*noun*), valley.

valoir (*verb*), to be worth (**cette maison vaut cent mille francs,** this house is worth a hundred thousand francs); to deserve, to merit (**ce livre vaut d'être lu,** this book deserves to be read); to remain valid (**cela vaudra toujours,** that will always hold good); (*impers.*) **il vaut mieux rester à la maison,** it is better to stay at home.

vanter (*verb*), to praise; **se vanter,** to boast, to brag.

vapeur *f.* (*noun*), steam, vapour; **à toute vapeur,** at full speed, full steam ahead.

vase *m.* (*noun*), vase, receptacle.

veau (*pl.* **veaux**) *m.* (*noun*), calf; veal.

véhicule *m.* (*noun*), vehicle.

veille *f.* (*noun*), vigil; watchfulness; eve (**la veille de Noël,** Christmas Eve).

veiller (*verb*), to sit up, to keep awake; to keep vigil.

veine *f.* (*noun*), vein; grain (of wood); seam (of coal).

vélo *m.* (*noun*), bicycle.

vendre (*verb*), to sell; **à vendre,** for sale.

vendredi *m.* (*noun*), Friday.

venir (*verb*), to come; **venir de,** to have just (**il vient de partir,** he has just left).

vent *m.* (*noun*), wind; **aller comme le vent,** to go like the wind.

ventilateur *m.* (*noun*), ventilator; ventilation hole.

ventiler (*verb*), to ventilate, to air.

ventre *m.* (*noun*), abdomen, belly, stomach.

ver *m.* (*noun*), worm; larva, grub.

verdoyant (*adj.*), verdant, green.

vérité *f.* (*noun*), truth; fact, scientific principle; sincerity; **en vérité,** indeed, truly, really.

verre *m.* (*noun*), glass; drinking glass.

verrou *m.* (*noun*), bolt; **fermer une porte au verrou,** to bolt a door.

vers (*prep.*), towards; at about, around (**vers cinq heures,** at about five o'clock).

verser (*verb*), to overturn, to tip, to turn over, to upset; to pour, to pour out.

vert (*adj.*), green.

veste *f.* (*noun*), jacket, coat.

veston *m.* (*noun*), lounge coat, jacket.

vêtement *m.* (*noun*), garment; (*pl.*) clothes, clothing.

viande *f.* (*noun*), meat; **viande de cheval,** horse-flesh.

victoire *f.* (*noun*), victory; win (at games).

vide (*adj.*), empty, unoccupied, vacant.

vider (*verb*), to empty, to clear out (a room); to vacate (premises); to drain (one's glass); **videz vos verres!** drink up!

vie *f.* (*noun*), life; living (**gagner sa vie,** to earn one's living).

vieillard *m.* (*noun*), old man.

vierge *f.* (*noun*), virgin, maid(en).

vieux (**vieil**) *m.*, **vieille** *f.* (*adj.*), old, aged (**un vieil homme,** an old man; **une vieille dame,** an old lady); shabby, worn (clothes); old-fashioned.

vif *m.*, **vive** *f.* (*adj.*), alive; quick, lively; spirited (animal).

vigne *f.* (*noun*), vine; **clos** *m.* **de vigne,** vineyard.

vigneron *m.* (*noun*), vine-grower.

vigoureux *m.*, **-euse** *f.* (*adj.*), vigorous, robust, sturdy; forceful.

vil (*adj.*), mean; vile, despicable.

village *m.* (*noun*), village.

ville *f.* (*noun*), town.

vin *m.* (*noun*), wine.

vinaigre *m.* (*noun*), vinegar.

vingt *m.* (*noun & adj.*), twenty; twentieth (**le vingt octobre,** the twentieth of October).
violent (*adj.*), violent; fierce; hot-headed.
violet *m.* (*noun*), violet (*colour*).
violette *f.* (*noun*), violet (*flower*).
violon *m.* (*noun*), violin; **jouer du violon,** to play the violin.
vis *f.* (*noun*), screw.
visage *m.* (*noun*), face.
visite *f.* (*noun*), visit, call; visitor, caller.
visiter (*verb*), to visit; to view, to look over.
vite (*adv.*), quickly, swiftly, fast.
vitesse *f.* (*noun*), speed, rapidity, swiftness.
viticulteur *m.* (*noun*), wine-grower.
vitre *f.* (*noun*), pane of glass; window-pane.
vitrine *f.* (*noun*), shop-window; glass cabinet; **sous vitrine,** under glass.
vivant (*adj.*), alive; lively (scene); vivid (description).
vivre (*verb*), to live; to be alive.
vogue *f.* (*noun*), vogue, fashion; **c'est la grande vogue,** it's all the rage.
voilà (*prep.*), there is, there are (*indicating something or someone*); that is, those are (**voilà ma sœur,** there is my sister, that is my sister).
voile *f.* (*noun*), sail (of boat); **bateau à voiles,** sailing-boat; **aller à la voile, faire de la voile,** to sail.
voir (*verb*), to see; to perceive, to notice, to observe.
voisin (*adj.*), neighbouring, nearby, adjacent; **voisin** *m.*, **voisine** *f.* (*noun*), neighbour.
voisinage *m.* (*noun*), neighbourhood.
voiture *f.* (*noun*), vehicle, conveyance, motor car; railway carriage.
voix *f.* (*noun*), voice; **parler à haute voix,** to speak aloud; **à voix haute,** in a loud voice; **à voix basse,** in a low voice.
volant *m.* (*noun*), steering wheel (of car).
voler (*verb*), (*of bird, aeroplane*) to fly; to go fast; to soar (in imagination); **le temps vole,** time flies; to steal, to rob.
voleur *m.*, **voleuse** *f.* (*noun*), robber, burglar, thief.
votre (*pl.* **vos**) (*adj.*), your (**votre maison,** your house; **votre père,** your father; **vos enfants,** your children).
vôtre: le, la vôtre (*sing.*), **les vôtres** (*pl.*) (*pron.*), yours.
vouloir (*verb*), to wish, to want; to intend; to have need of; **vouloir bien faire quelque chose,** to be willing to do something (**je veux bien vous aider,** I am willing to help you); **voulez-vous bien vous asseoir un moment,** would you kindly sit down a moment; **vouloir dire,** to mean to say, to mean (**le mot "garçon" veut dire "boy",** the word "garçon" means "boy").
vous (*pron.*), you; yourself (**vous vous regardiez dans la glace,** you were looking at yourself in the mirror); **vous-même(s)**, yourself, yourselves.
voyage *m.* (*noun*), journey, trip, voyage.
voyager (*verb*), to travel, to make a journey.
voyageur *m.*, **-euse** *f.* (*noun*), traveller, passenger.
voyelle *f.* (*noun*), vowel.
voyons! (*interj.*), see! look out!; **voyons! faites attention!** look what you are doing!
vrai (*adj.*), true; real, genuine.
vraiment (*adv.*), really, truly, indeed.
vue *f.* (*noun*), sight, eyesight; view, outlook.

W

wagon *m.* (*noun*), railway coach; railway truck.

wagon-lit *m.* (*noun*), sleeping-car; sleeper.

wigwam *m.* (*noun*), wigwam.

X

xylophone *m.* (*noun*), xylophone.

Y

y (*adv.*), there (**voulez-vous y aller?** do you want to go there?); in, at home (**il n'y était pas,** he was not in).

yacht *m.* (*noun*), yacht.

yeux: *pl. of* **œil.**

Z

zèbre *m.* (*noun*), zebra.

zéro *m.* (*noun*), zero, nought.

zigzag *m.* (*noun*), zigzag.

zoo *m.* (*noun*), zoo.

zoologique (*adj.*), zoological; **jardin zoologique,** zoological garden(s), zoo.

English–French

A

a (*indefinite article*), un *m.*, une *f.*; **to have a broken arm,** avoir le bras cassé; **twice a day,** deux fois par jour.
abandon (*verb*), abandonner, quitter.
abdicate (*verb*), abdiquer.
abdomen (*noun*), abdomen *m.*
ability (*noun*), aptitude *f.*; talent *m.*; capacité *f.* (**the ability to do something,** la capacité de faire quelque chose).
ablaze (*adv.*), en feu, en flammes; (*adj.*), enflammé.
able (*adj.*), capable, compétent; **to be able to do something,** pouvoir faire quelque chose.
abolish (*verb*), abolir; annuler.
abolition (*noun*), abolition *f.*
about (*adv.*), autour; environ (**they are about the same height,** ils ont environ la même taille); (*prep.*), autour de (**the forests about the town,** les forêts autour de la ville); au sujet de, à propos de (**we are talking about your letter,** nous parlons à propos de votre lettre).
above (*adv.*), en haut (**she can see them from above,** elle peut les voir d'en haut); (*prep.*), au-dessus de (**a mountain rises above the lake,** une montagne s'élève au-dessus du lac); **above all,** surtout.
abrupt (*adj.*), abrupt; brusque; (*hasty*) précipité.
absence (*noun*), absence *f.*
absent (*adj.*), absent.
academy (*noun*), académie *f.*; école *f.*, collège *m.*
accelerate (*verb*), accélérer; activer, hâter, précipiter.
acceleration (*noun*), accélération *f.*; (*of car*) reprise *f.*
accept (*verb*), accepter; se résigner à.
acceptable (*adj.*), acceptable; agréable (**to,** à).
accident (*noun*), (*mishap*) accident *m.*; (*chance event*) *hasard *m.*
accompany (*verb*), accompagner, aller avec.
accomplish (*verb*), accomplir, exécuter, achever.
according to (*prep.*), suivant, selon.
account (*noun*), compte *m.*, note *f.*
accumulate (*verb*), accumuler, amonceler, entasser.
accuse (*verb*), accuser.
achieve (*verb*), accomplir; exécuter, réaliser; atteindre (un but).
acorn (*noun*), gland *m.*
acquit (*verb*), acquitter; absoudre (**of,** de).
acrobat (*noun*), acrobate *m.* & *f.*
across (*prep.* & *adv.*), à travers (**the boy is walking across the field,** le garçon marche à travers le champ); **to go across a road,** traverser une rue; **to go across a bridge,** passer un pont; **Henry lives across the street,** Henri demeure de l'autre côté de la rue.
act (*noun*), acte *m.* (**act of kindness,** acte de bonté); action *f.* (**the act of eating,** l'action de manger); **act of Parliament,** loi *f.*; (*verb*), agir; jouer (au théâtre).
actor, actress (*noun*), acteur *m.*, actrice *f.*
add (*verb*), ajouter, joindre (**to,** à); **to add up,** additionner.
addition (*noun*), addition *f.*; **in addition,** en plus (**heating is in addition,** le chauffage est en plus); **in addition to,** en plus de (**there are four others in addition to him,** il y en a quatre en plus de lui).
address (*noun*), adresse *f.*; (*verb*), mettre l'adresse sur (une lettre).
administration (*noun*), administration *f.* (**of,** de); (*management*) gestion *f.*
admire (*verb*), admirer.
admit (*verb*), admettre, laisser entrer (**he admits everyone into his garden,** il admet tout le monde dans son jardin); **to admit the truth,** admettre la vérité.
advance (*noun*), avance *f.*, progression *f.*;

(*verb*), avancer, progresser; faire progresser.

advantage (*noun*), avantage *m.* (**of, over,** sur).

adventure (*noun*), aventure *f.*

advertise (*verb*), (*make known*) annoncer, faire savoir; (*to post up*) afficher (**to advertise a sale,** afficher une vente); faire de la réclame (**they are advertising their new soap,** ils font de la réclame pour leur nouveau savon).

advice (*noun*), avis *m.*, conseil(s) *m.* (*pl.*); **a piece of advice,** un conseil.

advise (*verb*), conseiller; (*inform*) avertir, aviser.

affair (*noun*), affaire *f.*

affect (*verb*), affecter; (*health*) atteindre; (*to produce a change in*) modifier.

affection (*noun*), affection *f.*, tendresse *f.* (**for,** pour).

affectionate (*adj.*), affectueux *m.*, -euse *f.*, tendre.

afloat (*adv.*), à flot, sur l'eau.

afraid: to be afraid (**of**) (*verb*), avoir peur (de).

after (*adv. & prep.*), après (**George arrives after Michael,** Georges arrive après Michel; **after three o'clock,** après trois heures; **you speak first; I will speak after,** parlez le premier; je parlerai après).

afternoon (*noun*), après-midi *m.*

again (*adv.*), encore; une fois de plus; de nouveau.

against (*prep.*), contre; en contraste avec.

age (*noun*), âge *m.* (**at my age,** à mon âge; **middle age,** âge mûr); époque *f.* (**in our age,** à notre époque); **old age,** vieillesse *f.*; **the Middle Ages,** le moyen âge.

aged (*adj.*), âgé, vieux (vieil) *m.*, vieille *f.*; **aged seven,** âgé de sept ans.

agitate (*verb*), agiter, troubler (quelqu'un); **to agitate against something,** faire de l'agitation contre quelque chose.

ago (*adv.*): **two months ago,** il y a deux mois.

agony (*noun*), angoisse *f.*, détresse *f.*; douleur *f.* intense.

agree (*verb*), consentir (à faire quelque chose); être d'accord (**with,** avec); **agreed!** d'accord!

agreeable (*adj.*), aimable, agréable, plaisant

agricultural (*adj.*), agricole.

agriculture (*noun*), agriculture *f.*

aid (*noun*), aide *f.*; secours *m.*; (*verb*), aider, venir à l'aide de.

ailment (*noun*), mal *m.*, indisposition *f.*, maladie *f.*

aim (*verb*), allonger (un coup); (*to take aim at*) viser.

air (*noun*), air *m.*; aspect *m.*; (*verb*), aérer, ventiler (une chambre).

aircraft (*noun*), avion *m.*; **aircraft carrier,** porte-avions *m.*

airport (*noun*), aéroport *m.*

ale (*noun*), bière *f.*, ale *f.*

alight (*verb*), mettre pied à terre; descendre (de cheval, de l'autobus); (*of bird*) se poser.

alike (*adj.*), pareil *m.*, -eille *f.*; semblable.

alive (*adj.*), vivant, en vie; plein de vie; éveillé; **look alive!** dépêchez-vous!

all (*adj. & pron.*), tout (**all my life,** toute ma vie; **all those people,** tous ces gens); entier *m.*, -ière *f.* (**all the world**, le monde entier); **that is all,** c'est tout; **we are all here,** nous sommes tous ici.

alley (*noun*), (*path*) allée *f.*; (*narrow street*) ruelle *f.*

allow (*verb*), admettre, concéder, accorder; permettre (**he allows us to smoke,** il nous permet de fumer).

almost (*adv.*), presque; à peu près (**almost everybody was there,** à peu près tout le monde était là); **almost always,** presque toujours.

alone (*adj.*), seul; **all alone,** tout seul; **leave me alone,** laisse-moi tranquille.

aloud (*adv.*), à haute voix (**to read aloud,** lire à haute voix).

alphabet (*noun*), alphabet *m.*

already (*adv.*), déjà.

also (*adv.*), aussi; également.

alter (*verb*), changer, modifier; retoucher (une robe).

alternate (*adj.*), alternatif *m.*, -ive *f.*; (*verb*), alterner (**with,** avec); se succéder.
although (*conj.*), bien que, quoique.
altogether (*adv.*), (*wholly*) entièrement; absolument; (*on the whole*) somme toute; tout compris (**how much altogether?** combien tout compris?).
always (*adv.*), toujours.
amaze (*verb*), stupéfier; étonner.
ambassador (*noun*), ambassadeur *m.*
ambition (*noun*), ambition *f.*
ambulance (*noun*), ambulance *f.*
amiable (*adj.*), aimable.
amid, amidst (*prep.*), parmi, au milieu de.
among, amongst (*prep.*), entre, parmi; chez.
amount (*noun*), somme *f.*; montant *m.*, total *m.*
amuse (*verb*), amuser, divertir; faire rire.
amusement (*noun*), amusement *m.*, divertissement *m.*
amusing (*adj.*), amusant, divertissant *f.*
ancestor (*noun*), ancêtre *m.*
anchor (*noun*), ancre *f.*; **to weigh anchor,** lever l'ancre.
ancient (*adj.*), (*of history, documents*) ancien *m.*, -ienne *f.*; (*old-fashioned*) antique.
and (*conj.*), et.
angel (*noun*), ange *m.*
angelic (*adj.*), angélique; **an angelic smile,** un sourire d'ange.
anger (*noun*), colère *f.*; (*verb*), irriter, mettre en colère.
angler (*noun*), pêcheur *m.* à la ligne.
angry (*adj.*), fâché; irrité; en colère.
anguish (*noun*), angoisse *f.*; douleur *f.*
animal (*noun*), animal *m.*; bête *f.*
ankle (*noun*), cheville *f.*; **ankle-sock,** socquette *f.*
anniversary (*noun*), anniversaire *m.*
announce (*verb*), annoncer; faire connaître (**he announced his decision,** il a fait connaître sa décision).
annoy (*verb*), ennuyer; (*to irritate*) agacer.
another (*adj.*), (*different*) un autre *m.*, une autre *f.*; (*additional*) encore un *m.*, encore une *f.*
answer (*noun*), réponse *f.*; solution *f.* (d'un problème); (*verb*), répondre.
ant (*noun*), fourmi *f.*
anticipate (*verb*), prévenir, devancer (quelqu'un, les ordres de quelqu'un); prévoir (une difficulté).
antique (*adj.*), antique, ancien *m.*, -ienne *f.*; (*noun*), (*work of art*) antique *f.*
antlers (*pl. noun*), les bois *m. pl.*
anxiety (*noun*), anxiété *f.*, inquiétude *f.*
any (*adj.*), de, du, de la, des (**have you any wool?** avez-vous de la laine?; **I haven't any milk,** je n'ai pas de lait); (*no matter which*) n'importe quel *m.*, quelle *f.* (**bring me any newspaper,** apportez-moi n'importe quel journal); **not any,** ne . . . aucun *m.*, aucune *f.*
anybody, anyone (*pron.*), quelqu'un (**has anyone seen him?** est-ce que quelqu'un l'a vu?); (*negative*) personne (**I haven't seen anyone,** je n'ai vu personne); n'importe qui (**anybody can do this work,** n'importe qui peut faire ce travail).
anything (*pron.*), quelque chose (**ask him if he has anything to say,** demandez-lui s'il a quelque chose à dire); rien (**he entered the room and didn't notice anything,** il est entré dans la salle et n'a rien remarqué); n'importe quoi (**he would do anything for me,** il ferait n'importe quoi pour moi).
ape (*noun*), grand singe *m.*
apologize (*verb*), s'excuser (**for,** de); faire des excuses (**to,** à).
appal (*verb*), horrifier, épouvanter.
appeal (*verb*), faire appel (**to,** à); lancer un appel (**for,** en faveur de); s'adresser (à quelqu'un); **that doesn't appeal to me,** cela ne me dit rien.
appear (*verb*), (*become visible*) apparaître; paraître; (*seem*) sembler.
apple (*noun*), pomme *f.*
appliance (*noun*), appareil *m.*, instrument *m.*
apply (*verb*), (*put on*) appliquer; s'appliquer (**that doesn't apply to literature,** cela ne s'applique pas à la littérature); **to apply to someone,** s'adresser à quelqu'un.

appoint (*verb*), nommer, désigner, préposer; (*a time or place*) assigner.
apprehend (*verb*), (*arrest*) saisir.
approach (*verb*), s'approcher (de quelqu'un), approcher (quelqu'un); aborder (une question).
approve (*verb*), approuver; **I don't approve of your friends,** vos amis ne me plaisent pas.
approximate (*adj.*), approximatif *m.*, -ive *f.*
apricot (*noun*), abricot *m.*
April (*noun*), avril *m.*
apron (*noun*), tablier *m.*
aptitude (*noun*), aptitude *f.* (**for,** à).
arch (*noun*), arc *m.*
argue (*verb*), discuter; faire des objections; plaider; (*indicate*) prouver.
argument (*noun*), argument *m.*, raisonnement *m.*; débat *m.*, discussion *f.*; controverse *f.*
arise (*verb*), s'élever; (*get up*); se lever; provenir (**from,** de).
ark (*noun*), arche *f.*; **Noah's Ark,** l'arche de Noé.
arm (*noun*), bras *m.*
armchair (*noun*), fauteuil *m.*
arms (*pl. noun*), (*weapons*) armes *f. pl.*
army (*noun*), armée *f.*
arrange (*verb*), arranger; (*set in order*) ranger.
arrears (*pl. noun*), arrérages *m. pl.*; **to get into arrears,** se mettre en retard.
arrest (*verb*), arrêter; (*noun*), arrêt *m.*
arrival (*noun*), arrivée *f.*
arrive (*verb*), arriver.
arrow (*noun*), flèche *f.*
art (*noun*), art *m.*
article (*noun*), article *m.*; clause *f.*
artist (*noun*), artiste *m.* & *f.*
as (*adv.* & *conj.*), comme; **as . . . as,** aussi . . . que.
aside (*adv.*), de côté, à part; (*theatre*) en aparté.
ask (*verb*), demander; **to ask a question,** poser une question.
asleep (*adv.*), endormi; **to be asleep,** dormir; **to fall asleep,** s'endormir.
ass (*noun*), âne *m.*; imbécile *m.* & *f.*
assailant (*noun*), assaillant *m.*, agresseur *m.*
assemble (*verb*), (s')assembler, se rassembler; monter (une machine).
assembly (*noun*), assemblée *f.*, réunion *f.*
assist (*verb*), aider, assister; seconder.
assistance (*noun*), aide *f.*, assistance *f.*, secours *m.*
assistant (*adj.*), auxiliaire; sous- (**assistant manager,** sous-directeur); (*noun*), aide *m.* & *f.*; adjoint *m.*, adjointe *f.*; employé *m.*, employée *f.*; assistant *m.*, assistante *f.*; vendeur *m.*, vendeuse *f.*
assure (*verb*), assurer.
assuredly (*adv.*), assurément, certainement.
astonish (*verb*), étonner.
astonishing (*adj.*), étonnant.
at (*prep.*), à (**at school,** à l'école; **at three o'clock,** à trois heures; **at full speed,** à toute allure); chez (**at my house,** chez moi).
attach (*verb*), attacher, fixer, lier (**to,** à).
attack (*verb*), attaquer; (*noun*), attaque *f.*
attempt (*verb*), tenter, essayer; (*noun*), essai *m.*; tentative *f.*
attend (*verb*), accompagner, escorter; soigner (un malade); aller à, assister à (un concert).
attention (*noun*), attention *f.*
attic (*noun*), grenier *m.*
attract (*verb*), attirer (**to,** à, vers).
attractive (*adj.*), attrayant, séduisant.
August (*noun*), août *m.*
aunt (*noun*), tante *f.*
authentic (*adj.*), authentique.
autumn (*noun*), automne *m.*
avenue (*noun*), avenue *f.*
aviator (*noun*), aviateur *m.*, aviatrice *f.*
avoid (*verb*), éviter.
await (*verb*), attendre.
awake (*verb*), éveiller, réveiller (quelqu'un); s'éveiller, se réveiller.
away (*adv.*), loin, au loin; **to go away,** partir; **to be away,** être absent, ne pas être là.
awful (*adj.*), épouvantable, terrible.
axe (*noun*), *hache *f.*
azure (*noun*), azur *m.*; (*adj.*), azuré.

B

baboon (*noun*), babouin *m.*
baby (*noun*), bébé *m.*
back (*noun*), dos *m.* (d'une personne, d'un animal); derrière *m.* (d'une maison); (*adj.*), de derrière (**back door,** porte de derrière); (*adv.*), **to come back,** revenir; **to be back,** être de retour.
backward (*adj.*), en arrière (**backward glance,** regard *m.* en arrière); attardé, arriéré (**backward child,** enfant arriéré).
backwards (*adv.*), en arrière (**to jump backwards,** sauter en arrière).
bacon (*noun*), lard *m.*
bad (*adj.*), mauvais; (*wicked*) méchant; (*serious*) grave (**a bad accident,** un grave accident).
badly (*adv.*), mal.
bag (*noun*) sac *m.*; **diplomatic bag,** valise *f.* diplomatique.
bake (*verb*), cuire; cuire au four.
baker (*noun*), boulanger *m.*, boulangère *f.*
bakery (*noun*), boulangerie *f.*
balance (*verb*), balancer (**the seal balances the ball on its nose,** le phoque balance le ballon sur le nez); (*noun*), (*scales*) balance *f.*
bald (*adj.*), chauve.
ball (*noun*), ballon *m.* (de football); balle *f.* (de tennis, de golf); pelote *f.* (de laine, de ficelle); (*dance*) bal *m.*; **ball-room,** salle *f.* de bal.
balloon (*noun*), ballon *m.*
banana (*noun*), banane *f.*
band (*noun*), bande *f.*, ruban *m.*; orchestre *m.*
bandage (*noun*), (*medical*) pansement *m.*; (*for blindfolding*) bandeau *m.*
bang (*noun*), détonation *f.*; claquement *m.* (de porte); (*verb*), claquer (**the door is banging,** la porte claque); **to bang on the door,** heurter à la porte.
bank (*noun*), (*finance*) banque *f.*; (*of river*) bord *m.*, rive *f.*
bar (*noun*), barre *f.* (de fer, de savon, de chocolat); barreau *m.* (**bars of a cage,** barreaux d'une cage); (*verb*), barricader; barrer.
barber (*noun*), coiffeur *m.*
bark (*verb*), aboyer; (*noun*), aboiement *m.* (d'un chien); écorce *f.* (d'un arbre).
barley (*noun*), orge *f.*
barn (*noun*), grange *f.*
barometer (*noun*), baromètre *m.*
barrel (*noun*), tonneau *m.*, baril *m.*; barrique *f.*
basic (*adj.*), fondamental.
basin (*noun*), bassin *m.*; (*washbasin*) cuvette *f.*; (*bowl*) bol *m.*
basket (*noun*), panier *m.*; corbeille *f.*
bat (*noun*), (*animal*) chauve-souris *f.*; batte *f.* (de cricket).
bath (*noun*), bain *m.* (**to have a bath,** prendre un bain); (*tub*) baignoire *f.*; **swimming bath,** la piscine.
bathroom (*noun*), salle *f.* de bains.
be (*verb*), être; (*impers.*) **there is, there are,** il y a (**there is an aircraft in the sky,** il y a un avion dans le ciel).
beach (*noun*), plage *f.*, grève *f.*
bead (*noun*), grain *m.*; perle *f.*; **string of beads,** collier *m.*
beam (*noun*), (*of light*) rayon *m.*; (*of building*) poutre *f.*
bean (*noun*), *haricot *m.*; **string bean,** haricot vert; **kidney bean,** haricot blanc.
bear (*noun*), ours *m.*
beard (*noun*), barbe *f.*
beast (*noun*), bête *f.*; brute *f.*
beautiful (*adj.*), beau (bel) *m.*, belle *f.*
beauty (*noun*), beauté *f.*
because (*conj.*), parce que; **because of,** à cause de.
become (*verb*), devenir; se faire (**to become a doctor,** se faire médecin).
bed (*noun*), lit *m.*; **to go to bed,** se coucher; **to put someone to bed,** coucher quelqu'un.
bedroom (*noun*), chambre *f.* à coucher.

bee (*noun*), abeille *f.*; **worker-bee,** abeille ouvrière; **bumble-bee,** bourdon *m.*
beef (*noun*), bœuf *m.*
beer (*noun*), bière *f.*
before (*adv. & prep.*) avant (**Mary left before Chantal,** Marie est partie avant Chantal; **the man had arrived three days before,** l'homme était arrivé trois jours avant); devant (**he stands before me,** il se tient devant moi).
beg (*verb*), mendier; **to beg for mercy,** demander grâce.
begin (*verb*), commencer; commencer à, se mettre à (**he began to read,** il se mit à lire); **to begin a conversation,** entamer une conversation; **to begin again,** recommencer.
beginning (*noun*), commencement *m.*; début *m.*; origine *f.*
behind (*adv.*), en arrière (**to stay behind,** rester en arrière); (*prep.*), derrière (**behind the house,** derrière la maison).
believe (*verb*), croire (**to believe in someone's word,** croire à la parole de quelqu'un; **to believe in God,** croire en Dieu); penser; estimer (**that,** que).
bell (*noun*), (*in church, etc.*) cloche *f.*; (*in house*) sonnette *f.*; (*fixed bell*) timbre *m.*
below (*adv.*), en bas, plus bas; (*prep.*), au-dessous de.
belt (*noun*), ceinture *f.*
bend (*verb*), courber, plier, ployer; (*noun*), (*of road*) tournant *m.*
benefit (*verb*), profiter; (*noun*), bénéfice *m.*; profit *m.*; avantage *m.*
berry (*noun*), baie *f.*
beside (*prep.*), à côté de, auprès de; comparé à.
besides (*adv.*), en outre, de plus.
best (*adj. & noun*), (le) meilleur, (la) meilleure, (*neuter*) le mieux (**it would be best to say nothing,** le mieux serait de ne rien dire); (*adv.*)**: he does it best,** c'est lui qui le fait le mieux.
bestow (*verb*), accorder, donner; conférer (un titre à quelqu'un).
better (*adj.*), meilleur (**than,** que); (*adv.*), mieux.
between (*prep.*), entre.
beware (*verb*), prendre garde, se méfier; (*interjection*), **beware!** gare!
bib (*noun*), bavette *f.*, bavoir *m.*
Bible (*noun*), Bible *f.*
bicycle (*noun*), bicyclette *f.*, vélo *m.*
big (*adj.*), (*bulky*) gros *m.*, grosse *f.*; (*tall, large*) grand; important; **to grow big,** grossir; grandir.
bill (*noun*), bec *m.* (d'oiseau); (*poster*) affiche *f.*; (*account*) note *f.*, addition *f.*; **bill of fare,** menu *m.*
bird (*noun*), oiseau *m.*
birth (*noun*), naissance *f.*
birthday (*noun*), anniversaire *m.* (de naissance).
biscuit (*noun*), biscuit *m.*
bite (*verb*), mordre; **to bite one's nails,** se ronger les ongles.
black (*noun*), noir *m.*; (*adj.*), noir.
blacksmith (*noun*), forgeron *m.*
blackboard (*noun*), tableau *m.* noir.
blade (*noun*), lame *f.* (de couteau); brin *m.* (d'herbe).
blanket (*noun*), couverture *f.*
blaze (*noun*), flambée *f.*, feu *m.*; éclat *m.* (de diamants); (*verb*), flamber, flamboyer; **to blaze up,** s'embraser.
bleed (*verb*), saigner.
blend (*verb*), (*with care and in definite quantities*) mélanger; (*general term, without special care*) mêler; fondre (des couleurs).
bless (*verb*), bénir.
blind (*adj.*), aveugle; **blind alley,** cul-de-sac *m.*; (*verb*), aveugler.
blond (*adj.*), blond; (*noun*), blonde *f.*
blood (*noun*), sang *m.*
blossom (*noun*), fleur *f.*
blossoming (*noun*), floraison *f.*
blot (*noun*), tache *f.*; (*of ink*) pâté *m.*; (*verb*), sécher l'encre; **to blot out,** effacer.
blouse (*noun*), corsage *m.*
blow (*verb*), souffler; **to blow one's nose,** se moucher; (*noun*), coup *m.*
blue (*noun*), bleu *m.*; (*adj.*), bleu.
board (*noun*), (*notice-board*) tableau *m.*; (*plank*) planche *f.*

boast (*verb*), se vanter.
boat (*noun*), bateau *m.*, canot *m.*; barque *f.*; **by boat,** en bateau.
body (*noun*), corps *m.*; (*dead*) cadavre *m.*; masse *f.* (de gens).
boil (*verb*), bouillir (**the water is boiling,** l'eau bout); faire bouillir (**to boil the water,** faire bouillir l'eau).
bolt (*noun*), verrou *m.* (de porte).
bone (*noun*), os *m.*; **fish-bone,** arête *f.*
bonnet (*noun*), bonnet *m.*, béret *m.*; béguin *m.* (d'enfant); (*of car*) capot *m.*
book (*noun*), livre *m.*
book-case, bibliothèque *f.*
book-shop, librairie *f.*
boot (*noun*), botte *f.*
bootee (*noun*), bottillon *m.*
booth (*noun*), baraque *f.*; **telephone booth,** cabine *f.* téléphonique.
border (*noun*), bord *m.*, côté *m.*; bordure *f.*; frontière *f.*, limite *f.*
born (*adj.*), né; **to be born,** naître.
borrow (*verb*), emprunter (**from,** à).
both (*adj. & pron.*), les deux, l'un(e) et l'autre; tous les deux.
bottle (*noun*), bouteille *f.*
bottom (*noun*), fond *m.* (**the bottom of the glass,** le fond du verre).
boulder (*noun*), roche *f.*; gros galet *m.*
bow (*noun*), arc *m.*; archet *m.* (de violon); (*greeting*) salut *m.*, révérence *f.*; (*verb*), ployer, plier; s'incliner, saluer.
bowl (*noun*), bol *m.*, bassin *m.*
box (*noun*), boîte *f.*; carton *m.*; (*verb*), boxer, faire de la boxe; **to box someone's ears,** gifler quelqu'un.
boy (*noun*), garçon *m.*
bracelet (*noun*), bracelet *m.*
branch (*noun*), branche *f.*
brassière (**bra**) (*noun*), soutien-gorge *m.*
brave (*adj.*), courageux *m.*, -euse *f.*, brave.
bread (*noun*), pain *m.*
breadth (*noun*), largeur *f.*
break (*verb*), casser, rompre, briser; interrompre (un voyage).
breakfast (*noun*), petit déjeuner *m.*; **to have breakfast,** prendre le petit déjeuner.
breathe (*verb*), respirer; souffler (**on,** sur).
bridge (*noun*), pont *m.*; **foot-bridge,** passerelle *f.*
bright (*adj.*), brillant; clair.
bring (*verb*), amener, mener, conduire; apporter (quelque chose); **to bring back** (**someone**), ramener (quelqu'un).
broad (*adj.*), large; **the road is broad,** la route est large; **the road is thirty foot broad,** la route a trente pieds de large; **in broad daylight,** en plein jour.
broken (*adj.*), cassé; brisé.
brooch (*noun*), broche *f.*
broom (*noun*), balai *m.*
brother (*noun*), frère *m.*
brush (*noun*), brosse *f.*; (*verb*), brosser; balayer (un tapis).
brutal (*adj.*), brutal.
bucket (*noun*), seau *m.*
buckle (*noun*), boucle *f.*; (*verb*), boucler.
bud (*noun*), bourgeon *m.*, bouton *m.*
buffet (*noun*), buffet *m.*
buffoon (*noun*), bouffon *m.*
build (*verb*), bâtir, construire, élever.
building (*noun*), bâtiment *m.*; immeuble *m.*; édifice *m.* (**public building,** édifice public).
bulb (*noun*), (*botanical*) bulbe *m.*; (*of lamp, thermometer*) ampoule *f.*
bull (*noun*), taureau *m.*
bumble-bee (*noun*), bourdon *m.*
bureau (*noun*), (*writing desk*) bureau *m.*; (*office*) bureau *m.*; **employment bureau,** bureau *m.* de placement.
burglar (*noun*), voleur *m.*, cambrioleur *m.*
burn (*noun*), brûlure *f.*; (*verb*), brûler.
burst (*noun*), éclatement *m.*, explosion *f.*; coup *m.* (de tonnerre); éclat *m.* (de rire); (*verb*), éclater, exploser, s'ouvrir.
bury (*verb*), enterrer, inhumer (quelqu'un).
bus (*noun*), autobus *m.*; **country bus,** autocar *m.*
business (*noun*), affaire *f.*; occupation *f.*
busy (*adj.*), occupé.
but (*conj.*), mais; (*adv.*), que (**none other but him,** nul autre que lui); ne . . . que (**he is but a child,** ce n'est qu'un enfant); excepté (**all but him,** tous excepté lui).

butcher (*noun*), boucher *m.*; **butcher's shop,** boucherie *f.*

butter (*noun*), beurre *m.*; (*verb*), beurrer.

butterfly (*noun*), papillon *m.*

button (*noun*), bouton *m.*

buy (*verb*), acheter.

by (*prep.*), par (**written by his friend,** écrit par son ami); près de (**by the fire,** près du feu).

C

cabbage (*noun*), chou *m.*
cabin (*noun*), cabane *f.*, case *f.*; (*at sea*) cabine *f.*
café (*noun*), café(-restaurant) *m.*
cage (*noun*), cage *f.*
cake (*noun*), gâteau *m.*; pain *m.* (de savon).
calculate (*verb*), calculer; arranger (**he calculated everything in advance,** il l'a tout arrangé d'avance); estimer (une distance).
calf (*pl.* **calves**) (*noun*), veau *m.*
calling (*noun*), appel *m.*; vocation *f.*; métier *m.*; profession *f.*
calm (*adj.*), calme; **calm down** (*verb*), se calmer.
camera (*noun*), appareil *m.* photographique.
camp (*noun*), camp *m.*; campement *m.*; **holiday camp,** colonie *f.* de vacances; (*verb*), camper.
canal (*noun*), canal *m.*
cancel (*verb*), annuler; rayer, barrer.
candid (*adj.*), franc *m.*, -anche *f.*, sincère; impartial.
candle (*noun*), (*wax*) bougie *f.*; (*tallow*) chandelle *f.*
canoe (*noun*), canoë *m.*, pirogue *f.*
cap (*noun*), (*with peak or visor*) casquette *f.*; (*brimless*) bonnet *m.*; (*for woman*) toque *f.*
capable (*adj.*), capable; compétent.
capacity (*noun*), capacité *f.*
capital (*adj.*), capital; principal; (*noun*), (*city, letter*) capitale *f.*; (*money*) capital *m.*
car (*noun*), voiture *f.*, automobile *f.*
caravan (*noun*), caravane *f.*; roulotte *f.*; (*touring*) remorque-camping *f.*
card (*noun*), carte *f.*; fiche *f.*
care (*noun*), (*watching over*) soin *m.*; (*anxiety, solicitude*) souci *m.*; inquiétude *f.*; (*verb*), (*worry*) se soucier, s'inquiéter; **to care for** (**an invalid**), soigner (un malade).
careful (*adj.*), attentif *m.*, -ive *f.*; soigneux *m.*, -euse *f.*; prudent.
caress (*noun*), caresse *f.*; (*verb*), caresser.
carpenter (*noun*), charpentier *m.*; (*joiner*) menuisier *m.*
carpet (*noun*), tapis *m.*
carriage (*noun*), voiture *f.*; transport *m.*
carrot (*noun*), carotte *f.*
carry (*verb*), porter.
carve (*verb*), sculpter.
casserole (*noun*), casserole *f.*, cocotte *f.*; ragoût *m.* en cocotte.
castle (*noun*), château *m.*
cat (*noun*), chat *m.*, chatte *f.*
catch (*verb*), attraper, saisir, prendre; (*prevent from falling*) soutenir.
cause (*noun*), cause *f.*, raison *f.*, sujet *m.*; (*verb*), causer, déterminer.
cave (*noun*), caverne *f.*
cavern (*noun*), caverne *f.*
ceiling (*noun*), plafond *m.*
cellar (*noun*), cave *f.*
cemetery (*noun*), cimetière *m.*
centimetre (*noun*), centimètre *m.*
centre (*noun*), centre *m.*
certain (*adj.*), certain; assuré; sûr; convaincu.
certify (*verb*), certifier, assurer; garantir.
chain (*noun*), chaîne *f.*
chair (*noun*), chaise *f.*
chalk (*noun*), craie *f.*
chance (*noun*), *hasard *m.*; chance *f.*; risque *m.*
change (*noun*), changement *m.*; (*verb*), changer, modifier, transformer.
chapter (*noun*), chapitre *m.*
character (*noun*), caractère *m.*; (*in play*) personnage *m.*
chart (*noun*), carte *f.* marine; tableau *m.*, diagramme *m.*, graphique *m.*
charwoman (*noun*), femme *f.* de ménage.
chase (*noun*), chasse *f.*, poursuite *f.*; (*verb*), chasser, pourchasser, poursuivre.
chat (*verb*), causer; bavarder; (*noun*), causerie *f.*
chauffeur (*noun*), chauffeur *m.*
cheap (*adj.*), bon marché, pas cher *m.*, pas chère *f.*

cheek (*noun*), (*of the face*) joue *f.*
cheerful (*adj.*), gai; riant.
cheese (*noun*), fromage *m.*
chemist (*noun*), pharmacien *m.*, pharmacienne *f.*; chimiste *m.*; **chemist's shop,** pharmacie *f.*
cheque (*noun*), chèque *m.*
cherry (*noun*), cerise *f.*
chest (*noun*), (*of body*) poitrine *f.*; caisse *f.*, boîte *f.*, coffre *m.*; **chest of drawers,** commode *f.*
chick (*noun*), poussin *m.*
chicken (*noun*), poulet *m.*
chief (*noun*), chef *m.*; patron *m.*; (*adj.*), principal; en chef.
child (*noun*), enfant *m. & f.*
chill (*verb*), glacer, geler, refroidir; (*noun*), refroidissement *m.*
chimney (*noun*), cheminée *f.*
chin (*noun*), menton *m.*
chocolate (*noun*), chocolat *m.*
choice (*noun*), choix *m.*; assortiment *m.*
choose (*verb*), choisir; faire choix de; opter pour.
chop (*verb*), trancher; couper à la hache, hacher.
Christian (*noun & adj.*), Chrétien *m.*, -ienne *f.*; **Christian name,** prénom *m.*
Christmas (*noun*), Noël *m.*; **Christmas Day,** le jour de Noël; **Father Christmas,** le Père Noël; **Christmas tree,** arbre *m.* de Noël.
chuckle (*noun*), gloussement *m.*; (*verb*), glousser.
church (*noun*), église *f.*
cigarette (*noun*), cigarette *f.*; **cigarette-lighter,** briquet *m.*
cinema (*noun*), cinéma *m.*
circle (*noun*), cercle *m.*; (*verb*), encercler, entourer.
circus (*noun*), cirque *m.*
city (*noun*), cité *f.*, ville *f.*
clap (*verb*), battre (des mains), applaudir; claquer; (*noun*), battement *m.* (de mains), applaudissements *m. pl.*
class (*noun*), classe *f.*, catégorie *f.*
claw (*noun*), (*of bird of prey*) serre *f.*; (*of small bird*) ongle *m.*; (*of crab*) pince *f.*; (*of wild animal*) griffe *f.*; (*verb*), (*clutch*) serrer; (*scratch*) griffer, égratigner; agripper.
clean (*adj.*), propre; net *m.*, nette *f.*; (*verb*), nettoyer; éplucher (les légumes).
clerk (*noun*), commis *m.*; employé *m.*, employée *f.* de bureau; (*solicitor's*) clerc *m.*
client (*noun*), client *m.*, cliente *f.*
cliff (*noun*), falaise *f.*
climb (*verb*), monter (une colline); monter à (une échelle); grimper (à un arbre).
clip (*verb*), tondre (un mouton); tailler (une haie).
clock (*noun*), (*large*) horloge *f.*; (*smaller*) pendule *f.*; **alarm-clock,** réveille-matin *m.*
close (*verb*), fermer.
cloth (*noun*), drap *m.*, tissu *m.*, étoffe *f.*; (*linen, cotton*) toile *f.*; (*for cleaning*) torchon *m.*
clothe (*verb*), habiller, vêtir (**with, in,** de).
clothes (*pl. noun*), vêtements *m. pl.*, habits *m. pl.*
cloud (*noun*), nuage *m.*
clown (*noun*), clown *m.*; bouffon *m.*
clump (*noun*), groupe *m.*, touffe *f.* (d'arbres); massif *m.*, bouquet *m.* (de fleurs).
coal (*noun*), charbon *m.*; **coal-bunker,** coffre *m.* à charbon.
coarse (*adj.*), grossier *m.*, -ière *f.*; vulgaire; (*of material*) gros *m.*, grosse *f.*
coast (*noun*), côte *f.*; rivage *m.*
coat (*noun*), (*man's jacket*) veston *m.*; (*overcoat*) pardessus *m.*, manteau *m.*; **dress coat,** habit *m.*; couche *f.* (de peinture).
cobbler (*noun*), cordonnier *m.*, savetier *m.*
cock (*noun*), coq *m.*
cockerel (*noun*), jeune coq *m.*
coffee (*noun*), café *m.*
coin (*noun*), pièce *f.* de monnaie.
cold (*adj.*), froid; **to be cold,** avoir froid; **it is cold,** (*of weather*) il fait froid; (*noun*), froid *m.*; (*illness*) rhume *m.*; **to catch a cold,** attraper un rhume; prendre froid.

collapse (*verb*), s'écrouler, s'effondrer; tomber.

collar (*noun*), col *m.* (de chemise); collier *m.* (de chien).

collect (*verb*), rassembler, réunir; (*gather up*) ramasser; collectionner (des timbres).

colour (*noun*), couleur *f.*

comb (*noun*), peigne *m.*; (*verb*), peigner; **to comb one's hair,** se peigner.

come (*verb*), venir, arriver.

comfort (*noun*), confort *m.*

comfortable (*adj.*), confortable; **this armchair is very comfortable,** ce fauteuil est très confortable.

command (*noun*), ordre *m.*; (*verb*), ordonner; commander.

commence (*verb*), commencer.

commerce (*noun*), commerce *m.*

common (*adj.*), commun; public *m.*, -ique *f.*; général.

communicate (*verb*), communiquer, transmettre (**to,** à).

companion (*noun*), compagnon *m.*, compagne *f.*

compartment (*noun*), compartiment *m.*; subdivision *f.*

compel (*verb*), contraindre, forcer, obliger; imposer, commander.

compete (*verb*), concourir, entrer en compétition.

competitor (*noun*), compétiteur *m.*, compétitrice *f.*

complain (*verb*), se plaindre (**against,** contre); formuler une plainte.

complete (*verb*), accomplir, finir, achever; (*adj.*), complet *m.*, -ète *f.*; entier *m.*, -ière *f.*

compose (*verb*), composer, constituer; arranger (**the artist has composed the figures in the picture,** l'artiste a arrangé les personnages du tableau).

conceal (*verb*), cacher, celer, dissimuler.

conceive (*verb*), concevoir; imaginer.

concentrate (*verb*), concentrer (**he concentrated his attention on the problem,** il concentra son attention sur le problème); se concentrer (**he concetnrated on the problem,** il se concentra sur le problème).

concern (*noun*), entreprise *f.*; rapport *m.*; (*worry*) inquiétude *f.*; (*verb*), concerner, intéresser; avoir rapport à.

condense (*verb*), condenser.

condition (*noun*), condition *f.*, stipulation *f.*, clause *f.*; état *m.*, situation *f.*

conduct (*noun*), conduite *f.*, attitude *f.* (envers quelqu'un); (*verb*), conduire, mener; diriger (un orchestre).

conductor (*noun*), conducteur *m.*, guide *m.*; chef *m.* d'orchestre; receveur *m.* (d'autobus).

confess (*verb*), avouer, confesser; **to confess to a crime,** avouer un crime; **to confess one's sins,** confesser ses péchés.

confidence (*noun*), confiance *f.* (**in,** en); confidence *f.* (**in confidence,** en confidence).

conflict (*noun*), conflit *m.*; (*verb*), être en conflit (**with,** avec).

confuse (*verb*), confondre (**with,** avec); rendre confus.

congratulate (*verb*), féliciter, complimenter.

congratulations (*noun*), félicitations *f. pl.*

connect (*verb*), connecter, mettre en contact; relier (**with,** avec).

conscientious (*adj.*), consciencieux *m.*, -euse *f.*

consequence (*noun*), conséquence *f.*; suites *f. pl.*

consider (*verb*), considérer, examiner, réfléchir à; regarder.

consist (*verb*) **of,** consister en; être composé de.

construct (*verb*), construire.

consume (*verb*), consumer; (*to use up*) consommer; (*to burn up*) brûler.

contain (*verb*), contenir, comporter.

contemplate (*verb*), contempler; méditer, réfléchir.

content (*adj.*), content; satisfait.

contents (*pl. noun*), matières *f. pl.*; contenu *m.* (*N.B. French singular*); (**table of**) **contents,** table *f.* des matières.

continue (*verb*), continuer; poursuivre (un travail).

contrary (*adj.*), contraire, opposé (**to,** à);

(*noun*), contraire *m.*; **on the contrary,** au contraire.
contribute (*verb*), contribuer; aider.
control (*verb*), régler (quelque chose); commander (aux hommes); (*noun*), autorité *f.*; pouvoir *m.* (**over,** sur).
convalesce (*verb*), être en convalescence.
convenient (*adj.*), commode.
converse (*verb*): **to converse with someone about something,** s'entretenir avec quelqu'un de quelque chose.
conversation (*noun*), conversation *f.*; entretien *m.*
convey (*verb*), transporter, apporter, porter; amener (quelqu'un); transmettre (des remerciements).
convince (*verb*), convaincre, persuader.
cook (*noun*), cuisinier *m.*, -ière *f.*; (*verb*), faire cuire, cuire.
cool (*adj.*), frais *m.*, fraîche *f.*; (*verb*), rafraîchir.
copy (*noun*), copie *f.*; reproduction *f.*; (*verb*), copier; imiter, reproduire.
cord (*noun*), corde *f.*
corn (*noun*), grain *m.*; (*wheat*) blé *m.*
corner (*noun*), coin *m.*, angle *m.*
corpse (*noun*), cadavre *m.*, corps *m.*
correct (*verb*), corriger; (*adj.*), correct; exact; bon *m.*, bonne *f.* (**speak in correct French,** parlez en bon français).
cost (*noun*), prix *m.*, coût *m.*; (*verb*), coûter.
cosy (*adj.*), confortable, chaud.
cot (*noun*), lit *m.* d'enfant, petit lit; berceau *m.*
cotton (*noun*), coton *m.*; (*thread*) (fil de) coton *m.*; (*cotton goods*) cotonnades *f. pl.*
couch (*noun*), couche *f.*; divan *m.*, sofa *m.*
cough (*noun*), toux *f.*; (*verb*), tousser.
counsel (*noun*), conseil *m.*, avis *m.*; (*barrister*) avocat *m.*; (*verb*), conseiller; donner un avis à.
count (*verb*), compter; calculer; (*noun*), compte *m.*, calcul *m.*
counter (*noun*), comptoir *m.*
counterpane (*noun*), couvre-lit *m.*
country (*noun*), pays *m.*; région *f.*; contrée *f.*; (*native country*) patrie *f.*
countryside (*noun*), campagne *f.*
courage (*noun*), courage *m.*
courageous (*adj.*), courageux *m.*, -euse *f.*; brave.
course (*noun*), (*of river, time*) cours *m.*; **of course,** naturellement.
court (*noun*), cour *f.*
cousin (*noun*), cousin *m.*, cousine *f.*
cover (*noun*), couverture *f.*; couvercle *m.*; (*verb*), couvrir; **to cover up,** recouvrir; dissimuler (la vérité).
cow (*noun*), vache *f.*
coward (*noun*), couard *m.*, poltron *m.*, lâche *m.* & *f.*
crab (*noun*), crabe *m.*
crack (*noun*), craquement *m.*, bruit *m.* sec; (*slit, chink*) fente *f.*; fissure *f.*; (*verb*), craquer; claquer (un fouet); émettre un bruit sec; fêler (un verre, une tasse).
crafty (*adj.*), rusé; astucieux *m.*, -euse *f.*
crane (*noun*), (*bird or machine*) grue *f.*
crave (*verb*), désirer intensément; implorer, solliciter.
crawl (*verb*), ramper; se traîner.
crazy (*adj.*), (*person*) fou (fol) *m.*, folle *f.*; **crazy paving,** dallage *m.* irrégulier.
cream (*noun*), crème *f.*
create (*verb*), créer.
crime (*noun*), crime *m.*
crop (*noun*), (*harvest*) récolte *f.*
cross (*noun*), croix *f.*; (*verb*), croiser (les jambes); traverser (la rue, la mer); **to cross out,** barrer, rayer.
cross-road (*noun*), chemin *m.* de traverse; **cross-roads** (*pl.*), carrefour *m.*, intersection *f.*
crowd (*noun*), foule *f.*, multitude *f.*
cruel (*adj.*), cruel *m.*, -elle *f.*
crush (*verb*), écraser.
cry (*noun*), cri *m.*; (*verb*), crier; (*weep*) pleurer, verser des larmes.
cube (*noun*), cube *m.*
culprit (*noun*), coupable *m.* & *f.*
cultivate (*verb*), cultiver.
culture (*noun*), culture *f.*
cup (*noun*), tasse *f.*
cupboard (*noun*), armoire *f.*; (*on wall*) placard *m.*

cure (*noun*), guérison *f.*; remède *m.*; cure *f.*; (*verb*), guérir (**of,** de).
curious (*adj.*), curieux *m.*, -euse *f.*
curl (*noun*), boucle *f.* (de cheveux); volute *f.* (de fumée); (*verb*), boucler; friser; **to curl one's lip,** retrousser la lèvre.
curtain (*noun*), rideau *m.*
cushion (*noun*), coussin *m.*
custom (*noun*), coutume *f.*; habitude *f.*; **customs** (*pl.*), douane *f.*
customer (*noun*), client *m.*, cliente *f.*
cut (*noun*), coupure *f.*; (*verb*), couper, tailler; trancher (du pain, la tête à quelqu'un).
cycle (*noun*), bicyclette *f.*, vélo *m.*
cygnet (*noun*), jeune cygne *m.*

D

dad, daddy (*noun*), papa *m.*
daily (*adj.*), journalier *m.*, -ière *f.*; quotidien *m.*, -ienne *f.*; (*noun*), **daily (help)**, femme *f.* de ménage; (*newspaper*) quotidien *m.*
damage (*noun*), dommage *m.*, dégâts *m. pl.*; (*verb*), endommager; abîmer.
damp (*adj.*), humide, moite.
dance (*noun*), danse *f.*; bal *m.*; (*verb*), danser.
dancer (*noun*), danseur *m.*, danseuse *f.*
danger (*noun*), danger *m.*
dangerous (*adj.*), dangereux *m.*, -euse *f.*
dare (*verb*), oser; **to dare someone to do something,** défier quelqu'un de faire quelque chose.
dark (*adj.*), sombre, obscur; foncé (**dark blue,** bleu foncé); **it is growing dark,** il se fait nuit.
darling (*noun & adj.*), chéri *m.*, chérie *f.*
dart (*noun*), fléchette *f.*; **to play darts,** jouer aux fléchettes.
daughter (*noun*), fille *f.*; **daughter-in-law,** belle-fille *f.*
dawn (*noun*), aube *f.*, aurore *f.*
day (*noun*), jour *m.*; **day-time,** journée *f.*; **all day long,** toute la journée.
dead (*adj.*), mort; (*pl. noun*), morts *m. pl.*; **dead person,** mort *m.*, morte *f.*
deaf (*adj.*), sourd.
dealer (*noun*), marchand *m.*, marchande *f.*
dear (*adj.*), cher *m.*, -ère *f.*; précieux *m.*, -euse *f.*; (*noun*), **my dear,** mon cher *m.*, ma chère *f.*
death (*noun*), mort *f.*
decay (*noun*), délabrement *m.* (d'un bâtiment); carie *f.* (des dents); (*verb*), délabrer; détériorer; (*of teeth*) se carier.
deceive (*verb*), tromper, duper.
December (*noun*), décembre *m.*
decide (*verb*), décider, résoudre (de faire quelque chose).
decision (*noun*), décision *f.*
deck (*noun*), pont *m.*; **lower deck,** premier pont *m.*; **deckhand,** homme *m.* de pont.
declare (*verb*), déclarer.
decline (*verb*), décliner; baisser (**prices are declining,** les prix baissent).
decorate (*verb*), décorer (une salle, un soldat).
decrease (*verb*), diminuer, amoindrir, décroître.
deed (*noun*), action *f.*; exploit *m.*; fait *m.*
deep (*adj.*), profond.
deer (*noun*), cerf *m.*
defeat (*noun*), défaite *f.*; insuccès *m.*; échec *m.*; (*verb*), défaire, vaincre.
defence (*noun*), défense *f.*
defend (*verb*), défendre, protéger; soutenir (une proposition).
defy (*verb*), défier; braver.
dejected (*adj.*), déprimé; abattu.
delay (*noun*), retard *m.*; délai *m.*; (*verb*), retarder (quelqu'un); tarder (à faire quelque chose); s'attarder.
delicacy (*noun*), délicatesse *f.*; (*tit-bit*) friandise *f.*
delicate (*adj.*), délicat; fin; doux *m.*, douce *f.*; fragile; raffiné.
delicious (*adj.*), délicieux *m.*, -euse *f.*
delightful (*adj.*), délicieux, -euse, charmant.
deliver (*verb*), délivrer; livrer (un paquet); **to deliver letters,** distribuer des lettres.
delivery (*noun*), remise *f.* (d'un paquet); livraison *f.*; distribution *f.* (des lettres); **delivery van,** camionnette *f.*
demand (*verb*), exiger, réclamer.
demolish (*verb*), démolir.
den (*noun*), antre *f.*, tanière *f.*; fosse *f.*
denote (*verb*), dénoter, marquer; signifier.
dense (*adj.*), dense; épais *m.*, -aisse *f.*; (*packed tight*) tassé.
dentist (*noun*), dentiste *m.*
deny (*verb*), démentir; nier; refuser; renier.
depart (*verb*), partir, s'en aller.
departure (*noun*), départ *m.*

deprive (*verb*), priver (**of,** de); déposséder (de).
descend (*verb*), descendre; **to descend to,** s'abaisser à.
desert (*noun*), (*waste land*) désert *m.*; (*verb*), abandonner, quitter.
deserve (*verb*), mériter.
design (*noun*), dessein *m.*, projet *m.*; intention *f.*; (*verb*), (*draw*) dessiner; (*plan, contemplate*) projeter; créer (une robe).
desire (*noun*), désir *m.*; (*verb*), désirer; (*wish*) souhaiter.
desk (*noun*), (*at school*) pupitre *m.*; (*in office*) bureau *m.*
despair (*noun*), désespoir *m.*; (*verb*), désespérer.
dessert (*noun*), dessert *m.*
destination (*noun*), destination *f.*
destroy (*verb*), détruire, démolir.
detach (*verb*), détacher, séparer.
detect (*verb*), discerner, apercevoir; découvrir.
detest (*verb*), détester.
develop (*verb*), développer, amplifier; exploiter; contracter (une maladie).
devil (*noun*), diable *m.*
devoted (*adj.*), dévoué, attaché (**to,** à).
diagram (*noun*), diagramme *m.*, graphique *m.*
diamond (*noun*), diamant *m.*
dice (*pl. noun*), (*game*) dés *m. pl.*
dictionary (*noun*), dictionnaire *m.*
die (*verb*), mourir; s'éteindre.
difference (*noun*), différence *f.*
different (*adj.*), différent (**from,** de); autre (**that is a different matter,** ça, c'est une autre affaire).
difficult (*adj.*), difficile, dur.
difficulty (*noun*), difficulté *f.*; obstacle *m.*
dig (*verb*), bêcher, retourner le sol; **to dig a hole,** creuser un trou; **to dig (with a pick),** piocher.
dignified (*adj.*), plein de dignité, imposant.
dignity (*noun*), dignité *f.*
din (*noun*), fracas *m.*, tapage *m.*, vacarme *m.*
dine (*verb*), dîner.
dinner (*noun*), dîner *m.*
dip (*verb*), tremper, plonger; baisser (**to dip the head-lights,** baisser les phares).
direction (*noun*), direction *f.*; orientation *f.*; conduite *f.* (**he is responsible for the direction of State affairs,** il est responsable de la conduite des affaires de l'État).
director (*noun*), directeur *m.*, administrateur *m.*
dirty (*adj.*), sale.
disadvantage (*noun*), désavantage *m.*
disagree (*verb*), être en désaccord; ne pas s'accorder, ne pas être d'accord (**with,** avec); différer d'opinion.
disappear (*verb*), disparaître.
disappoint (*verb*), désappointer (quelqu'un), décevoir; **to disappoint someone's expectations,** tromper les espérances de quelqu'un.
disapprove (*verb*), désapprouver; exprimer sa désapprobation.
disarrange (*verb*), déranger.
disaster (*noun*), désastre *m.*; catastrophe *f.*
discontinue (*verb*), discontinuer, interrompre; mettre fin à.
discover (*verb*), découvrir, trouver; révéler.
discovery (*noun*), découverte *f.*
discretion (*noun*), discrétion *f.*; **to reach the age of discretion,** atteindre l'âge de raison *f.*
discuss (*verb*), discuter, s'entretenir de, échanger des vues sur.
disease (*noun*), maladie *f.*; mal *m.*
dish (*noun*), plat *m.*
dishonest (*adj.*), malhonnête.
dismount (*verb*), descendre (de cheval); mettre pied à terre.
disobey (*verb*), désobéir (à).
dispensary (*noun*), dispensaire *m.*
dispense (*verb*), dispenser; administrer; exempter (**from,** de); **to dispense with something,** se passer de quelque chose.
display (*noun*), exposition *f.*; déploiement *m.*; étalage *m.*; (*verb*), exposer; déployer, étaler.

dispute (*noun*), débat *m.*, contestation *f.*; dispute *f.*; **industrial dispute,** conflit *m.* ouvrier; (*verb*), discuter, disputer; débattre (quelque chose avec quelqu'un).
distance (*noun*), distance *f.*; **in the distance,** au loin.
distrust (*noun*), défiance *f.*; (*verb*), se défier de (quelqu'un).
ditch (*noun*), fossé *m.*
diver (*noun*), plongeur *m.*, plongeuse *f.*
division (*noun*), division *f.*, séparation *f.*; (*sharing out*) répartition *f.*
do (*verb*), faire; accomplir.
doctor (*noun*), médecin *m.*, docteur *m.*
dodge (*verb*), esquiver (un coup); éluder (une difficulté); éviter (quelqu'un).
dog (*noun*), chien *m.*, chienne *f.*
doll (*noun*), poupée *f.*
door (*noun*), porte *f.*
double (*adj.*), double; deux (**double s,** deux s) ; **double bed,** lit *m.* à deux places.
doubt (*noun*), doute *m.*; **no doubt,** sans doute.
doubtless (*adv.*), sans doute.
downward, downwards (*adv.*), en bas, vers le bas, en descendant.
drain (*verb*), vider (**to drain one's glass,** vider son verre).
drawing (*noun*), dessin *m.*
dream (*noun*), rêve *m.*; (*verb*), rêver.
dress (*noun*), habillement *m.*; habits *m. pl.*; vêtements *m. pl.*; costume *m.*, robe *f.*; (*verb*), habiller; (*dress oneself*) s'habiller.
drink (*noun*), boisson *f.*; (*verb*), boire.
drive (*verb*), conduire (une auto); enfoncer (**to drive in a nail,** enfoncer un clou).
driver (*noun*), conducteur *m.* (d'auto, d'autobus); chauffeur *m.* (de taxi); **engine driver,** mécanicien *m.*
drizzle (*noun*), bruine *f.*; crachin *m.*; (*verb*), bruiner.
drop (*noun*), goutte *f.* (**a drop of water,** une goutte d'eau); (*verb*), tomber; laisser tomber (quelque chose); **to drop dead,** tomber mort; **to be ready to drop,** tomber de fatigue.
drum (*noun*), tambour *m.*
drummer (*noun*), tambour *m.*
dry (*adj.*), sec *m.*, sèche *f.*; (*verb*), sécher.
duck (*noun*), (*drake*) canard *m.*; (*female*) cane *f.*
dumb (*adj.*), muet *m.*, -ette *f.*
dump (*noun*), amas *m.*, tas *m.*; **refuse dump,** dépotoir *m.*; (*verb*), décharger, déverser; jeter au rebut.
during (*prep.*), pendant, durant.
dust (*noun*), poussière *f.*; poudre *f.*; (*verb*), épousseter; saupoudrer (**with,** de).
duster (*noun*), torchon *m.*
duty (*noun*), devoir *m.*; droit *m.* (**customs duty,** droit(s) de douane); **to be on duty,** être de service.
dwell (*verb*), habiter, demeurer, résider (**in,** à, dans); rester; **to dwell on a subject,** s'étendre sur un sujet.

E

each (*adj.*), chaque; (*pron.*), chacun *m.*, chacune *f.*
eagle (*noun*), aigle *m.*
ear (*noun*), (*of body*) oreille *f.*; (*of corn*) épi *m.*
early (*adv.*), de bonne heure; tôt; **early in,** au début de (**early in the year,** au début de l'année).
earn (*verb*), gagner (de l'argent); mériter (l'admiration de quelqu'un).
earth (*noun*), terre *f.*; monde *m.*; (*ground*) sol *m.*
ease (*noun*), aise *f.*; aisance *f.*; **with ease,** facilement; aisément.
east (*noun*), est *m.*, levant *m.*, orient *m.*
Easter (*noun*), Pâques *m.*; **Easter Sunday** le jour de Pâques.
easy (*adj.*), aisé; simple; facile; confortable.
eat (*verb*), manger; **to eat into,** ronger.
economic(al) (*adj.*), économique; (*thrifty*) économe.
economy (*noun*), économie *f.*, épargne *f.*
edge (*noun*), bord *m.*; (*of blade*) fil *m.*
educate (*verb*), éduquer; faire l'éducation de, instruire.
efface (*verb*), effacer (**from,** de).
efficient (*adj.*) (*person*) compétent, capable; (*work*) efficace.
effort (*noun*), effort *m.*
egg (*noun*), œuf *m.*
eight (*noun & adj.*), *huit *m.*
eighteen (*noun & adj.*), dix-huit *m.*
eighth (*noun & adj.*), *huitième *m.* (**Henry the Eighth,** Henri Huit).
eighty (*noun & adj.*), quatre-vingts *m.*; **eighty-one,** quatre-vingt-un.
either (*adv.*), non plus (**nor I either,** ni moi non plus); (*pron.*), l'un(e) ou l'autre; (*conj.*), **either . . . or,** ou . . . ou.
eject (*verb*), éjecter; émettre; expulser (**from,** de).
elbow (*noun*), coude *m.*
eldest (*adj.*), aîné; le plus âgé *m.*, la plus âgée *f.*
electric (*adj.*), électrique.
electrician (*noun*), électricien *m.*
electricity (*noun*), électricité *f.*
elephant (*noun*) éléphant *m.*
eleven (*noun & adj.*), onze *m.*
embark (*verb*), embarquer; s'embarquer.
embrace (*verb*), embrasser; s'embrasser.
emerge (*verb*), émerger (**from,** de) (**the workman emerges from the hole,** l'ouvrier émerge du trou); ressortir (**from these facts it emerges that you are right,** de ces faits il ressort que vous avez raison); découler (**we know the evils which emerge from war,** nous savons les maux qui découlent de la guerre).
emit (*verb*), émettre; dégager; exhaler (une odeur); débiter (de la fumée, de l'eau).
emperor (*noun*), empereur *m.*
employ (*verb*), employer, utiliser.
employee (*noun*), employé *m.*, employée *f.*
employer (*noun*), employeur *m.*, employeuse *f.*; patron *m.*, patronne *f.*
empty (*adj.*), vide; (*verb*), vider.
enable (*verb*), rendre capable, permettre à (**that enables my mother to earn some money,** cela permet à ma mère de gagner de l'argent).
enclose (*verb*), enclore; enfermer; (*encircle*) entourer; (*contain*) renfermer.
enclosure (*noun*), clôture *f.*; (*document*) pièce *f.* jointe.
encourage (*verb*), encourager; (*hearten*) remonter.
end (*noun*), fin *f.*; terme *m.* (d'un voyage); bout *m.* (**at the end of the road,** au bout de la rue); extrémité *f.*; (*verb*), finir, terminer.
endanger (*verb*), mettre en danger, exposer au danger, mettre en péril; risquer (la vie de quelqu'un).
endeavour (*noun*), effort *m.*; (*verb*), essayer de; s'efforcer de; faire tous ses efforts (pour faire quelque chose).

enemy (*noun*), ennemi *m.*
energetic (*adj.*), énergique, vigoureux *m.*, -euse *f.*
engine (*noun*), machine *f.*; moteur *m.*; locomotive *f.*
engineer (*noun*), (*technician*) ingénieur *m.*; (*workman*) mécanicien *m.*
England (*noun*), Angleterre *f.*
enjoy (*verb*), prendre plaisir à (faire quelque chose); jouir de (**to enjoy good health,** jouir d'une bonne santé).
enlarge (*verb*), agrandir, développer; grossir.
enough (*adv.*), assez, suffisamment.
enrich (*verb*), enrichir (**with,** de).
ensure (*verb*), assurer.
entangle (*verb*), embrouiller, entortiller.
enter (*verb*), entrer, pénétrer (**into,** dans).
entertain (*verb*), divertir, amuser; donner une réception.
entice (*verb*), attirer, tenter.
entire (*adj.*), entier *m.*, -ière *f.*; total; complet *m.*, -ète *f.*
entrance (*noun*), entrée *f.*; admission *f.*
entry (*noun*), entrée *f.*; inscription *f.*
enumerate (*verb*), énumérer.
envelop (*verb*), envelopper.
envelope (*noun*), enveloppe *f.*
envious (*adj.*), envieux *m.*, -euse *f.*
envy (*noun*), envie *f.*
episode (*noun*), épisode *m.*
equal (*adj.*), égal (**to,** à); sur le même plan.
equip (*verb*), équiper; outiller; installer.
equivalent (*noun*), équivalent *m.*; (*adj.*): **to be equivalent to,** équivaloir à.
erase (*verb*), effacer; (*cross out*) raturer; (*scratch out*) gratter; (*rub out*) gommer.
erect (*adj.*), droit, debout.
errand (*noun*), commission *f.*, course *f.*
error (*noun*), erreur *f.*, méprise *f.*, opinion *f.* fausse.
escalator (*noun*), escalier *m.* roulant.
escape (*noun*), action *f.* de s'échapper, fuite *f.*; (*verb*), s'échapper, s'enfuir, s'évader; éviter.
especially (*adv.*), surtout, spécialement.
essential (*adj.*), essentiel *m.*, -ielle *f.*
establish (*verb*), établir, instituer, fonder, installer; prouver.
estimate (*noun*), évaluation *f.*, estimation *f.*; (*verb*), estimer, évaluer.
etcetera (*phrase*), et caetera.
evade (*verb*), éluder, éviter, échapper à.
evening (*noun*), soir *m.*; (*duration of evening*) soirée *f.*; **good evening,** bonsoir.
ever (*adv.*), jamais, toujours; **for ever and ever,** à jamais, à perpétuité.
every (*adj.*), chaque; tous les *m. pl.*, toutes les *f. pl.*; **every day of the week,** chaque jour (*or* tous les jours) de la semaine; **every third day,** tous les trois jours.
everywhere (*adv.*), partout.
evidence (*noun*), évidence *f.*; indication *f.*; (*witness*) témoignage *m.*
evil (*adj.*), mauvais; dépravé; méchant; (*noun*), mal *m.*
exact (*adj.*), précis; juste; exact.
exaggerate (*verb*), exagérer.
examine (*verb*), examiner (**the student is examining the specimen,** l'étudiant examine le spécimen); interroger (**the judge is examining the witness,** le juge interroge le témoin).
example (*noun*), exemple *m.*; **for example,** par exemple; **to set an example,** donner l'exemple.
excavate (*verb*), excaver; (*to dig*) creuser.
exceed (*verb*), dépasser; excéder; surpasser (**Henry exceeded George in intelligence,** Henri surpassait Georges par l'intelligence).
excellent (*adj.*), excellent.
except (*prep.*), excepté, sauf.
exchange (*verb*), échanger, troquer (**for,** contre); interchanger.
excite (*verb*), exciter, stimuler.
excuse (*noun*), prétexte *m.*, excuse *f.* (**for,** à); (*verb*), excuser, exempter.
execute (*verb*), exécuter, accomplir; remplir (son devoir).
exercise (*noun*), exercice *m.*; devoir *m.*; (*verb*), exercer.
exert (*verb*), employer (la force); déployer (son talent); exercer (une influence); **to exert oneself,** se dépenser.
exist (*verb*), exister, être; vivre.

exit (*noun*), sortie *f.*
exonerate (*verb*), exonérer (**from,** de); dispenser (**from,** de), exempter (**from,** de).
expand (*verb*), (*spread out*) déployer; étendre; élargir; se détendre.
expect (*verb*), attendre (quelqu'un); s'attendre à (**I was expecting that,** je m'attendais à cela); (*rely on*) compter sur.
expensive (*adj.*), coûteux *m.*, -euse *f.*, cher *m.*, -ère *f.*
explain (*verb*), expliquer, donner l'explication de.
explanation (*noun*), explication *f.*
explode (*verb*), exploser, détoner.
explore (*verb*), explorer; (*medical*) sonder.
explosion (*noun*), explosion *f.*, détonation *f.*
export (*noun*), exportation *f.*; (*verb*), exporter.
expose (*verb*), exposer; dévoiler (un crime).
express (*noun*), (*train*) rapide *m.*; (*verb*), exprimer, émettre; **to express oneself,** s'exprimer.
exquisite (*adj.*), exquis; délicat.
exterior (*noun*), extérieur *m.*
extinguish (*verb*), éteindre.
extraordinary (*adj.*), extraordinaire.
extricate (*verb*), dégager; libérer.
eye (*noun*), œil *m.* (*pl.* yeux).

F

fable (*noun*), fable *f.*
fabric (*noun*), tissu *m.*; étoffe *f.*
face (*noun*), figure *f.*; visage *m.*
fact (*noun*), fait *m.*; réalité *f.*
factory (*noun*), usine *f.*, fabrique *f.*
fail (*verb*), faillir, manquer (**in one's duty,** à son devoir); **to fail to do something,** négliger de faire quelque chose; **to fail in an examination,** être refusé à un examen, échouer à un examen.
fair (*adj.*), beau (bel) *m.*, belle *f.*; (*of hair*) blond; juste; (*noun*), foire *f.*
fairy (*noun*), fée *f.*
faith (*noun*), foi *f.*, confiance *f.*; croyance *f.* (**in,** en).
fall (*verb*), tomber.
false (*adj.*), faux *m.*, fausse *f.*; artificiel *m.*, -elle *f.*
falsehood (*noun*), mensonge *m.*
familiar (*adj.*), familier *m.*, -ère *f.*; intime; bien connu.
family (*noun*), famille *f.*
famous (*adj.*), fameux *m.*, -euse *f.*, célèbre.
fan (*noun*), éventail *m.*
fancy (*verb*), s'imaginer, se figurer; avoir envie de (**I fancy a walk,** j'ai envie de me promener).
fantastic (*adj.*), fantastique, bizarre.
far (*adv.*), loin (**from,** de); **Peter is far from home,** Pierre est loin de chez lui; **far from being angry, he is pleased with the plan,** loin d'être en colère, il est content du projet; **Henry is not here, he is far away,** Henri n'est pas ici, il est loin.
farewell (*noun*), adieu *m.*
farm (*noun*), ferme *f.*; (*small farm*) métairie *f.*
farmer (*noun*), fermier *m.*; cultivateur *m.*
fashion (*noun*), façon *f.*; mode *f.*; (*shape*) forme *f.*; manière *f.*
fast (*adj.*), rapide, vite; (*of clock*) en avance; (*firm*) ferme, stable.
fasten (*verb*), attacher, fixer.
fat (*adj.*), gras *m.*, grasse *f.*; gros *m.*, grosse *f.*; (*noun*), graisse *f.*
father (*noun*), père *m.*
fatigue (*noun*), fatigue *f.*
fault (*noun*), défaut *m.*; imperfection *f.*; faute *f.*
faulty (*adj.*), imparfait, défectueux *m.*, -euse *f.*
favour (*noun*), faveur *f.*
fear (*noun*), peur *f.*, crainte *f.*; (*verb*), avoir peur, craindre.
feast (*noun*), fête *f.*
feather (*noun*), plume *f.*
February (*noun*), février *m.*
feeble (*adj.*), faible, débile.
feed (*verb*), nourrir; donner à manger à.
feel (*verb*), toucher, palper, tâter; sentir; **to feel tired,** se sentir fatigué.
fence (*noun*), clôture *f.*; barrière *f.*; (*paling*) palissade *f.*
fetch (*verb*), aller chercher; atteindre (**the painting fetched 300 francs at the auction,** la peinture a atteint 300 francs aux enchères); **to fetch a high price,** se vendre cher.
fête (*noun*), fête *f.*
fever (*noun*), fièvre *f.*
few (*adj.*), peu de (**she has few friends,** elle a peu d'amis); **a few,** quelques (*pl.*) (**in a few minutes,** dans quelques minutes; **a few of us,** quelques-un(e)s d'entre nous); **she is one of the few people I like,** elle est une des rares personnes que j'aime.
field (*noun*), champ *m.*; terrain *m.*
fierce (*adj.*), féroce; sauvage; violent; (*of storm*) furieux *m.*, -euse *f.*
fifteen (*noun & adj.*), quinze *m.*
fifteenth (*adj.*), quinzième; **Louis the Fifteenth,** Louis Quinze.
fifth (*adj.*), cinquième.
fifty (*noun & adj.*), cinquante *m.*
fight (*verb*), se battre; combattre; (*noun*), lutte *f.*, bataille *f.*, combat *m.*

figure (*noun*), forme *f.*, silhouette *f.*; figure *f.*; (*number*) chiffre *m.*
fill (*verb*), remplir (**with,** de); boucher (un trou); **to fill a position,** occuper un poste.
film (*noun*), (*for photographs*) pellicule *f.*; (*cinema*) film *m.*
find (*verb*), trouver; découvrir.
fine (*adj.*), superbe, excellent; fin; delicat; beau (bel) *m.*, belle *f.*
finger (*noun*), doigt *m.*
finish (*verb*), finir, terminer.
fire (*noun*), feu *m.*, incendie *m.*; **fire-alarm,** avertisseur *m.* d'incendie; (*verb*), (*shoot*) tirer.
first (*adv.*), d'abord; (*adj.*), premier *m.*, -ière *f.*; **first aid,** soins *m. pl.* d'urgence.
fir-tree (*noun*), sapin *m.*
fish (*noun*), poisson *m.*; (*verb*), pêcher.
fisherman (*noun*), pêcheur *m.*
fish-hook (*noun*), hameçon *m.*
fishing (*noun*), pêche *f.*
fist (*noun*), poing *m.*
fit (*adj.*), bon, propre (**for something,** à quelque chose); (*medical*) en bonne santé; (*verb*), aller à (**this dress does not fit you,** cette robe ne vous va pas); ajuster (**she will fit this dress on the lady,** elle ajustera cette robe à la dame).
five (*noun & adj.*), cinq *m.*
flabby (*adj.*), flasque; mou *m.*, molle *f.*; (*of character*) avachi.
flag (*noun*), drapeau *m.*
flame (*noun*), flamme *f.*
flan (*noun*), tarte *f.* aux fruits.
flannel (*noun*), flanelle *f.*; **flannel trousers,** pantalon *m.* de flanelle.
flash (*noun*), éclair *m.*; éclat *m.* brusque.
flat (*adj.*), plat; **to fall flat,** tomber à plat; (*noun*), appartement *m.*
flee (*verb*), fuir, s'enfuir.
flesh (*noun*), chair *f.*; (*meat*) viande *f.*
float (*verb*), flotter; faire flotter.
floor (*noun*), plancher *m.*, parquet *m.*; (*storey*) étage *m.*
florist (*noun*), fleuriste *m. & f.*
flour (*noun*), farine *f.*
flow (*verb*), couler.
flower (*noun*), fleur *f.*
fly (*noun*), mouche *f.*; (*verb*), voler (**birds fly,** les oiseaux volent); faire voler (**to fly a kite,** faire voler un cerf-volant); **to fly away,** s'envoler.
fog (*noun*), brouillard *m.*
fold (*noun*), pli *m.*; (*verb*), plier.
follow (*verb*), suivre; (*come after*) succéder à.
following (*adj.*), suivant.
fond (*adj.*), tendre, affectueux *m.*, -euse *f.*; **to be fond of someone (something),** aimer quelqu'un (quelque chose), être attaché à quelqu'un (quelque chose).
food (*noun*), nourriture *f.*; aliments *m. pl.*; ravitaillement *m.*
fool (*noun*), sot *m.*, sotte *f.*; imbécile *m. & f.*; dupe *f.*; (*jester*) bouffon *m.*
foolish (*adj.*), sot *m.*, sotte *f.*; stupide; absurde.
foot (*noun*), pied *m.*; **on foot,** à pied.
footpath (*noun*), sentier *m.*; piste *f.* pour piétons; (*pavement*) trottoir *m.*
for (*prep.*), pour (**he works for his father,** il travaille pour son père); depuis (**I have been in Paris for a week,** je suis à Paris depuis une semaine); pendant (**he stayed in Paris for a week,** il est resté à Paris pendant une semaine).
for (*conj.*), car.
forbid (*verb*), interdire, défendre; empêcher (**my work forbids my seeing you,** mon travail m'empêche de vous voir).
force (*noun*), force *f.*, violence *f.*
forceful (*adj.*), puissant; vigoureux *m.*, -euse *f.*
forehead (*noun*), front *m.*
foreigner (*noun*), étranger *m.*, étrangère *f*
forest (*noun*), forêt *f.*
foretell (*verb*), (*predict*) prédire, pronostiquer; (*portend*) présager, augurer.
forge (*noun*), forge *f.*; (*verb*), forger; (*counterfeit*) contrefaire.
forget (*verb*), oublier.
forgive (*verb*), pardonner; remettre (une dette).
forgiveness (*noun*), pardon *m.*; remise *f.* (d'une dette).

fork (*noun*), fourchette *f.* (de table); (*agriculture*) fourche *f.*
form (*noun*), (*shape*) forme *f.*; (*bench*) banc *m.*; (*in school*) classe *f.*; **to fill in a form,** remplir une fiche.
fortify (*verb*), fortifier, renforcer.
fortunate (*adj.*), fortuné, heureux *m.*, -euse *f.*
fortune (*noun*), fortune *f.*, chance *f.*; richesse *f.*
forty (*noun & adj.*), quarante *m.*
forward, forwards (*adv.*), (*onward*) en avant, vers l'avant.
fountain (*noun*), fontaine *f.*
four (*noun & adj.*), quatre *m.*; **on all fours,** à quatre pattes.
fourteen (*noun & adj.*), quatorze *m.*
fourteenth (*adj.*), quatorzième; **Louis the Fourteenth,** Louis Quatorze.
fourth (*adj.*), quatrième; **Henry the Fourth,** Henri Quatre.
fox (*noun*), renard *m.*
fracture (*noun*), fracture *f.*
fragile (*adj.*), fragile.
fragment (*noun*), fragment *m.*
frame (*noun*), cadre *m.* (de tableau); monture *f.* (de lunettes).
franc (*noun*), franc *m.*
France (*noun*), France *f.*
frank (*adj.*), franc *m.*, franche *f.*; sincère.
free (*adj.*), libre, en liberté; indépendant; gratuit; (*verb*), libérer, délivrer; dégager; exempter.
freedom (*noun*), liberté *f.*
freeze (*verb*), geler, se geler.
French (*adj.*), français.
frequent (*adj.*), fréquent; nombreux *m.*, -euse *f.*
frequently (*adv.*), fréquemment; souvent.
fresh (*adj.*), frais *m.*, fraîche *f.*; spontané; nouveau (nouvel) *m.*, -elle *f.* (**fresh proof,** nouvelle preuve); récent; **fresh water,** (*freshly drawn*) eau fraîche; (*not salt*) eau douce.
freshen (*verb*), rafraîchir.
Friday (*noun*), vendredi *m.*
friend (*noun*), ami *m.*, amie *f.*
friendly (*adj.*), amical; favorable (**she was friendly towards the idea,** elle était favorable à l'idée).
fright (*noun*), frayeur *f.*; peur *f.*; effroi *m.*
frighten (*verb*), effrayer, fair peur à (**the tiger frightens him,** le tigre lui fait peur); **to be, feel frightened,** avoir peur (**the small boy is frightened of the tiger,** le petit garçon a peur du tigre).
frivolous (*adj.*), frivole; futile.
frock (*noun*), robe *f.*
frog (*noun*), grenouille *f.*
from (*prep.*), de; **from morning till night,** du matin au soir.
front (*noun*), (*military*) front *m.*; (*front part*) devant *m.* (**the front of the dress,** le devant de la robe); façade *f.* (d'une maison); **in front of,** devant, en face de.
frontier (*noun*), frontière *f.*
frost (*noun*), gelée *f.*
fruit (*noun*), fruit *m.*
fry (*verb*), frire.
full (*adj.*), plein, rempli; entier *m.*, -ière *f.*; complet *m.*, -ète *f.*
full-stop, point *m.*
funnel (*noun*), entonnoir *m.*; cheminée *f.*
funny (*adj.*), drôle, comique, bizarre; étrange.
fur (*noun*), fourrure *f.*; **fur coat,** manteau *m.* de fourrure.
furious (*adj.*), furieux *m.*, -euse *f.*; **to become furious,** entrer en fureur.
furnace (*noun*), fourneau *m.*; four *m.*; (*hot place*) fournaise *f.*
furniture (*noun*), meubles *m. pl.*, ameublement *m.*; **piece of furniture,** meuble *m.*
further (*adv.*), plus loin, plus avant; (*more*) davantage.
futile (*adj.*), futile, vain.
future (*noun*), futur *m.*, avenir *m.*; **in future,** à l'avenir.

G

gain (*verb*), gagner, trouver avantage (**by,** à); (*noun*), (*increase, growth*) accroissement *m.*; bénéfice *m.*, profit *m.*, avantage *m.*
game (*noun*), jeu *m.*; partie *f.* (**a game of cards, of billiards, of tennis,** une partie de cartes, de billard, de tennis).
garage (*noun*), garage *m.*; (*verb*), garer, mettre au garage.
garden (*noun*), jardin *m.*; **flower garden,** jardin d'agrément; **vegetable garden,** jardin potager; **garden-city,** cité-jardin *f.*
garment (*noun*), vêtement *m.*
gas (*noun*), gaz *m.*
gate (*noun*), barrière *f.*; porte *f.* (d'une ville); (*of park*) grille *f.*
gather (*verb*), assembler; amasser; cueillir (des fleurs).
gay (*adj.*), gai; joyeux *m.*, -euse *f.*
generous (*adj.*), généreux *m.*, -euse *f.*; libéral; abondant.
gentle (*adj.*), doux *m.*, douce *f.*; modéré; léger *m.*, -ère *f.* (**a gentle tap,** un coup léger).
germinate (*verb*), germer; faire germer.
get (*verb*), procurer, obtenir, prendre, atteindre; recevoir; (*become*) devenir; **to get to a place,** arriver à un endroit.
giant (*noun*), géant *m.*
gift (*noun*), don *m.*; cadeau *m.*, présent *m.*
girdle (*noun*), ceinture *f.*
girl (*noun*), fille *f.*, jeune fille *f.*; **little girl,** fillette *f.*, petite fille *f.*
give (*verb*), donner, offrir; remettre (un message); **to give back,** rendre, restituer.
glad (*adj.*), content; heureux *m.*, -euse *f.*
glass (*noun*), verre *m.*; **pane of glass,** vitre *f.*; **wine-glass,** verre à vin.
glide (*verb*), glisser, avancer en glissant; (*of aircraft*) planer.
glider (*noun*), (*aircraft*) planeur *m.*
glisten (*verb*), (*of water*) miroiter; scintiller, briller.
gloomy (*adj.*), (*of person*) morose; (*of place*) sombre, obscur.
glory (*noun*), gloire *f.*, honneur *m.*
glove (*noun*), gant *m.*
glue (*noun*), colle *f.*; (*verb*), coller.
go (*verb*), aller; partir, s'en aller; **to go out,** sortir; **to go across,** traverser.
goat (*noun*), bouc *m.*; chèvre *f.*
God (*noun*), Dieu *m.*; **the gods,** les dieux.
gold (*noun*), or *m.*; **gold-fish,** poisson rouge *m.*
good (*adj.*), bon *m.*, bonne *f.*; (*well-behaved*) sage; **to be good at,** être fort en.
good-bye (*noun*), au revoir *m.*
goose (*noun*), oie *f.*
government (*noun*), gouvernement *m.*; régime *m.*; administration *f.* (**local government,** administration *f.* départementale).
grab (*verb*), saisir, agripper.
grain (*noun*), (*of corn, sand, leather*) grain *m.*
grammar-school (*noun*), lycée *m.*
gramophone (*noun*), électrophone *m.*, gramophone *m.*, phonographe *m.* (*see* **record-player**).
grandchildren (*pl. noun*), petits-enfants *m. pl.*
grand-daughter (*noun*), petite-fille *f.*
grandfather (*noun*), grand-père *m.*
grandmother (*noun*), grand-mère *f.*
grandparents (*pl. noun*), grands-parents *m. pl.*
grandson (*noun*), petit-fils *m.*
grange (*noun*), grange *f.*; manoir *m.*
grape (*noun*), grain *m.* de raisin; **bunch of grapes,** grappe *f.* de raisin.
grasp (*verb*), saisir, empoigner; étreindre.
grass (*noun*), herbe *f.*; **blade of grass,** brin *m.* d'herbe.
grateful (*adj.*), reconnaissant (**to someone,** envers quelqu'un); réconfortant.
grave (*adj.*), grave, sérieux *m.*, -euse *f.*
graveyard (*noun*), cimetière *m.*
grease (*noun*), graisse *f.*; lubrifiant *m.*; (*verb*), graisser.

great (*adj.*), grand; éminent; illustre; fameux *m.*, -euse *f.*; **a great big man,** un homme de haute taille; **a great big balloon,** un énorme ballon.

greedy (*adj.*), avide; gourmand.

green (*adj.*), vert; verdoyant; (*noun*), vert *m.*

greengrocer (*noun*), marchand *m.* de légumes, fruitier *m.*

greenhouse (*noun*), serre *f.*

greet (*verb*), saluer, accueillir (**with,** avec, par).

greetings! (*interjection*), salut!

grey (*adj.*), gris.

grief (*noun*), chagrin *m.*; affliction *f.*

grip (*noun*), prise *f.*, étreinte *f.* (**he held his friend's hand in a firm grip,** il tenait la main de son ami dans une étreinte ferme); (*verb*), étreindre, empoigner.

grocer (*noun*), épicier *m.*, épicière *f.*; **at the grocer's,** à l'épicerie *f.*, chez l'épicier.

ground (*noun*), terre *f.*; terrain *m.*, sol *m.*; **ground-floor,** rez-de-chaussée *m.*

groundnut (*noun*), arachide *f.*

group (*noun*), groupe *m.*

grow (*verb*), pousser, croître; grandir.

guard (*noun*), garde *m.*; chef *m.* de train; (*verb*), garder, escorter; **to guard against,** se méfier de.

guess (*noun*), conjecture *f.*; (*verb*), deviner, conjecturer; estimer.

guide (*noun*), guide *m.*; **girl-guide,** éclaireuse *f.*; (*verb*), guider, diriger.

guitar (*noun*), guitare *f.*

gum (*noun*), gomme *f.*; résine *f.*; (*glue*) colle *f.*

gun (*noun*), (*rifle*) fusil *m.*; canon *m.*

H

habit (*noun*), habitude *f.*; costume *m.*
hail (*verb*): **it is hailing,** il grêle.
hair (*noun*), (*single hair*), cheveu *m.*; cheveux (*pl.*) (**she has fair hair,** elle a les cheveux blonds); (*of animals*) poil *m.*
hairdresser (*noun*), coiffeur *m.*, coiffeuse *f.*
half (*noun*), moitié *f.* (**of,** de); (*adj.*), demi (**half an hour,** une demi-heure; **two and a half hours,** deux heures et demie; **half a dozen,** une demi-douzaine; **a loaf and a half,** un pain et demi).
halt (*noun*), *halte *f.*; (*verb*), faire halte, s'arrêter; **halt!** halte!
hammer (*noun*), marteau *m.*
hand (*noun*), main *f.*; (*of watch*) aiguille *f.*; **hand-towel,** essuie-mains *m.*
handkerchief (*noun*), mouchoir *m.*
handle (*noun*), (*of door*) poignée *f.*; (*of basket*) anse *f.*; (*of broom, knife, etc.*) manche *m.*; (*of pan*) queue *f.*
handwriting (*noun*), écriture *f.*
hang (*verb*), pendre; **to hang up,** suspendre, accrocher; **to hang out the washing,** étendre le linge; **to hang wall-paper,** coller du papier peint.
happen (*verb*), arriver (**an accident happened,** il est arrivé un accident; **what has happened to him?** qu'est-ce qui lui est arrivé?).
happy (*adj.*), heureux *m.*, -euse *f.*; content.
harbour (*noun*), port *m.*
hard (*adj.*), dur, ferme; difficile; (*of fate, weather*) sévère, rigoureux *m.*, -euse *f.*
harm (*noun*), (*hurt*) mal *m.*, tort *m.*; (*verb*), faire du mal à, faire du tort à.
harvest (*noun*), moisson *f.*, récolte *f.*; (*verb*), moissonner, récolter; faire la moisson.
haste (*noun*), *hâte *f.*
hasten (*verb*), *hâter, accélérer, presser; se dépêcher, se *hâter.
hasty (*adj.*), *hâtif *m.*, -ive *f.*; précipité; rapide; vif *m.*, vive *f.*
hat (*noun*), chapeau *m.*; **hat-shop,** (*for men*) chapellerie *f.*; (*for women*) boutique *f.* de modiste.
hatchet (*noun*), *hachette *f.*
hate (*verb*), *haïr, détester, exécrer.
hatred (*noun*), *haine *f.*
have (*verb*), avoir, posséder; tenir; **to have to do something,** devoir faire quelque chose.
hay (*noun*), foin *m.*
he (*pron.*), il; lui *m.* (**he and she,** lui et elle; ***he* has said nothing,** lui n'a rien dit; **he, a doctor!** lui médecin!); **he is my father,** c'est mon père.
head (*noun*), tête *f.*; chevet *m.* (de lit).
headache (*noun*), mal *m.* de tête; **to have a headache,** avoir mal à la tête.
headmaster (*noun*), principal *m.*, directeur *m.*
heal (*verb*), (se) guérir; (*of a wound*) (se) cicatriser.
health (*noun*), santé *f.*; **good health!** à votre santé!
heap (*noun*), tas *m.*, amas *m.*, amoncellement *m.*
hear (*verb*), entendre; écouter (**to hear a lesson,** écouter une leçon); **to hear the truth,** apprendre la vérité.
heart (*noun*), cœur *m.*; centre *m.*
hearth (*noun*), foyer *m.*, âtre *m.*
heat (*noun*), chaleur *f.*; (*verb*), chauffer.
heating (*noun*), chauffage *m.*; **central heating,** chauffage *m.* central.
heave (*verb*), lever, soulever; **to heave a sigh,** pousser un soupir.
heaven (*noun*), ciel *m.*
heavy (*adj.*), lourd; pesant; (*of weather*) gros *m.*, grosse *f.*; (*of blow*) violent.
hedge (*noun*), *haie *f.*
height (*noun*), hauteur *f.*; taille *f.* (de quelqu'un); altitude *f.*; élévation *f.*
hello! (*interj.*), bonjour! salut!; (*on telephone*) allô!; tiens! (**hello! here is the key I lost,** tiens! voici la clef que j'avais perdue).

help (*verb*), aider; faciliter; venir en aide à; **help yourself,** servez-vous; **help!** au secours!
hen (*noun*), poule *f.*
her (*pron.*), la (**look at her,** regardez-la!); lui (**take her this letter,** apportez-lui cette lettre); elle (**I am thinking of her,** je pense à elle); (*adj.*), son *m.*, sa *f.*, ses *pl.* (**her brother,** son frère; **her sister,** sa sœur; **her children,** ses enfants).
herb (*noun*), herbe *f.*
here (*adv.*), ici,; **here is, here are,** *etc.*, voici (**here is the theatre,** voici le théâtre; **here I am,** me voici).
hers (*pron.*), le sien, *m.*, la sienne *f.*, les siens *m. pl.*, les siennes *f. pl.*; à elle (**the house is hers,** la maison est à elle).
herself (*pron.*), elle-même.
hesitate (*verb*), hésiter.
hide (*noun*), (*leather*) cuir *m.*; (*skin*) peau *f.*; (*verb*), cacher; tenir secret; **hide-and-seek** (*noun*), cache-cache *m.*
high (*adj.*), *haut; grand; (*of price*) élevé.
highway (*noun*), grande route *f.*; route *f.* principale; chaussée *f.*
hill (*noun*), colline *f.*; (*on road*) côte *f.*
him (*pron.*), le, l' (**she loves him,** elle l'aime); lui (**tell him all,** dites-lui tout; **I think of him,** je pense à lui).
himself (*pron.*), lui-même.
hinder (*verb*), gêner, entraver, retarder.
hire (*verb*), louer; **to hire out,** louer; donner en location; (*noun*), location *f.*; gages *m. pl.*; **hire-purchase,** vente *f.* à tempérament; vente *f.* à crédit.
his (*adj.*), son *m.*, sa *f.*, ses *pl.* (**his brother,** son frère; **his sister,** sa sœur; **his children,** ses enfants); (*pron.*), le sien *m.*, la sienne *f.*, les siens *m. pl.*, les siennes *f. pl.*; à lui (**the pen is his,** le stylo est à lui).
history (*noun*), histoire *f.*
hit (*noun*), coup *m.*; (*verb*), frapper, heurter; atteindre.
hoar-frost (*noun*), gelée *f.* blanche.
hold (*verb*), tenir; **to be held,** se tenir (**the exhibition is held in September,** l'exposition se tient au mois de septembre).
hole (*noun*), trou *m.*
holiday (*noun*), congé *m.*; vacances *f. pl.*
hollow (*noun*), creux *m.*; (*in tooth*) cavité *f.*
holly (*noun*), *houx *m.*
home (*noun*), demeure *f.*; maison *f.*; domicile *m.*; **at home,** à la maison, chez soi.
honest (*adj.*), honnête; intègre.
honey (*noun*), miel *m.*
honour (*noun*), honneur *m.*; (*verb*), honorer.
hook (*noun*), crochet *m.*; (*fishing*) hameçon *m.*; (*verb*), accrocher (**to hook a fish,** accrocher un poisson).
hope (*noun*), espoir *m.*; espérance *f.*; (*verb*), espérer.
horn (*noun*), (*of cattle*), corne *f.*; (*of car*) klaxon *m.*, avertisseur *m.*
horrible (*adj.*), horrible, affreux *m.*, -euse *f.*
horse (*noun*), cheval *m.*
hospital (*noun*), hôpital *m.*
hot (*adj.*), très chaud; brûlant.
hotel (*noun*), hôtel *m.*
hour (*noun*), heure *f.*; **half an hour,** une demi-heure; **an hour and a half,** une heure et demie.
house (*noun*), maison *f.*
household (*noun*), ménage *m.*
housewife (*noun*), ménagère *f.*; maîtresse *f.* de maison.
how (*adv.*), comment (**how are you?** comment allez-vous?); (*in exclamations*) comme, que (**how kind of you!** que vous êtes aimable!); **how much, how many,** combien (de).
hug (*noun*), embrassement *m.*, étreinte *f.*; (*verb*), embrasser, étreindre.
hundred (*noun & adj.*), cent *m.*; **a hundred and one,** cent un(e); **about a hundred,** une centaine.
hunger (*noun*), faim *f.*
hungry (*adj.*), affamé; **to be hungry,** avoir faim.
hunt (*noun*), chasse *f.*; (*verb*), chasser; faire la chasse (**after, for,** à).

hunter (*noun*), chasseur *m.*
hurl (*verb*), précipiter, jeter.
hurry (*noun*), *hâte *f.*, précipitation *f.*; (*verb*), *hâter, presser; se *hâter, se dépêcher, se presser.
hurt (*verb*), blesser, faire du mal à (**the boy's teeth hurt him,** les dents du garçon lui font mal); faire du tort à.
husband (*noun*), mari *m.*
hut (*noun*), hutte *f.*, cabane *f.*

I

I (*pron.*), je; moi (**it is I,** c'est moi).
ice (*noun*), glace *f.*; (*verb*), glacer (un gâteau).
ice-cream (*noun*), glace *f.*
idea (*noun*), idée *f.*
identify (*verb*), identifier.
identity (*noun*), identité *f.*
idle (*adj.*), inoccupé; paresseux *m.*, -euse *f.*
if (*conj.*), si.
ignore (*verb*), ne tenir aucun compte de (quelque chose); ne pas vouloir reconnaître (quelqu'un).
ill (*adj.*), malade (**with,** de); mauvais (**ill health,** mauvaise santé *f.*; **ill deed,** mauvaise action *f.*); (*adv.*), mal (**ill-founded,** mal fondé; **ill-informed,** mal renseigné).
illness (*noun*), maladie *f.*
illuminate (*verb*), éclairer; illuminer.
illustrate (*verb*), illustrer (un livre).
imagine (*verb*), imaginer; se représenter, se figurer.
imitate (*verb*), imiter.
immense (*adj.*), immense; formidable.
impassable (*adj.*), (*of river*) impassable; (*of road*) impraticable; infranchissable.
imply (*verb*), (*without malice*) impliquer; sous-entendre; (*with malice*) insinuer.
import (*verb*), (*commercially*) importer (**into,** dans).
important (*adj.*), important.
impossible (*adj.*), impossible.
improve (*verb*), améliorer.
in (*prep.*), dans (**in the garden,** dans le jardin); **in there,** là-dedans; en (**in England,** en Angleterre); à (**in Paris,** à Paris); **in good health,** en bonne santé; **each in his own way,** chacun à sa manière; **blind in one eye,** aveugle d'un œil; **in alphabetical order,** par ordre alphabétique.
inaccurate (*adj.*), inexact.
inactive (*adj.*), inactif *m.*, -ive *f.*
incapable (*adj.*), incapable.
include (*verb*), renfermer, comprendre.
inconvenient (*adj.*), incommode; gênant; (*of time*) mal choisi.
indeed (*adv.*), en vérité, vraiment, en effet.
Indian (*adj.*), indien *m.*, -ienne; (*noun*), Indien *m.*, Indienne *f.*
indoors (*adv.*), à l'intérieur; à la maison.
industrial (*adj.*), industriel *m.*, -ielle *f.*, d'industrie.
industrious (*adj.*), travailleur *m.*, -euse *f.*
industry (*noun*), industrie *f.*; (*effort*) application *f.*
inefficient (*adj.*), (*of person*) incapable, incompétent; inefficace.
infant (*noun*), petit enfant *m.*; bébé *m.*
inform (*verb*), informer; avertir (**of,** de); **to keep oneself informed,** se tenir au courant.
inhale (*verb*), (*medical*) inhaler; avaler (la fumée d'une cigarette).
injure (*verb*), blesser; faire du tort à, nuire à (quelqu'un); endommager (quelque chose).
injury (*noun*), (*medical*) blessure *f.*; (*to character*) tort *m.*, préjudice *m.*; dommage *m.*
ink (*noun*), encre *f.*; **ink-well,** encrier *m.*
inn (*noun*), auberge *f.*; hôtellerie *f.*; (*in town*) hôtel *m.*
inoculate (*verb*), vacciner, inoculer (quelqu'un contre une maladie).
inquiry (*noun*), investigation *f.*, enquête *f.*
insect (*noun*), insecte *m.*
inside (*adv. & prep.*), à l'intérieur (de); (*adv.*), dedans; (*prep.*), dans.
insist (*verb*), insister; **to insist on doing something,** insister pour faire quelque chose, vouloir absolument faire quelque chose.
install (*verb*), installer.
instant (*adj.*), immédiat; (*noun*), instant *m.*
instruct (*verb*), instruire; enseigner; donner des instructions.

intact (*adj.*), intact.
intellect (*noun*), intelligence *f.*
intelligent (*adj.*), intelligent.
intend (*verb*), avoir l'intention de; destiner (**for,** à).
interest (*noun*), intérêt *m.*; profit *m.*; (*verb*), intéresser.
interesting (*adj.*), intéressant.
interior (*adj.*), intérieur; (*noun*), intérieur *m.*
interrupt (*verb*), interrompre.
interval (*noun*), intervalle *m.*; (*theatre*) entracte *m.*
into (*prep.*), dans (**to go into a house,** entrer dans une maison); en (**to burst into tears,** fondre en larmes).
introduce (*verb*), introduire; présenter (quelqu'un à quelqu'un).
invade (*verb*), envahir.
invent (*verb*), inventer.
investment (*noun*), placement *m.*; **to make investments,** faire des placements.
iron (*noun*), fer *m.*; (*verb*), repasser.
ironworks (*pl. noun*), forges *f. pl.*
irritate (*verb*), irriter.
island (*noun*), île *f.*; **small island,** îlot *m.*
it (*pron.*), il, elle (**the garden is small but it is pretty,** le jardin est petit mais il est joli), le, la (**he took the apple and ate it,** il prit la pomme et la mangea); ce, cela, ça (**who is it?** qui est-ce?; **it doesn't matter,** cela (*ou* ça) ne fait rien).
item (*noun*), article *m.*

J

jacket (*noun*), (*woman's*) jaquette *f.*; (*man's*) veston *m.*
jam (*noun*), confiture *f.*; **traffic jam,** embouteillage *m.*
January (*noun*), janvier *m.*
jar (*noun*), pot *m.*
jealous (*adj.*), jaloux *m.*, -ouse *f.* (**of,** de).
jelly (*noun*), gelée *f.*; **jelly-fish,** méduse *f.*
jetty (*noun*), jetée *f.*
jewel (*noun*), bijou *m.*, joyau *m.*
join (*verb*), joindre, unir; rejoindre (quelqu'un).
joiner (*noun*), menuisier *m.*
joke (*noun*), plaisanterie *f.*; (*verb*), plaisanter.
journalist (*noun*), journaliste *m. & f.*
journey (*noun*), voyage *m.*; trajet *m.*
joy (*noun*), joie *f.*
judge (*noun*), juge *m.*; (*verb*), juger.
jug (*noun*), (*earthenware*) cruche *f.*; (*for milk, water*) pot *m.*; (*large*) broc *m.*
juggle (*verb*), faire de la prestidigitation.
juggler (*noun*), prestidigitateur *m.*; jongleur *m.*
juice (*noun*), jus *m.*
July (*noun*), juillet *m.*
jump (*verb*), sauter, bondir.
jumper (*noun*), (*athlete*) sauteur *m.*, sauteuse *f.*; (*pullover*) pull(-over) *m.*
June (*noun*), juin *m.*
just (*adj.*), juste; (*adv.*), précisément, justement; **to have just . . .,** venir de . . . (**he has just left,** il vient de partir); **he just missed the train,** il a manqué de peu le train; **just by the gate,** tout près de la porte; **just as the door was opening,** au moment même où la porte s'ouvrait.
justice (*noun*), justice *f.*

K

kangaroo (*noun*), kangourou *m.*
keep (*verb*), tenir (**she kept her house clean,** elle tenait sa maison propre; **to keep a diary,** tenir un journal); garder (**you can keep your money,** tu peux garder ton argent; **the girl kept her secret,** la fille a gardé son secret).
kettle (*noun*), bouilloire *f.*
key (*noun*), clef *f.*, clé *f.*
kick (*noun*), coup *m.* de pied; (*verb*), donner des coups de pied.
kill (*verb*), tuer; abattre (une bête).
kind (*adj.*), gentil *m.*, -ille *f.*; aimable; **give her my kind regards,** faites-lui mes amitiés; (*noun*), espèce *f.*, genre *m.*; **nothing of the kind,** rien de la sorte.
kindness (*noun*), bonté *f.*, amabilité *f.*
king (*noun*), roi *m.*
kingdom (*noun*), royaume *m.*; **the United Kingdom,** le Royaume-Uni.
kiss (*noun*), baiser *m.*; (*verb*), embrasser, donner un baiser à.
kitchen (*noun*), cuisine *f.*
kite (*noun*), cerf-volant *m.*
kitten (*noun*), chaton *m.*, petit chat *m.*, petite chatte *f.*
knee (*noun*), genou *m.*
kneel (*verb*), s'agenouiller, se mettre à genoux.
knickers (*pl. noun*), culotte *f.* (*N.B. singular*).
knife (*noun*), couteau *m.*
knit (*verb*), tricoter.
knitting (*noun*), tricot *m.*
knob (*noun*), bouton *m.* (de porte).
knock (*verb*), frapper, cogner; **to knock someone down,** renverser quelqu'un.
knot (*noun*), nœud *m.*; (*coil of hair*) chignon *m.*
know (*verb*), (*a fact*) savoir; (*a person*) connaître.
knowledge (*noun*), savoir *m.*; connaissance *f.*

L

label (*noun*), étiquette *f.*; (*verb*), étiqueter.
labourer (*noun*), ouvrier *m.*, travailleur *m.*
lace (*noun*), dentelle *f.*; lacet *m.* (de soulier); (*verb*), lacer (un soulier).
ladder (*noun*), échelle *f.*; **I have a ladder in my stocking,** j'ai une maille qui file; (*verb*), (*of stocking*) démailler.
ladle (*noun*), louche *f.*
lady (*noun*), dame *f.*
lake (*noun*), lac *m.*
lamb (*noun*), agneau *m.*
lamp (*noun*), lampe *f.*
lamp-post (*noun*), réverbère *m.*
land (*noun*), terre *f.*; pays *m.*; (*verb*), débarquer; (*from ship*) descendre; (*of plane*) atterrir.
language (*noun*), (*in general*) langage *m.*; (*of a particular country*) langue *f.*
large (*adj.*), (*spacious*) grand *m.*; fort *m.*; (*big*) gros *m.*, grosse *f.*
lark (*noun*), alouette *f.*
last (*adj.*), dernier *m.*, -ière *f.*; **the last week (of the year),** la dernière semaine (de l'année); **last week,** la semaine dernière; **at last,** enfin; (*verb*), durer.
late (*adv.*), tard; en retard; **later, later on,** plus tard; (*adj.*), retardé; avancé (**at a late hour,** à une heure avancée).
laugh (*verb*), rire; **to laugh at,** se moquer de.
laughter (*noun*), rire *m.*
lavatory (*noun*), cabinets *m. pl.*; (*on train*) toilette *f.*
law (*noun*), loi *f.*; législation *f.*; droit (**to study law,** étudier le droit; **criminal law,** le droit criminel).
lawn (*noun*), pelouse *f.*, gazon *m.*; **lawn-mower,** tondeuse *f.* (de gazon).
lay (*verb*), mettre, poser, placer; **to lay an egg,** pondre un œuf.
lazy (*adj.*), paresseux *m.*, -euse *f.*; indolent.
lead (*verb*), mener, conduire.
leader (*noun*), guide *m.*; conducteur *m.*; chef *m.*
leaf (*noun*), feuille *f.*
lean (*verb*), s'appuyer (**on,** sur; **against,** contre); **to lean back against,** s'adosser à; (*adj.*), maigre.
learn (*verb*), apprendre.
leather (*noun*), cuir *m.*
leave (*noun*), (*holiday*) congé *m.*; permission *f.*; autorisation *f.*; (*verb*), laisser; quitter (un endroit, quelqu'un); partir, s'en aller.
left (*adj.*), gauche; **the left hand,** la gauche; (*adv.*), à gauche.
leg (*noun*), jambe *f.*; (*of animal*) patte *f.*; (*of table*) pied *m.*; **leg of chicken,** cuisse *f.* de poulet; **leg of pork,** jambon *m.*; **leg of mutton,** gigot *m.*
leisure (*noun*), loisir *m.*
lemon (*noun*), citron *m.*
lend (*verb*), prêter; **to lend a hand,** donner un coup de main.
length (*noun*), (*size*) longueur *f.*
less (*adv.*), moins (**less than five,** moins de cinq); (*adj.*), moindre (**of less value,** de moindre valeur).
lesson (*noun*), leçon *f.*
letter (*noun*), lettre *f.*; **letter-box,** boîte *f.* aux lettres.
level (*adj.*), plat; plan; de niveau (**with,** avec); égal; horizontal; **level crossing,** passage *m.* à niveau; (*verb*), niveler.
liberate (*verb*), libérer.
liberation (*noun*), libération *f.*
library (*noun*), bibliothèque *f.*
lick (*verb*), lécher.
lid (*noun*), couvercle *m.*
lie (*noun*), mensonge *m.*; (*verb*), mentir; **to lie down,** se coucher, s'étendre.
life (*noun*), vie *f.*; **life-boat,** canot *m.* de sauvetage.
lift (*noun*), (*for people*) ascenseur *m.*; (*verb*), lever (la tête, etc.); soulever (un poids).
light (*noun*), lumière *f.*; éclairage *m.*; (*verb*), allumer (un feu); éclairer (une rue, une pièce); (*adj.*), (*in weight*) léger *m.*, -ère; (*in colour*) clair.

lightning (*noun*), éclair *m.*; foudre *f.*
like (*verb*), aimer (**I like to see them,** j'aime à les voir); **I like this music,** cette musique me plaît; **he doesn't like these ornaments at all,** ces ornements ne lui plaisent pas du tout; (*adj.*), pareil *m.*, -eille *f.*, semblable; (*prep.*), comme.
line (*noun*), ligne *f.*; (*row*) rangée *f.*; (*railway*) voie *f.*
linen (*noun*), linge *m.*; (*cloth*) toile *f.*; **linen-basket,** panier *m.* à linge.
lion, lioness (*noun*), lion *m.*, lionne *f.*
lip (*noun*), lèvre *f.*
liquid (*noun*), liquide *m.*
listen (*verb*), écouter.
little (*adj.*), (*size*) petit; (*quantity*) peu de; **a little,** un peu (**do you want some cake? Yes, a little please,** veux-tu du gâteau? Oui, un peu s'il te plaît); **little by little,** peu à peu.
live (*verb*), vivre; habiter, demeurer (**he lives in the country,** il demeure à la campagne, il habite la campagne).
load (*noun*), fardeau *m.*; (*weight*) poids *m.*; (*burden*) charge *f.*; (*verb*), charger.
loaf (*noun*), pain *m.*; (*round loaf*) miche *f.*
local (*adj.*), local, régional (**local authorities,** autorités *f.pl.* locales; **local anaesthetic,** anesthésique *m.* local; **local agricultural show,** concours *m.* agricole régional).
locality (*noun*), localité *f.*; région *f.*; **in this locality,** dans ces parages *m. pl.*
locate (*verb*), localiser; découvrir.
lock (*noun*), (*on door*) serrure *f.*; (*on canal*) écluse *f.*; (*verb*), fermer à clef.
lodge (*noun*), (*of caretaker*) loge *f.*; (*verb*), loger, être logé.
loft (*noun*), grenier *m.*
lonely (*adj.*), (*of person*) solitaire; **to feel very lonely,** se sentir bien seul; (*of place*) isolé.
long (*adj.*), long *m.*, longue *f.*; étendu; (*adv.*), longtemps.
look (*verb*), regarder (**to look out of the window,** regarder par la fenêtre); paraître; **he looks sad,** il a l'air triste; sembler; **look out!** (*interj.*), attention!; (*noun*), (*glance*) regard *m.*; aspect *m.*
lorry (*noun*), camion *m.*
lose (*verb*), perdre; égarer (quelque chose).
loud (*adj.*), fort; (*of applause*) vif *m.*, vive *f.*
loudly (*adv.*), à voix haute, haut, fort.
lounge (*noun*), (*in house*) salon *m.*; (*in hotel*) hall *m.*; (*verb*), flâner.
love (*noun*), amour *m.*; (*verb*), aimer.
lovely (*adj.*), beau (bel) *m.*, belle *f.*; charmant.
low (*adj.*), bas *m.*, basse *f.*
lower (*verb*), abaisser; baisser (la voix); s'abaisser.
loyal (*adj.*), loyal; fidèle (**to,** à).
lubricant (*noun*), lubrifiant *m.*
lubricate (*verb*), lubrifier; graisser.
luck (*noun*), chance *f.*; hasard *m.*; **good luck,** bonne chance, bonheur *m.*; **bad luck,** malchance *f.*, malheur *m.*
luggage (*noun*), bagages *m. pl.*
lump (*noun*), (*of coal*) boulet *m.*; (*of earth*) motte *f.*; (*of sugar*) morceau *m.*; tas *m.*, bloc *m.*
lunatic (*noun*), fou *m.*, folle *f.*; aliéné *m.*
luxurious (*adj.*), luxueux *m.*, -euse *f.*; somptueux *m.*, -euse *f.*

M

machine (*noun*), machine *f.*, appareil *m.*
mad (*adj.*), fou (fol) *m.*, folle *f.*; (*of action*) insensé; (*angry*) furieux *m.*, -euse *f.*
madam (*noun*), madame *f.*, mademoiselle *f.*
madman (*noun*), fou *m.*, dément *m.*, aliéné *m.*
magistrate (*noun*), magistrat *m.* (*used widely in France, but in a more restricted way in Britain*); (*J.P.*) juge *m.* de paix.
magnify (*verb*), grossir; amplifier (un son); exagérer (**he magnified the dangers,** il exagérait les dangers).
maid (*noun*), (*servant*) bonne *f.*, domestique *f.*; (*maiden*) vierge *f.*, jeune fille *f.*
maize (*noun*), maïs *m.*
make (*verb*), faire; fabriquer.
mallet (*noun*), maillet *m.*
man (*noun*), homme *m.*, être *m.* humain.
manage (*verb*), (*in industry*) diriger, gérer, administrer; s'arranger, se débrouiller.
manager (*noun*), directeur *m.*, gérant *m.*, administrateur *m.*
mandate (*noun*), mandat *m.*
manipulate (*verb*), manipuler, manœuvrer.
manner (*noun*), manière *f.*, façon *f.*; **in this manner,** de cette façon; *pl.* (*behaviour*) manières *f. pl.*, comportement *m.*; (**good**) **manners,** savoir-vivre *m.*; (*customs*) usages *m. pl.*; mœurs *f. pl.*
manor (*noun*), manoir *m.*
mantelpiece (*noun*), manteau *m.* de cheminée.
manufacture (*noun*), fabrication *f.*, produit *m.*; (*verb*), fabriquer, manufacturer.
many (*adj.*), beaucoup de, bien des; un grand nombre de.
map (*noun*), carte *f.*
March[1] (*noun*), mars *m.*
march[2] (*noun*), marche *f.*
march[3] (*verb*), faire une marche, marcher; **to march past,** défiler.
mariner (*noun*), marin *m.*, matelot *m.*
market (*noun*), marché *m.*; **market-day,** jour *m.* de marché.
marry (*verb*), marier (**the priest married them,** le curé les a mariés); **to get married,** se marier; (s')épouser.
mason (*noun*), maçon *m.*
mass[1] (*noun*), amas *m.*, tas *m.*, masse *f.*; **a mass of people,** une foule de gens.
mass[2] (*noun*), (*church*) messe *f.*
mast (*noun*), mât *m.*
master (*noun*), maître *m.*; patron *m.*, chef *m.*; (*schoolmaster*) maître *m.*, professeur *m.*
mat (*noun*), (*of straw*) natte *f.*; (*carpet*) tapis *m.*; (*door-mat*) tapis-brosse *m.*, paillasson *m.*; (*table-mat*) dessous *m.* de plat.
match[1] (*noun*), allumette *f.*; **match-box,** boîte *f.* à allumettes; **box of matches,** boîte *f.* d'allumettes.
match[2] (*noun*), (*sport*) match *m.* (**football match,** match de football); partie *f.* (**tennis match,** partie de tennis).
material (*noun*), (*fabric*) étoffe *f.*, tissu *m.*; (*in general*) matière *f.*
mattress (*noun*), matelas *m.*; **interior sprung mattress,** matelas à ressort(s); sommier *m.*
mature (*adj.*), mûr; (*verb*), mûrir.
May[1] (*noun*), mai *m.*
may[2] (*verb*): **with luck I may succeed,** avec de la chance je peux réussir; **may I?** puis-je?; **you may go,** vous pouvez partir; **however that may be,** quoi qu'il en soit.
maybe (*adv.*), peut-être.
mayor (*noun*), maire *m.*
me (*pron.*), me (**they see me,** ils me voient); moi (**listen to me!** écoutez-moi!).
meadow (*noun*), pré *m.*; prairie *f.*
meagre (*adj.*), maigre.
meal (*noun*), repas *m.*; **meal-time,** heure *f.* du repas.
mean (*adj.*), vil; misérable (**a mean street,** une rue misérable); (*miserly*) avare; (*verb*), avoir l'intention; signifier; vouloir dire; (*intend*) se proposer.

means (*noun*), moyen *m.*; ressources *f. pl.*; **by all means!** mais certainement!
meanwhile (*adv.*), pendant ce temps, dans l'intervalle, en attendant.
measure (*noun*), mesure *f.*; (*verb*), mesurer.
meat (*noun*), viande *f.*
mechanic (*noun*), mécanicien *m.*; ouvrier *m.*
medicine (*noun*), (*general term*) médecine *f.*; (*for ailments*) médicament *m.*, remède *m.*
meet (*verb*), rencontrer; faire la connaissance de; **to meet again: when shall we meet again?** quand nous reverrons-nous?; **fancy meeting you again!** comme on se retrouve!
meeting (*noun*), rencontre *f.*
melody (*noun*), mélodie *f.*
melt (*verb*), fondre.
memory (*noun*), mémoire *f.*; (*recollection*) souvenir *m.*
mend (*verb*), réparer; raccommoder (des vêtements); (*darn*) repriser; **to mend one's ways,** changer de conduite *f.*
menu (*noun*), menu *m.*
merry (*adj.*), gai; joyeux *m.*, -euse *f.*
metal (*noun*), métal *m.*; (*adj.*), métallique.
method (*noun*), méthode *f.*
midday (*noun*), midi *m.*
middle (*noun*), milieu *m.*; (*adj.*), moyen *m.*, moyenne *f.* (**the middle classes,** les classes moyennes; **middle-sized,** de grandeur moyenne; **the Middle Ages,** le Moyen Age).
midnight (*noun*), minuit *m.*
mild (*adj.*), doux *m.*, douce *f.*; clément; (*of remedy, weather*) bénin *m.*, -igne *f.*; (*of punishment*) léger *m.*, -ère *f.*
mile (*noun*), mille *m.* (= 1·6 km.).
milk (*noun*), lait, *m.*; (*verb*), traire.
milkman (*noun*), laitier *m.*, crémier *m.*
mill (*noun*), moulin *m.*; (*factory*) usine *f.*
million (*noun*), million *m.*; **a million men,** un million d'hommes.
mind (*noun*), esprit *m.*; raison *f.*, intelligence *f.*; opinion *f.*, pensée *f.*
mine (*pron.*), le mien *m.*, la mienne *f.*, les miens *m. pl.*, les miennes *f. pl.*; (*noun*), mine *f.* (**coal-mine,** mine de *houille *f.*).
minus (*prep.*), moins; sans; (*adj.*), négatif *m.*, -ive *f.* (**a minus quantity,** une quantité négative).
minute (*adj.*), minime, infime; (*detailed*) minutieux *m.*, -euse *f.*; (*noun*), minute *f.*; moment *m.*; **minutes of a meeting,** procès-verbal *m.* d'une séance.
mirror (*noun*), miroir *m.*, glace *f.*
misbehave (*verb*), se mal conduire.
mischief (*noun*), tort *m.*, mal *m.*, dommage *m.*; espièglerie *f.*
mischievous (*adj.*), méchant, malfaisant; (*of child*) malicieux *m.*, -euse *f.*, espiègle.
misfortune (*noun*), infortune *f.*; malheur *m.*
miss (*noun*), mademoiselle *f.*; coup *m.* manqué; (*verb*), manquer (**he missed the train,** il a manqué le train); **I missed my holiday this year,** je n'ai pas eu de vacances cette année.
mistake (*noun*), erreur *f.*; (*misunderstanding*) méprise *f.*
mitten (*noun*), mitaine *f.*, moufle *f.*
mix (*verb*), (*in specific quantities*) mélanger; (*generally*) mêler.
moan (*verb*), gémir, se lamenter.
mob (*noun*), (*unruly*) cohue *f.*; (*crowd*) foule *f.*; **the mob,** la populace; (*rabble*) canaille *f.*
mock (*verb*), ridiculiser; se moquer de.
modern (*adj.*), moderne.
modest (*adj.*), modeste.
moist (*adj.*), humide; (*of skin*) moite; (*of lips, eyes; soil*) mouillé.
moment (*noun*), moment *m.*, instant *m.*
Monday (*noun*), lundi *m.*
money (*noun*), argent *m.*; **money-box,** tirelire *f.*; **money-order,** mandat *m.*
monkey (*noun*), singe *m.*; **monkey-nut,** arachide *f.*, cacahuète *f.*
month (*noun*), mois *m.*
moon (*noun*), lune *f.*; **moon rocket,** fusée *f.* lunaire.
moonlight (*noun*), clair *m.* de lune.
more (*adv.*), plus (**more easily,** plus facilement); davantage (**you are happy but he is more so,** vous êtes heureux mais il l'est davantage); **once more,**

encore une fois; **more intelligent than me,** plus intelligent que moi; **more than twenty,** plus de vingt.

morning (*noun*), matin *m.*; matinée *f.*; **good morning!** bonjour!

morsel (*noun*), morceau *m.*

mosquito (*noun*), moustique *m.*; **mosquito-bite,** piqûre *f.* de moustique.

mother (*noun*), mère *f.*; **mother-in-law,** belle-mère *f.*; **Mothers' Day,** la Fête des Mères.

motion (*noun*), mouvement *m.*; (*verb*), faire signe (**to,** à).

motor (*noun*), moteur *m.*; **motor-car,** auto *f.*; voiture *f.*; **motor-cycle,** motocyclette *f.*; **motor-bike,** moto *f.*

mountain (*noun*), montagne *f.*

mouse (*noun*), souris *f.*

mouth (*noun*), bouche *f.*; (*of a river*) embouchure *f.*; **mouth-organ,** harmonica *m.* (à bouche).

mouthful (*noun*), bouchée *f.*

move (*verb*), remuer; déplacer; **to move back,** reculer; faire reculer; **to move forward,** avancer; faire avancer; **to move house,** déménager.

Mr. (*noun*), monsieur *m.*

Mrs. (*noun*), madame *f.*

much (*adv.*), beaucoup; **how much?** combien?; **as much,** autant; **too much,** trop.

mummy (*noun*), maman *f.*; (*preserved body*) momie *f.*

mushroom (*noun*), champignon *m.*

music (*noun*), musique *f.*

mutton (*noun*), mouton *m.*; **leg of mutton,** gigot *m.*

my (*adj.*), mon *m.*, ma *f.*, mes *pl.*

myself (*pron.*), moi-même.

mysterious (*adj.*), mystérieux *m.*, -euse *f.*

N

nail (*noun*), clou *m.*; (*fingernail*) ongle *m.*; **nail-brush,** brosse *f.* à ongles.
nail (up) (*verb*), clouer.
name (*noun*), nom *m.*; appellation *f.*; **Christian name,** prénom *m.*; (*verb*), nommer.
narrow (*adj.*), étroit; **narrow-minded,** borné.
nationality (*noun*), nationalité *f.*
natural (*adj.*), naturel *m.*, -elle *f.*; inné; natif *m.*, -ive *f.*
naturally (*adv.*), naturellement.
nature (*noun*), nature *f.*; essence *f.*; caractère *m.*
near (*adj.*), (*of relative*) proche; (*of friend*) intime; (*adv.*), près; (*prep.*), près de, auprès de.
nearly (*adv.*), près de; à peu près, presque; **it is nearly nine o'clock,** il est à peu près neuf heures.
necessary (*adj.*), nécessaire, indispensable.
neck (*noun*), cou *m.*; (*of bottle*) goulot *m.*, col *m.*; (*of dress*) encolure *f.*
necklace (*noun*), collier *m.*
needle (*noun*), aiguille *f.*
needlework (*noun*), (*as school subject*) couture *f.*
neighbour (*noun*), voisin *m.*, voisine *f.*
neighbourhood (*noun*), voisinage *m.*; **in the neighbourhood of the town,** aux alentours *m. pl.* de la ville.
neither (*adv. & conj.*): **neither . . . nor,** ni . . . ni (**neither one nor the other,** ni l'un ni l'autre); non plus (**if you do not go, neither shall I,** si vous n'y allez pas, je n'irai pas non plus).
nephew (*noun*), neveu *m.*
nest (*noun*), nid *m.*
net (*noun*), filet *m.*; (*material*) tulle *m.*; (*adj.*), (*of weight, price*) net *m.*, nette *f.*
never (*adv.*), jamais (**never again,** jamais plus); ne . . . jamais (**I never go there,** je n'y vais jamais).
new (*adj.*), nouveau (nouvel) *m.*, -elle *f.*; (*brand new*) neuf *m.*, neuve *f.*; **new bread,** pain *m.* frais; **new-laid egg,** œuf *m.* frais pondu.
news (*noun*), nouvelles *f. pl.*; **piece of news,** nouvelle *f.*; **the news,** (*radio*) les informations *f. pl.*; (*cinema, T.V.*) les actualités *f. pl.*
newspaper (*noun*), journal *m.*
next (*adj.*), prochain; (*of place*) le plus proche *m.*, la plus proche *f.*; (*of time*) suivant; (*adv.*), après, ensuite; **next to,** près de, à côté de.
nibble (*verb*), grignoter; **to nibble at the bait,** mordre à l'hameçon *m.*
nice (*adj.*), gentil *m.*, -ille *f.*; aimable; agréable; joli; bon *m.*, bonne *f.*
nickel (*noun*), (*metal*) nickel *m.*
niece (*noun*), nièce *f.*
night (*noun*), nuit *f.*; **night has fallen,** la nuit est tombée); **last night,** la nuit dernière; **night-dress, night-gown,** chemise *f.* de nuit.
nightmare (*noun*), cauchemar *m.*
nine (*adj. & noun*), neuf *m.*
nineteen (*adj. & noun*), dix-neuf *m.*
ninety (*adj. & noun*), quatre-vingt-dix *m.*
ninth (*adj.*), neuvième.
no (*adv.*), non; (*adj.*), aucun *m.*, aucune *f.*; nul *m.*, nulle *f.*; pas de; **no more,** ne . . . plus (**I have no more worries,** je n'ai plus de soucis; **no more worries!** plus de soucis!).
nobody (*pron.*), personne (**nobody saw me,** personne ne m'a vu; **I saw nobody,** je n'ai vu personne; **who is there? Nobody,** qui est là? Personne).
noise (*noun*), bruit *m.*, tapage *m.*
none (*pron.*), aucun, nul (**none can tell,** nul ne le sait); **none of you knows,** personne d'entre vous ne le sait; **none at all,** pas un seul.
north (*noun*), nord *m.*; (*adv.*), au nord; (*adj.*), du nord (**the north wind,** le vent du nord); (*facing north*) exposé au nord.

nose (*noun*), nez *m.*

nosebleed (*noun*), saignement *m.* de nez.

not (*adv.*), ne . . . pas; **I am not rich,** je ne suis pas riche; **not yet,** pas encore; **I think not,** je crois que non; **not at all,** pas du tout.

note (*noun*), note *f.*; marque *f.*; billet *m.*; **note-book,** carnet *m.*; **note-paper,** papier *m.* à lettres; (*verb*), noter, remarquer.

nothing (*pron.*), rien (**nothing is easier,** rien n'est plus facile; **I see nothing,** je ne vois rien); **nothing easier,** rien de plus facile; **nothing serious,** rien de grave.

notice (*noun*), avis *m.*; notification *f.*; **notice-board,** (*in schools*) tableau *m.* d'annonces; (*on a wall*) écriteau *m.*; (*verb*), remarquer, faire attention à.

nourish (*verb*), nourrir, alimenter (**with, on,** de).

nourishment (*noun*), nourriture *f.*

November (*noun*), novembre *m.*

now (*adv.*), maintenant, à présent, en ce moment; **well now!** eh bien!; **come now!** voyons!

number (*noun*), nombre *m.*; numéro *m.*; (*verb*), compter, dénombrer; numéroter.

nun (*noun*), sœur *f.*, religieuse *f.*

nurse (*noun*), infirmière *f.*, garde-malade *f.*; (*nursemaid*) bonne *f.* d'enfants; (*verb*), soigner; **to nurse a child,** bercer un enfant.

nut (*noun*), noix *f.* (*in general*); **hazel-nut,** noisette *f.*; (*screw-nut*) écrou *m.*

nylon (*noun*), nylon *m.*; **nylon stockings,** bas *m. pl.* nylon.

O

oak (*noun*), chêne *m.*; (*adj.*), de chêne, en chêne.

oar (*noun*), rame *f.*

obedient (*adj.*), obéissant, soumis, docile.

obey (*verb*), obéir (à).

object (*noun*), objet *m.*, chose *f.*; (*aim*) but *m.*; (*verb*), faire des objections *f. pl.* (**to,** à); **to object to someone,** avoir des objections à faire contre quelqu'un; **to object to doing something,** se refuser à faire quelque chose.

oblige (*verb*), obliger, contraindre (quelqu'un à faire quelque chose); **to be obliged to someone,** être obligé à quelqu'un; **I am much obliged to you for your kindness,** je vous suis bien reconnaissant de votre bonté.

observe (*verb*), observer, regarder; noter.

occupy (*verb*), occuper habiter (une maison); donner du travail à (quelqu'un).

occur (*verb*), se présenter, arriver; venir à l'esprit (**it occurs to me,** il me vient à l'esprit).

ocean (*noun*), océan *m.*

October (*noun*), octobre *m.*

odour (*noun*), odeur *f.*; (*fragrance*) parfum *m.*

of (*prep.*), de (*possession:* **the mother of my friends,** la mère de mes amis; *quantity:* **a pound of coffee,** une livre de café); **he died of thirst,** il est mort de soif; en (**a ring of gold,** un anneau en or); entre (**he of all men,** lui entre tous).

offer (*noun*), offre *f.*; (*verb*), offrir; proposer.

office (*noun*), bureau *m.*

often (*adv.*), souvent, fréquemment.

oh! (*interj.*), oh!

oil (*verb*), huiler, graisser; (*noun*), huile *f.*; **paraffin oil,** pétrole *m.*

oilcloth (*noun*), toile *f.* cirée.

ointment (*noun*), onguent *m.*, pommade *f.*

old (*adj.*), vieux (vieil) *m.*, vieille *f.*; ancien *m.*, -ienne *f.*; âgé; **old man,** vieillard *m.*

omit (*verb*), omettre; **to omit to do something,** omettre de faire quelque chose.

on (*prep.*), sur; (*adv.*): **later on,** plus tard.

once (*adv.*), une fois (**once again,** encore une fois); (*formerly*) autrefois; **at once,** tout de suite.

one (*adj. & noun*), un *m.*, une *f.*; (*pron.*), on (**one cannot always be right,** on ne peut pas toujours avoir raison).

onion (*noun*), oignon *m.*; **spring onion,** petit oignon.

only (*adv.*), seulement, ne . . . que (**Mary has six francs, but Paul has only three francs,** Marie a six francs, mais Paul n'a que trois francs).

open (*adj.*), ouvert; accessible (**to,** à); **in the open air,** en plein air; (*verb*), ouvrir.

operate (*verb*), opérer.

operation (*noun*), opération *f.*

opinion (*noun*), opinion *f.*, avis *m.*; **in my opinion,** à mon avis.

oppose (*verb*), s'opposer à; opposer, mettre en opposition.

opposite (*adj.*), opposé; contraire; (*prep.*), en face de; vis-à-vis (**to,** de).

or (*conj.*), ou.

orange (*noun*), orange *f.*; (*adj.*), orange.

orchestra (*noun*), orchestre *m.*

order (*noun*), ordre *m.*; commande *f.*; (*verb*), ordonner, mettre en ordre; régler; commander (à quelqu'un de faire quelque chose).

organ (*noun*), orgue *m.*; **organ-grinder,** joueur *m.* d'orgue de Barbarie; (*of the body*) organe *m.*

organize (*verb*), organiser.

other (*adj.*), autre.

ought (*auxiliary verb*): *use parts of* devoir, falloir: **one ought never to be unkind,** il ne faut (*or* on ne doit) jamais être malveillant; **you ought to have**

taken an umbrella, vous auriez dû prendre un parapluie; **you ought to have said so,** il fallait le dire.

our (*adj.*), notre; (*pl.*) nos.

ours (*pron.*), le nôtre *m.*, la nôtre *f.*; les nôtres (*pl.*).

ourselves (*pron.*), nous-mêmes.

out (*adv.*), dehors; **to go out,** sortir; **day out,** jour *m.* de sortie; **out of the question,** hors de question; **five out of nine,** cinq sur neuf; **out of fashion,** passé de mode.

outfit (*noun*), (*suit*) habit *m.*; (*of clothing*) trousseau *m.*

outside (*adv.*), dehors (**I've left my dog outside,** j'ai laissé mon chien dehors); (*prep.*), en dehors de (**outside the house,** en dehors de la maison).

oven (*noun*), four *m.*; **drying oven,** étuve *f.*

over (*prep.*), sur (**his hat over one ear,** le chapeau sur l'oreille); par-dessus (**to throw something over the wall,** jeter quelque chose par-dessus le mur); au-dessus de (**numbers over a hundred,** numéros *m. pl.* au-dessus de cent); (*adv.*), dessus.

overcoat (*noun*), pardessus *m.*

overtake (*verb*), atteindre, rattraper (quelqu'un); (*sports*) dépasser; (*driving*) doubler.

overture (*noun*), ouverture *f.*

overturn (*verb*), renverser; faire verser, faire capoter (une auto).

owe (*verb*), devoir (**I owe you five francs,** je vous dois cinq francs).

owing to (*prep.*), à cause de, en raison de, par suite de.

owl (*noun*), *hibou *m.*

ox (*noun*), bœuf *m.*; **ox-tail,** queue *f.* de bœuf; **ox-tongue,** langue *f.* de bœuf.

P

pace (*noun*), (*step*) pas *m.*; allure *f.* (**the boy walks at a brisk pace,** le garçon marche à une vive allure); (*verb*), marcher à pas mesurés; **at a walking pace,** au pas.

pack (*verb*), empaqueter, emballer (quelque chose); faire ses malles.

packet (*noun*), paquet *m.*, colis *m.*

page (*noun*), (*of book*) page *f.*; (*at court*) page *m.*

pail (*noun*), seau *m.*

pain (*noun*), douleur *f.*; (*mental*) peine *f.*; mal *m.*; **to have a pain,** avoir mal.

paint (*noun*), peinture *f.*; **box of paints,** boîte *f.* de couleurs; (*verb*), peindre.

painting (*noun*), peinture *f.*; tableau *m.*

pair (*noun*), paire *f.*; **a pair of trousers,** un pantalon.

pal (*noun*), camarade *m.* & *f.*, copain *m.*, copine *f.*

palace (*noun*), palais *m.*

palate (*noun*), palais *m.*

pale (*adj.*), pâle, blême; **a pale blue dress,** une robe bleu clair; **to turn pale,** pâlir.

pancake (*noun*), crêpe *f.*

pane (*noun*), vitre *f.*; carreau *m.* (de fenêtre).

paper (*noun*), papier *m.*; document *m.*; (*newspaper*) journal *m.*; (*verb*), tapisser.

parachute (*noun*), parachute *m.*; **parachute drop,** parachutage *m.*; (*verb*), parachuter.

paraffin (*noun*), paraffine *f.*; **liquid paraffin,** huile *f.* de paraffine; pétrole *m.*

parcel (*noun*), paquet *m.*; colis *m.*; (*verb*), (*pack*) empaqueter; **to parcel up,** emballer; **to parcel out,** distribuer, morceler, diviser.

pardon (*noun*), pardon *m.*; (*verb*), pardonner, excuser.

parent (*noun*), père *m.*, mère *f.*; (*pl.*) parents *m.*

park (*noun*), parc *m.*; **car-park,** parc à voitures; (*verb*), parquer, garer; stationner.

parrot (*noun*), perroquet *m.*

part (*noun*), partie *f.*; part *f.* (**he had no part in it whatsoever,** il n'y a pris aucune part); portion *f.*; (*theatre*) rôle *m.*

parting (*noun*), séparation *f.*; (*in the hair*) raie *f.*

pass (*noun*), défilé *m.* (de montagne); permis *m.*; (*verb*), passer; (*of time*) s'écouler; (*march past*) défiler.

passenger (*noun*), voyageur *m.*, voyageuse *f.*; (*by sea or air*) passager *m.*, passagère *f.*

passport (*noun*), passeport *m.*

past (*noun*), passé *m.*; (*prep.*), au delà de; plus loin que; (*adj.*), passé *m.*

paste (*verb*), coller; (*noun*), colle *f.*

pastry (*noun*), (*dough*) pâte *f.*; (*cake*) pâtisserie *f.*

pat (*noun*), petite tape *f.*; coup *m.* léger; (*verb*), taper.

patch (*noun*), pièce *f.* (pour raccommoder); parcelle *f.* (de terre); carré *m.* (**cabbage-patch,** carré de choux); (*verb*), rapiécer, raccommoder.

path (*noun*), sentier *m.*, chemin *m.*; (*in a garden*) allée.

patience (*noun*), patience *f.*

patient (*adj.*), patient; endurant; (*noun*), malade *m.* & *f.*; patient *m.*, patiente *f.*

pavement (*noun*), pavé *m.*; trottoir *m.*

paw (*noun*) patte *f.*

pawn (*noun*), (*chess*) pion *m.*; (*verb*), mettre en gage.

pay (*noun*), paie *f.*, salaire *m.*; (*verb*), payer; **to pay someone a visit,** rendre une visite à quelqu'un; **to pay a bill,** régler un compte; **to pay attention,** faire attention.

pea (*noun*), pois *m.*; **garden-peas,** petits pois *m.*

peace (*noun*), paix *f.*; tranquillité *f.*; calme *m.*

peach (*noun*), pêche *f.*

peanut (*noun*), arachide *f.*; **roasted peanuts,** cacahuètes *f. pl.*
pear (*noun*), poire *f.*
pearl (*noun*), perle *f.*
peasant (*noun*), paysan *m.*, paysanne *f.*
pebble (*noun*), caillou *m.*; (*on beach*) galet *m.*
peel (*noun*), pelure *f.* (de pomme); peau *f.*, écorce *f.* (d'orange); (*verb*), peler (un fruit); éplucher (des pommes de terre).
pen (*noun*), plume *f.*; **fountain-pen,** stylo *m.*; **ball-point pen,** stylo *m.* à bille.
pencil (*noun*), crayon *m.*; **pencil box,** plumier *m.*; **pencil-sharpener,** taille-crayon *m.*
people (*noun*), (*in general*) gens *m. or f. pl.*; (*populace*) peuple *m.*; **a thousand people,** mille personnes *f. pl.*
pepper (*noun*), poivre *m.*
perceive (*verb*), percevoir (un son); s'apercevoir de (quelque chose).
perfect (*adj.*), parfait.
perform (*verb*), exécuter, faire, accomplir; s'acquitter de (son devoir); (*theatre*) jouer.
perhaps (*adv.*), peut-être; **perhaps not,** peut-être que non.
permit (*noun*), permis *m.*, autorisation *f.*; (*verb*), permettre.
persevere (*verb*), persévérer.
persist (*verb*), persister, s'obstiner.
person (*noun*), personne *f.*; individu *m.*; personnage *m.*
persuade (*verb*), persuader, convaincre (**of,** de).
petrol (*noun*), essence *f.*; **petrol-can,** bidon *m.* à essence.
petticoat (*noun*), jupon *m.*
photo(graph) (*noun*), photo(graphie) *f.*; (*verb*), photographier.
photographer (*noun*), photographe *m.*
photography (*noun*), photographie *f.*
piano (*noun*), piano *m.*; **grand piano,** piano à queue; **upright piano,** piano droit.
pick (*noun*), (*pickaxe*) pioche *f.*, pic *m.*; (*choice*) choix *m.*; (*verb*), choisir; ronger (un os); cueillir (des fruits); **to pick up,** (*from the ground*) ramasser.
picnic (*noun*), pique-nique *m.*
picture (*noun*), image *f.*, tableau *m.*; gravure *f.*; illustration *f.*; peinture *f.*
pie (*noun*), (*fruit*) tourte *f.*; (*meat*) pâté *m.* en croûte.
piece (*noun*), (*part*) pièce *f.*, partie *f.*; (*bit*) morceau *m.*; **to take to pieces,** défaire (une robe), démonter (une machine); (*verb*), **to piece together,** joindre, rassembler.
pig (*noun*), cochon *m.*, porc *m.*
pigeon (*noun*), pigeon *m.*
pigsty (*noun*), porcherie *f.*
pigtail (*noun*), queue *f.*, natte *f.* (de cheveux).
pile (*noun*), (*stake*) pieu *m.*; (*stack*) pile *f.*; (*heap*) tas *m.*, monceau *m.*
pile up (*verb*), empiler; entasser.
pill (*noun*), pilule *f.*; **pill-box,** (*medical*) boîte *f.* à pilules; (*military*) abri *m.* en béton.
pillow (*noun*), oreiller *m.*; **pillow-slip, pillow-case,** taie *f.* d'oreiller.
pimple (*noun*), bouton *m.*
pin (*noun*), épingle *f.*; **rolling-pin,** rouleau *m.* à pâte; (*verb*), épingler.
pinafore (*noun*), tablier *m.*
pineapple (*noun*), ananas *m.*
pink (*adj.*), rose.
pipe (*noun*), (*for smoking*) pipe *f.*; (*tube*) conduit *m.*, tuyau *m.*; **pipe of peace,** calumet *m.* de paix.
pit (*noun*), fosse *f.*; (*quarry*) carrière *f.*; **pit of the stomach,** creux *m.* de l'estomac; (*verb*), **to pit oneself against,** se mesurer contre; **to pit someone against someone,** opposer quelqu'un à quelqu'un.
pity (*noun*), pitié *f.*, compassion *f.*; **what a pity!** quel dommage!; (*verb*), plaindre, avoir pitié de.
place (*noun*), place *f.* (**to put a book back in its place,** remettre un livre à sa place); localité *f.*, lieu *m.*, endroit *m.*; (*verb*), placer, mettre.
placing (*noun*), placement *m.*
plain (*adj.*), clair, évident; simple; franc *m.*, franche *f.*; (*noun*), plaine *f.*

plainly (*adv.*), simplement, évidemment, clairement, franchement.
plan (*noun*), plan *m.*; projet *m.*; (*verb*), faire le plan de, projeter.
plank (*noun*), planche *f.*; (*beam*) madrier *m.*
plant (*noun*), plante *f.*; (*in factory*) installation *f.*; (*verb*), planter.
plate (*noun*), assiette *f.*; (*photography*) plaque *f.*; (*silver*) argenterie *f.*
platform (*noun*), (*railway*) quai *m.*; (*for public speakers*) tribune *f.*
play (*noun*), activité *f.*; récréation *f.*; jeu *m.*, amusement *m.*; (*theatre*) pièce *f.*; (*verb*), jouer (**to play cards,** jouer aux cartes; **to play the piano,** jouer du piano).
playpen (*noun*), parc *m.* pour enfants.
plead (*verb*), plaider, intercéder (**for,** pour).
pleasant (*adj.*), agréable, aimable.
please (*verb*), être agréable; plaire (à), faire plaisir (à).
pleased (*adj.*), content (**I am very pleased to see you,** je suis très content de vous voir).
pleasure (*noun*), plaisir *m.*
plenty (*noun*), abondance *f.*; **plenty of,** beaucoup de.
plough (*noun*), charrue *f.*; (*verb*), labourer (un champ); creuser (un sillon).
ploughman (*noun*), laboureur *m.*
plum (*noun*), prune *f.*; **plum-tree,** prunier *m.*
pocket (*noun*), poche *f.*; **pocket-book,** calepin *m.*; **pocket money,** argent *m.* de poche; (*verb*), empocher.
poem (*noun*), poème *m.*
poet (*noun*), poète *m.*
point (*noun*), point *m.*; détail *m.*; pointe *f.* (d'une aiguille); **to point at** (*verb*), indiquer du doigt; **to point the way,** indiquer le chemin.
pointed (*adj.*), pointu.
police (*noun*), police *f.*
policeman (*noun*), agent *m.* de police; (*in country districts*) gendarme *m.*
polish (*verb*), polir; (*shoes*) cirer; (*furniture*) faire reluire.
polite (*adj.*), poli, courtois.
pond (*noun*), étang *m.*
ponder (*verb*), peser; réfléchir (**on, over,** à); considérer; méditer.
pony (*noun*), poney *m.*; **pony-tail,** queue *f.* de cheval.
pool (*noun*), (*stagnant*) mare *f.*; (*for swimming*) piscine *f.*
poor (*adj.*), pauvre; **a poor man,** un homme pauvre; **poor man!** pauvre homme!
porcelain (*noun*), porcelaine *f.*
pork (*noun*), porc *m.*; **pork-butcher,** charcutier *m.*, charcutière *f*
port (*noun*), (*harbour*) port *m.*; bâbord *m.*; **on the port side,** à bâbord; (*wine*) porto *m.*
position (*noun*), position *f.*; (*in class*) place *f.*; (*rank*) rang *m.* social.
possess (*verb*), posséder.
possible (*adj.*), possible.
post (*noun*), (*mail*) poste *f.*; **post-office,** bureau *m.* de poste; (*employment*) poste *m.*; (*stake*) poteau *m.*; **winning post,** poteau d'arrivée.
postal-order (*noun*), mandat *m.*
postman (*noun*), facteur *m.*
postpone (*verb*), remettre, ajourner,
pot (*noun*), pot *m.* (**pot of jam,** pot de confiture; **flower-pot,** pot à fleurs); (*for cooking*) marmite *f.*
potato (*noun*), pomme *f.* de terre; **baked potato,** pomme (de terre) au four; **mashed potatoes,** purée *f.* de pommes (de terre).
pound (*noun*), livre *f.* (= 1 lb 1½ oz.); **pound (sterling),** livre (sterling).
pour (*verb*), verser (un liquide); **it is pouring,** il pleut à verse.
power (*noun*), puissance *f.*; pouvoir *m.*; capacité *f.*; force *f.*
pray (*verb*), prier.
prayer (*noun*), prière *f.*
precaution (*noun*), précaution *f.*
precious (*adj.*), précieux *m.*, -euse *f.*
prefer (*verb*), préférer (quelque chose à quelque chose); aimer mieux.
prepare (*verb*), préparer, arranger, organiser.
present (*noun*), cadeau *m.*, don *m.*,

présent *m.*; **the present** (**time**), le (temps) présent; (*verb*), présenter; donner.

presently (*adv.*), tout à l'heure.

preserve (*verb*), préserver, protéger (**from,** contre); conserver.

press (*noun*), presse *f.*; (*verb*), presser; (*to press down*) appuyer; **to press the button,** appuyer sur le bouton.

pretend (*verb*), simuler, feindre, faire semblant (de); **to pretend to be,** avoir la prétention d'être, prétendre être.

pretty (*adj.*), joli; beau (bel) *m.*, belle *f.*; gentil *m.*, -ille *f.*

prevent (*verb*), empêcher (**from,** de).

price (*noun*), prix *m.*; **cost price,** prix coûtant; **market price,** prix courant.

prick (*noun*), piqûre *f.*; (*verb*), piquer; crever (un ballon).

priest (*noun*), prêtre *m.*

prince (*noun*), prince *m.*

princess (*noun*), princesse *f.*

print (*verb*), imprimer; **to print a negative,** tirer une épreuve d'un cliché.

prison (*noun*), prison *f.*

private (*adj.*), privé, particulier *m.*, -ière *f.*

prize (*noun*), (*reward*) prix *m.*; (*in a lottery*) lot *m.*; (*verb*), priser, estimer.

probable (*adj.*), probable.

probably (*adv.*), sans doute, probablement.

produce (*noun*), produits *m. pl.*; denrées *f. pl.*; (*verb*), produire; fournir.

profession (*noun*), profession *f.*, métier *m.*

profit (*noun*), profit *m.*, avantage *m.*, bénéfice *m.*; (*verb*), profiter, bénéficier (**by,** de).

profound (*adj.*), profond.

progress (*noun*), progrès *m.*, avancement *m.*; (*verb*), progresser, faire des progrès (**with,** dans); s'avancer.

promise (*noun*), promesse *f.*; (*verb*), promettre.

prompt (*adj.*), prompt; immédiat; (*verb*), (*theatre*) souffler.

propose (*verb*), (se) proposer.

proprietor (*noun*), propriétaire *m.* & *f.*

protect (*verb*), protéger; **to protect someone's interests,** sauvegarder les intérêts de quelqu'un.

prove (*verb*), prouver, établir, démontrer; (*to check proof*) vérifier.

provide (*verb*), pourvoir, munir (**with,** de); fournir; se prémunir, se pourvoir (**against,** contre).

provisions (*noun*), provisions *f. pl.*; vivres *m. pl.*

prudent (*adj.*), prudent; circonspect; avisé.

public (*noun*), public *m.*; (*adj.*), public *m.*, -ique *f.*

pull (*verb*), tirer; **to pull up,** s'arrêter; **to pull down,** (*demolish*) démolir.

pullet (*noun*), poulette *f.*; poulet *m.*

pullover (*noun*), pullover *m.*, pull *m.*

pulp (*noun*), pulpe *f.*; **paper-pulp,** pâte *f.* à papier.

pumpkin (*noun*), potiron *m.*, citrouille *f.*

punish (*verb*), punir; châtier.

pup, puppy (*noun*), petit chien *m.*, jeune chien *m.*

pupil (*noun*), élève *m.* & *f.*; écolier *m.*, écolière *f.*

purchase (*noun*), emplette *f.*, achat *m.*; (*verb*), acheter, acquérir.

pure (*adj.*), pur; **pure-bred,** de race.

purpose (*noun*), dessein *m.*, but *m.*, intention *f.*; **on purpose,** exprès, à dessein.

purse (*noun*), porte-monnaie *m.*; bourse *f.*

push (*verb*), pousser; **to push the button,** appuyer sur le bouton; **to push back,** repousser.

puss, pussy (*noun*), minet *m.*, minette *f.*

put (*verb*), mettre, placer, poser; **to put in electricity,** installer l'électricité; **to put aside,** mettre de côté; **to put off** (**doing something**), différer (de faire quelque chose), tarder (à faire quelque chose); **to put down,** déposer; **to put away,** serrer, ranger; rentrer; **to put by,** économiser; **to put up with,** souffrir, se contenter de; **to put out** éteindre (le feu); **to put on,** (*clothes*) mettre.

pyjamas (*pl. noun*), pyjama *m.* (*N.B. French singular*).

Q

qualify (*verb*), qualifier (**as,** de; **for,** pour); rendre capable de; modifier.
quality (*noun*), qualité *f.*
quantity (*noun*), quantité *f.*
quarrel (*noun*), querelle *f.*, dispute *f.*, altercation *f.*; (*verb*), se quereller, se disputer, se brouiller.
quarter (*noun*), quart *m.*; quartier *m.* (d'une ville); **from all quarters,** de toutes parts.
quay (*noun*), quai *m.*
queen (*noun*), reine *f.*
question (*noun*), question *f.*; **without question,** sans aucun doute *m.*; (*verb*), questionner, interroger; douter de.
queue (*noun*), queue *f.*; (*verb*), faire la queue.
quick (*adj.*), rapide; vif *m.*, vive *f.*; agile; prompt.
quickly (*adv.*), vite, rapidement, vivement; sans délai.
quiet (*noun*), calme *m.*; silence *m.*; repos *m.*; tranquillité *f.*; (*adj.*), tranquille, calme, reposant.
quieten (*verb*), tranquilliser, calmer, apaiser.
quite (*adv.*), absolument; tout à fait, complètement, entièrement.

R

rabbit (*noun*), lapin *m.*; **rabbit-hutch,** clapier *m.*

race (*noun*), (*sport*) course *f.*; (*human*) race *f.*; (*verb*), faire une course avec, faire courir (un cheval).

radio (*noun*), radio *f.*, T.S.F. *f.*; **radio set,** poste *m.* de T.S.F.

rag (*noun*), chiffon *m.*; lambeau *m.*; (*verb*), brimer (un camarade); chahuter (un professeur).

rage (*noun*), fureur *f.*, rage *f.*; **it's all the rage,** c'est la grande vogue; (*verb*), être furieux; tempêter (**against,** contre).

rail (*noun*), balustrade *f.*; barre *f.*; (*of chair, fence*) barreau *m.*; (*railway*) rail *m.*; **hand-rail,** (*of stairs*) rampe *f.*

railway (*noun*), chemin *m.* de fer; voie *f.* ferrée; **railway guard,** chef *m.* de train.

rain (*noun*), pluie *f.*; (*verb*), pleuvoir.

rainbow (*noun*), arc-en-ciel *m.*

raise (*verb*), lever; élever; (*to increase*) augmenter.

rap (*noun*), tape *f.*; petit coup *m.* sec (*ou* léger); (*verb*), frapper; donner un coup sec à.

rare (*adj.*), rare; exceptionnel *m.*, -elle *f.*; précieux *m.*, -euse *f.*

rat (*noun*), rat *m.*

rather (*adv.*), plutôt (**the weather was rather cold,** il faisait plutôt froid); assez (**she is rather pretty,** elle est assez jolie).

raw (*adj.*), cru (**raw meat,** viande *f.* crue).

rayon (*noun*), rayonne *f.*; soie *f.* artificielle.

razor (*noun*), rasoir *m.*

reach (*verb*), atteindre, gagner; arriver à.

read (*verb*), lire; (*at university*) étudier (**to read French,** étudier le français).

ready (*adj.*), prêt; **ready-cooked,** tout cuit; **ready-made clothes,** le prêt-à-porter, confection *f.*

realize (*verb*), se rendre compte (de quelque chose).

reason (*noun*), raison *f.*; motif *m.*; (*verb*), raisonner.

receive (*verb*), recevoir; (*welcome*) accueillir.

recent (*adj.*), récent; nouveau (nouvel) *m.*, nouvelle *f.*

recite (*verb*), réciter; raconter; déclamer.

recognize (*verb*), reconnaître (**by,** à); identifier (**by,** par).

record (*noun*), disque *m.*; document *m.*; dossier *m*; **record-player,** électrophone *m.*, tourne-disques *m.*; (*verb*), enregistrer; relater.

recount (*verb*), raconter.

recover (*verb*), retrouver, recouvrer; **to recover one's health,** guérir, recouvrer sa santé; **to recover lost time,** rattraper le temps perdu.

red (*noun & adj.*), rouge (*m.*).

reduce (*verb*), réduire (**to,** à); (*lessen*) diminuer; (*lose weight*) maigrir.

reflect (*verb*), (se) réfléchir, (se) refléter; penser; méditer.

refreshment (*noun*), rafraîchissement *m.*; (*pl.*) rafraîchissements; **refreshment-room,** buffet *m.*

refrigerator (*noun*), réfrigérateur *m.*

refuse (*noun*), ordures *f. pl.* (**household refuse,** ordures ménagères); (*verb*), refuser; rejeter; repousser.

regard (*noun*), attention *f.*, considération *f.*; estime *f.*; **to send one's kind regards,** envoyer le bonjour; **give my regards to . . .,** faites mes amitiés à . . .; **with regard to . . .,** quant à . . .; pour ce qui concerne . . .; (*verb*), regarder, considérer.

region (*noun*), région *f.*

reindeer (*noun*), renne *m.*

reject (*verb*), rejeter, repousser.

relation (*noun*), relation *f.*, rapport *m.*; (*relative*) parent *m.*

relax (*verb*), (se) relâcher, (se) reposer, (se) détendre, (se) délasser.

release (*verb*), (*let go*) lâcher; (*set free*) délivrer, libérer; décharger (**to release**

someone from an obligation, décharger quelqu'un d'une obligation).
religion (*noun*), religion *f.*
remain (*verb*), rester.
remember (*verb*), se rappeler, se souvenir de.
remind (*verb*), rappeler; faire penser (**of,** à); **that reminds me!** à propos!
remove (*verb*), enlever, effacer; **to remove a stain,** faire partir une tache.
renounce (*verb*), renoncer à.
repair (*noun*), réparation *f.*; raccommodage *m.* (de vêtements); (*verb*), réparer; raccommoder (des vêtements).
repay (*verb*), rembourser; récompenser.
repeat (*verb*), répéter.
replace (*verb*), remplacer (**by,** par); (*put back in place*) replacer, remettre en place.
reply (*noun*), réponse *f.*; (*verb*), répondre.
report (*noun*), rapport *m.*; bulletin *m.*; (*rumour*) bruit *m.*; (*verb*), rapporter; déclarer, annoncer; faire un reportage.
reporter (*noun*), journaliste *m.* & *f.* reporter *m.*; correspondant *m.*
represent (*verb*), représenter.
reproduce (*verb*), (se) reproduire.
republic (*noun*), république *f.*
request (*noun*), requête *f.*, demande *f.*, prière *f.*; (*verb*), demander (quelque chose à quelqu'un), solliciter (quelque chose de quelqu'un); prier (quelqu'un de faire quelque chose).
rescue (*noun*), secours *m.*, sauvetage *m.*; délivrance *f.*; (*verb*), secourir, sauver, délivrer.
resemble (*verb*), ressembler à.
resign (*verb*), résigner; se démettre de; donner sa démission.
rest (*noun*), repos *m.*; (*remainder*) reste *m.*; (*verb*), se reposer; (*remain*) rester.
restaurant (*noun*), restaurant *m.*
result (*noun*), résultat *m.*; conséquence *f.*; (*verb*), résulter, s'ensuivre (**from,** de).
retreat (*noun*), retraite *f.*; (*verb*), reculer; se retirer; battre en retraite.
return (*noun*), retour *m.*; renvoi *m.*; **many happy returns (of the day)!** bon anniversaire!; (*verb*), revenir, retourner, rentrer; rendre; remettre; restituer.
reverse (*verb*), renverser, retourner; (*a car*) faire marche arrière.
reward (*noun*), récompense *f.*; rémunération *f.*; (*verb*), récompenser, rémunérer.
ribbon (*noun*), ruban *m.*
rice (*noun*), riz *m.*; **rice-field,** rizière *f.*
rich (*adj.*), riche; somptueux *m.*, -euse *f.*
ride (*noun*), tour *m.*, promenade *f.* (à cheval, à bicyclette, en auto); voyage *m.* (en auto, en autobus); (*verb*), monter à cheval, se promener à cheval.
rifle (*noun*), fusil *m.*; **rifle-range,** tir *m.*
right (*adj.*), juste; exact; bon (**to arrive at the right moment,** arriver au bon moment); droit; **on the right,** à droite; **turn right,** tournez à droite; **right away,** tout de suite; **you are right,** vous avez raison.
ring (*noun*), (*plain*) anneau *m.*; (*jewelled*) bague *f.*; (*of people*) cercle *m.*; (*of bell*) sonnerie *f.*; (*verb*), sonner; faire sonner.
ripe (*adj.*), mûr; **ripe cheese,** fromage *m.* fait.
rise (*noun*), (*slope*) montée *f.*; côte *f.*; (*hill*) élévation *f.*; (*of wages*) augmentation *f.*; (*verb*), se lever; se soulever; s'élever; monter.
river (*noun*), (*large or main river*) fleuve *m.*; (*tributary, smaller river*) rivière *f.*
riverside (*noun*), rivage *m.*
road (*noun*), route *f.*; (= *street*) rue *f.*
roar (*noun*), rugissement *m.*; **a roar of laughter,** un gros éclat *m.* de rire; (*verb*), rugir; (*gunfire, thunder*) gronder.
rob (*verb*), voler; piller.
robber (*noun*), voleur *m.*, voleuse *f.*
robin (*noun*), rouge-gorge *m.*; **Robin Hood,** Robin des Bois.
rock (*noun*), rocher *m.*, roc *m.*; (*small*) roche *f.*; (*verb*), bercer (un enfant); se bercer, se balancer; **to rock with laughter,** se tordre de rire.
rocket (*noun*), fusée *f.*
rod (*noun*), baguette *f.*; (*for punishment*) verge *f.*; (*for curtains, stairs*) tringle *f.*
roll (*noun*), rouleau *m.* (de papier); (*bread*) petit pain *m.*; **roll of thunder,** roulement *m.* du tonnerre; (*verb*), rouler;

(*of thunder*) gronder, rouler.
roller (*noun*), rouleau *m.*, cylindre *m.*
roof (*noun*), toit *m.*; (*roofing*) toiture *f.*
room (*noun*), (*space*) place *f.*; espace *m.*; pièce *f.*, salle *f.*, chambre *f.*; **to make room,** faire place.
root (*noun*), racine *f.*; source *f.*, origine *f.*
rope (*noun*), corde *f.*; cordage *m.*; (*verb*), corder; **to rope climbers together,** encorder des alpinistes.
rose (*noun*), rose *f.*
rotate (*verb*), tourner; faire tourner; pivoter; (*of crops*) alterner.
rough (*adj.*), rude; inégal; (*of manners*) grossier *m.*, -ière *f.*; (*of voice*) rauque.
round (*adj.*), rond, circulaire; (*rounded*) arrondi; (*adv.*), autour (**a garden with a wall right round,** un jardin avec un mur tout autour); (*prep.*), autour de (**seated round the table,** assis autour de la table).
rouse (*verb*), réveiller; **to rouse someone to action,** inciter quelqu'un à agir.
route (*noun*), route *f.*; itinéraire *m.*; **bus route,** parcours *m.* d'un autobus.
row[1] (*noun*), rangée *f.*, rang *m.*; promenade *f.* en bateau; (*verb*), ramer.
row[2] (*noun*), querelle *f.*; (*verb*), se quereller (**with,** avec).
rub (*verb*), frotter; **to rub out,** effacer.
rubber (*noun*), caoutchouc *m.*; (*eraser*) gomme *f.*
rug (*noun*), (*on floor*) tapis *m.*; **travelling rug,** couverture *f.* de voyage; **bedside rug,** descente *f.* de lit.
rule (*verb*), régler (du papier); **to rule over,** gouverner, régner sur.
ruler (*noun*), (*person*) souverain *m.*; (*instrument*) règle *f.*
run (*verb*), courir; **to run over,** écraser; **to run away,** se sauver, s'enfuir.
rung (*noun*), (*of ladder*) échelon *m.*
rusk (*noun*), biscotte *f.*

S

sack (*noun*), sac *m.*
sad (*adj.*), triste; (*of place*) lugubre; (*of news*) désolant.
safe (*noun*), coffre-fort *m.*; caisse *f.*; (*adj.*), solide; intact; sûr; **safe and sound,** sain et sauf.
sail (*noun*), voile *f.*; promenade *f.* à la voile; voyage *m.* en mer; (*verb*), voguer, faire voile, naviguer.
sailor (*noun*), marin *m.*, matelot *m.*
saint (*noun*), saint *m.*, sainte *f.*; **All Saints' Day,** la Toussaint.
salad (*noun*), salade *f.*
salary (*noun*), traitement *m.*; appointements *m. pl.*
salt (*noun*), sel *m.*; **salt-cellar,** salière *f.*; (*verb*), saler.
salute (*noun*), salut *m.*; **to fire a salute,** tirer une salve; (*verb*), saluer.
same (*adj. & pron.*), même; (*adv.*), **just the same, all the same,** quand même, tout de même.
sand (*noun*), sable *m.*
sandwich (*noun*), sandwich *m.*; **ham sandwich,** sandwich au jambon.
satchel (*noun*), (*for books*) cartable *m.*
Saturday (*noun*), samedi *m.*
saucepan (*noun*), casserole *f.*
saucer (*noun*), soucoupe *f.*; **flying saucer,** soucoupe volante.
savage (*adj.*), (*of blow*) brutal; (*not civilized*) sauvage; (*of animal*) féroce.
save (*verb*), sauver, délivrer; économiser, épargner.
saw (*noun*), scie *f.*; (*verb*), scier.
say (*verb*), dire; réciter (une prière); **to say again,** répéter.
scale (*noun*), (*for weighing*) plateau *m.*; (*on fish*) écaille *f.*; (**pair of**) **scales,** balance *f.*
scholar (*noun*), (*at school*) élève *m. & f.*, écolier *m.*, écolière *f.*; (*learned man*) savant *m.*
school (*noun*), école *f.*; **school begins at nine,** les classes commencent à neuf heures; **schoolboy,** écolier *m.*, élève *m.*; **schoolgirl,** écolière *f.*, élève *f.*; **schoolmaster, schoolmistress,** professeur *m.*
science (*noun*), science *f.*
scissors (*pl. noun*), ciseaux *m. pl.*
scratch (*noun*), égratignure *f.*; (*by a person*) coup *m.* d'ongle; (*verb*), (se) gratter.
scream (*noun*), (*of fear*) cri *m.* perçant; (*of pain*) hurlement *m.*; (*verb*), crier, pousser des cris perçants; (*with pain*) hurler.
screw (*noun*), vis *f.*
screwdriver (*noun*), tournevis *m.*
scrub (*verb*), frotter; récurer (une casserole).
sculpt (*verb*), sculpter.
sculptor (*noun*), sculpteur *m.*
sculpture (*noun*), sculpture *f.*
scuttle (*verb*), saborder (un navire).
sea (*noun*), mer *f.*; **in the open sea, out at sea,** en pleine mer; **sea-shell,** coquille *f.*; (*shell-fish, mollusc*) coquillage *m.*; **sea-shore,** bord *m.* de la mer; littoral *m.*; côte *f.*
seal[1] (*noun*), (*on documents*) sceau *m.*
seal[2] (*noun*), (*animal*) phoque *m.*
season (*noun*), saison *f.*; période *f.*
second (*adj.*), second; deuxième; **Charles the Second,** Charles Deux; (*noun*), seconde *f.*, instant *m.* (**I'll be back in a second,** je reviens dans un instant); (*verb*), seconder; appuyer; soutenir.
secondhand (*adj.*), d'occasion (**secondhand car,** voiture *f.* d'occasion); **secondhand bookseller,** bouquiniste *m. & f.*
see (*verb*), voir; (*perceive*) apercevoir; **to see again,** revoir.
seed (*noun*), graine *f.*; semence *f.*
seek (*verb*), chercher.
seem (*verb*), sembler; paraître; (*impers.*) **it seems he has plenty of money,** il paraît qu'il a beaucoup d'argent.

seesaw (*noun*), bascule *f.*
seize (*verb*), saisir; prendre; s'emparer de.
seldom (*adv.*), rarement, peu souvent.
select (*verb*), choisir (**from,** parmi).
self (*pron.*): **himself, herself, itself, themselves, oneself,** se (**he washes himself,** il se lave); **myself,** me; **yourself,** te, vous; **ourselves,** nous; **yourselves,** vous.
sell (*verb*), vendre; se vendre (**what are the roses selling at?** à combien se vendent les roses?); **to sell off,** liquider.
send (*verb*), envoyer, expédier (un colis); **to send away,** renvoyer; **to send for,** faire venir, envoyer chercher,
sense (*noun*), sens *m.* (**the five senses,** les cinq sens; **in this sense,** dans ce sens); sentiment *m.* (**to have a sense of time,** avoir le sentiment de l'heure); (*verb*), sentir; avoir le sens de.
September (*noun*), septembre *m.*
serious (*adj.*), sérieux *m.*, -euse *f.*; grave; (*earnest*) sincère.
serve (*verb*), servir, être au service de, rendre service à.
service (*noun*), service *m.*; **at your service,** à votre service.
serviette (*noun*), serviette *f.* de table.
set (*verb*), poser, placer, mettre; régler (une pendule); **to set an example,** donner un exemple; **to set out (again),** (re)partir; (*noun*), jeu *m.* (**set of dominoes,** jeu de dominos; **set of tools,** jeu d'outils); **tea-set,** service *m.* à thé; **wireless set,** poste *m.* de T.S.F.; (*hairdressing*) mise *f.* en plis; (*theatre*) décor *m.*
seven (*adj. & noun*), sept *m.*
seventeen (*adj. & noun*), dix-sept *m.*
seventeenth (*adj.*), dix-septième; **the seventeenth of June,** le dix-sept juin.
seventh (*adj.*), septième; **the seventh of August,** le sept août.
seventy (*adj. & noun*), soixante-dix *m.*
seventy-one (*adj. & noun*), soixante et onze.
several (*adj.*), plusieurs.
sew (*verb*), coudre; **sewing** (*noun*), couture *f.*; **sewing machine,** machine *f.* à coudre.
shade (*noun*), ombre *f.*; (*window-blind*) store *m.*; **shade of meaning,** nuance *f.*
shadow (*noun*), ombre *f.*
shake (*verb*), secouer (un tapis), ébranler (une table); trembler; **to shake hands with someone,** serrer la main à quelqu'un.
shape (*noun*), forme *f.*; configuration *f.*; (*verb*), former, façonner; **shaped like,** en forme de.
share (*noun*), part *f.*, portion *f.*; action *f.* (**to hold shares,** posséder des actions); (*verb*), partager, diviser en parts; répartir.
sharp (*adj.*), (*of knife*) affilé; (*of needle*) pointu; (*of edge*) tranchant; (*of cry*) aigu *m.*, aiguë *f.*
shave (*verb*), raser (quelqu'un); se raser.
she (*pron.*), elle (**she is pretty,** elle est jolie; **it is she,** c'est elle); celle (**she who . . .,** celle qui . .).
sheep (*noun*), mouton *m.*
sheet (*noun*), drap *m.* (de lit); feuille *f.* (de papier, de verre); **sheet-metal,** tôle *f.*
shelf (*noun*), tablette *f.*; rayon *m.* (de bibliothèque); **set of shelves,** étagère *f.*
shell (*noun*), coquille *f.* (d'œuf, de noix).
shine (*verb*), (*of sun*) briller; (*of a surface*) luire, reluire; **shiny** (*adj.*), brillant; luisant.
ship (*noun*), (*in general*) bateau *m.*; (*merchant ship*) navire *m.*; (*for war*) bâtiment *m.* vaisseau *m.*
shirt (*noun*), chemise *f.*
shocking (*adj.*), choquant; scandaleux *m.*, -euse *f.*; horrifiant; (*of news*) atterrant; (*of weather*) exécrable.
shoe (*noun*), soulier *m.*, chaussure *f.*; **shoe-horn,** corne *f.*; **shoe-string, shoe-lace,** lacet *m.*
shoot (*verb*), tirer (**at,** sur); **to shoot ahead,** s'élancer en avant; **to shoot down,** abattre.

shop (*noun*), (*large*) magasin *m.*; (*small*) boutique *f.*

shopkeeper (*noun*), commerçant *m.*, marchand *m.*

shopping (*noun*), achats *m. pl.*, commissions *f. pl.*, emplettes *f. pl.*; **to go shopping,** faire ses emplettes.

short (*adj.*), court; bref *m.*, brève *f.*; **to take a short cut,** prendre au plus court.

shorts (*pl. noun*), culotte *f.* (*N.B. French singular*).

shoulder (*noun*), épaule *f.*

shout (*noun*), cri *m.*; clameur *f.*; éclat *m.* (de rire); (*verb*), crier.

shovel (*noun*), pelle *f.*; (*verb*), pelleter.

show (*verb*), montrer.

shower (*noun*), (*of rain*) averse *f.*; (*shower-bath*) douche *f.*; **to take a shower,** prendre une douche.

shrewd (*adj.*), sagace; pénétrant; judicieux *m.*, -euse *f.*; perspicace.

shut (*verb*), fermer.

sick (*adj.*), malade; **sick person,** malade *m.* & *f.*; **to be sick,** vomir; **to be sick of something,** être las *m.*, lasse *f.*, de quelque chose.

side (*noun*), côté *m.*; bord *m.*; flanc *m.* (d'un animal, d'une montagne); **side of bacon,** flèche *f.* de lard.

sideboard (*noun*), buffet *m.*

siege (*noun*), siège *m.*

sight (*noun*), vue *f.*

sign (*noun*), signe *m.*; symbole *m.*; (*commercial*) enseigne *f.*; **sign-post,** poteau *m.* indicateur; (*verb*), signer (son nom).

signature (*noun*), signature *f.*

signify (*verb*), signifier.

silence (*noun*), silence *m.*; (*verb*), faire taire; imposer silence à.

silent (*adj.*), silencieux *m.*, -euse *f.*; muet *m.*, -ette *f.*; **to be silent,** se taire.

silk (*noun*), soie *f.*

silkworm (*noun*), ver *m.* à soie.

silver (*noun*), argent *m.*

similar (*adj.*), pareil *m.*, -eille *f.*, semblable (**to,** à).

simple (*adj.*), simple; naturel *m.*, -elle *f.*; sans affectation.

since (*conj.*), depuis que (**since I have been here,** depuis que je suis ici); (*seeing that*) puisque (**since he is not of age,** puisqu'il est mineur); (*prep.*), depuis (**since yesterday,** depuis hier).

sing (*verb*), chanter.

single (*adj.*), seul, unique; individuel *m.*, -elle *f.*; (*opposite of double*) simple; (*not married*) célibataire.

sink (*noun*), évier *m.*; (*verb*), (*of ship*) couler au fond; s'enfoncer (**into,** dans); s'abaisser.

sister (*noun*), sœur *f.*; **sister-in-law,** belle-sœur *f.*

sit (*verb*), s'asseoir; (*be seated*) être assis.

six (*adj. & noun*), six *m.*

sixteen (*adj. & noun*), seize *m.*

sixteenth (*adj. & noun*), seizième; **Louis the Sixteenth,** Louis Seize; **the sixteenth of March,** le seize mars.

sixth (*adj.*), sixième; **the sixth of May,** le six mai.

sixty (*adj. & noun*), soixante *m.*

skate (*noun*), patin *m.*; (*verb*), patiner.

skater (*noun*), patineur *m.*, patineuse *f.*

skilful (*adj.*), adroit; ingénieux *m.*, -euse *f.*; habile.

skin (*noun*), peau *f.*

skirt (*noun*), jupe *f.*

sky (*noun*), ciel *m.*

skylark (*noun*), alouette *f.*

skyscraper (*noun*), gratte-ciel *m.*

slacken (*verb*), lâcher, relâcher.

sledge (*noun*), traîneau *m.*; (*verb*), aller en traîneau.

sleep (*noun*), sommeil *m.*; (*verb*), dormir, être endormi; **to go to sleep,** s'endormir; **sleeping-car** (*noun*), wagon-lit *m.*

sleeve (*noun*), manche *f.*

slice (*noun*), tranche *f.*; **slice of bread and butter,** tartine *f.* de beurre.

slide (*noun*), glissade *f.*; (*for children*) glissoire *f.*; (*verb*), glisser; faire glisser.

slim (*adj.*), mince, svelte.

slipper (*noun*), pantoufle *f.*

slow (*adj.*), lent; ralenti; (*of clock*) en retard; **slow train,** train *m.* omnibus.

slowly (*adv.*), lentement.
small (*adj.*), petit.
smash (*verb*), briser; écraser; **to smash into,** emboutir.
smell (*noun*), odeur *f.*, parfum *m.*; (*verb*), flairer (quelque chose); sentir (une fleur); **to smell nice,** sentir bon.
smile (*noun*), sourire *m.*; (*verb*), sourire.
smithy (*noun*), forge *f.*
smoke (*noun*), fumée *f.*; (*verb*), fumer.
snail (*noun*), escargot *m.*; colimaçon *m.*
snake (*noun*), serpent *m.*
sneeze (*noun*), éternuement *m.*; (*verb*), éternuer.
snow (*noun*), neige *f.*; (*verb*), neiger.
snowman (*noun*), bonhomme *m.* de neige.
snug (*adj.*), confortable.
snuggle (*verb*)**: to snuggle up to someone,** se pelotonner contre quelqu'un; **to snuggle down in bed,** se blottir dans son lit.
so (*adv.*), tellement (**she is not so beautiful,** elle n'est pas tellement belle); si (**it is so fine today,** il fait si beau aujourd'hui); aussi (**he's right and so are you,** il a raison et vous aussi); **so far,** jusqu'à présent; **so many,** tant de; **so that,** pour que, afin que, de façon que; **so as,** de façon que (**speak slowly so as to be understood,** parlez lentement de façon qu'on vous comprenne).
soap (*noun*), savon *m.*
sock (*noun*), chaussette *f.*
sofa (*noun*), canapé *m.*, sofa *m.*, divan *m.*
soft (*adj.*), mou *m.*, molle *f.*
soil (*noun*), sol *m.*, terrain *m.*, terre *f.*
soldier (*noun*), soldat *m.*
solely (*adv.*), seulement, uniquement.
solid (*adj.*), solide; bien construit; (*of gold, silver*) massif *m.*, - ive *f.*
solve (*verb*), résoudre (un problème).
sombre (*adj.*), sombre.
some (*adj. & pron.*), quelque (**some distance away,** à quelque distance de là; **some days ago,** il y a quelques jours; **some of the shops,** quelques-uns des magasins); des (**some apples,** des pommes); de, du, de la (**have some tea!** prenez du thé!); en (**I have some,** j'en ai).
somebody, someone (*pron.*), quelqu'un, *pl.* quelques-uns.
something (*pron.*), quelque chose; **something good,** quelque chose de bon.
sometimes (*adv.*), quelquefois.
somewhere (*adv.*), quelque part.
son (*noun*), fils *m.*; **son-in-law,** gendre *m.*, beau-fils *m.*
song (*noun*), chanson *f.*; chant *m.*; **song-book,** recueil *m.* de chansons.
soon (*adv.*), bientôt; **as soon as,** aussitôt que.
sorcerer (*noun*), sorcier *m.*
sore (*adj.*), douloureux *m.*, -euse *f.*; endolori; enflammé; (*noun*), plaie *f.*; (*graze*) écorchure *f.*
sort (*noun*), genre *m.*, sorte *f.*, espèce *f.*; catégorie *f.*; (*verb*), assortir, trier.
sound (*noun*), bruit *m.*, son *m.*; (*verb*), sonner, résonner.
soup (*noun*), soupe *f.*, potage *m.*
source (*noun*), source *f.* (d'un fleuve); origine *f.*
south (*noun*), sud *m.*; **to the south of,** au sud de; (*adj.*), du sud.
souvenir (*noun*), souvenir *m.*
sow (*verb*), semer.
space (*noun*), espace *m.*
spade (*noun*), bêche *f.*; (*child's*) pelle *f.*
speak (*verb*), parler.
spectacles (*pl. noun*), lunettes *f. pl.*
speed (*noun*), vitesse *f.*, vélocité *f.*, rapidité *f.*, célérité *f.*; (*verb*), aller vite, se hâter; expédier, dépêcher.
spend (*verb*), dépenser (de l'argent); (*of time*) passer (**to spend a week in London,** passer une semaine à Londres).
spendthrift (*noun*), dépensier *m.*, dépensière *f.*; prodigue *m.* & *f.*
spider (*noun*), araignée *f.*
spill (*verb*), renverser, répandre; **to spill blood,** verser du sang.
spirit (*noun*), esprit *m.*, âme *f.*; spectre *m.*, fantôme *m.*; verve *f.*, vigueur *f.*

spoil (*verb*), gâter (un enfant, quelque chose), abîmer (quelque chose).
sponge (*noun*), éponge *f.*; **sponge-cake,** gâteau *m.* de Savoie; (*verb*), éponger.
spoon (*noun*), cuiller *f.*, cuillère *f.*
sport (*noun*), sport *m.*; jeu *m.*, amusement *m.*
spot (*noun*), (*place*) endroit *m.*, lieu *m.*; (*stain*) tache *f.*; (*on face*) bouton *m.*
spring (*noun*), (*season*) printemps *m.*; (*of car, watch*) ressort *m.*; (*leap*) bond *m.*, saut *m.*; (*verb*), bondir, sauter, s'élancer.
square (*noun*), carré *m.*; (*in a city*) place *f.*; (*adj.*), carré.
squeeze (*verb*), serrer.
squirrel (*noun*), écureuil *m.*
stain (*noun*), tache *f.*; (*verb*), tacher, se tacher.
staircase (*noun*), escalier *m.*
stamp (*noun*), (*postage*) timbre-poste *m.*; **stamp collector,** collectionneur *m.* de timbres-poste.
stand (*verb*), être debout; se tenir debout; se lever; **to stand back,** reculer; **to stand by,** se tenir prêt; **to stand up,** se lever, se mettre debout.
star (*noun*), étoile *f.*
stare (*noun*), regard *m.* fixe; (*verb*), regarder fixement; **to stare at someone,** fixer quelqu'un, regarder quelqu'un fixement.
start (*noun*), commencement *m.*; départ *m.*; sursaut *m.* (**to wake with a start,** se réveiller en sursaut); (*verb*), commencer; partir; sursauter.
starving (*adj.*), affamé.
state (*noun*), état *m.*; **the State,** l'État; (*verb*), déclarer (**that,** que), affirmer; spécifier.
station (*noun*), poste *m.*, place *f.*, position *f.*; (*railway*) gare *f.*
stationary (*adj.*), stationnaire.
stationery (*noun*), papeterie *f.*; fournitures *f. pl.* de bureau.
stay (*verb*), rester; demeurer quelque temps (dans un endroit).
steal (*verb*), voler.
steam (*noun*), (*from boiling water*) vapeur *f.*; (*from cooking*) fumée *f.*
steamer (*noun*), paquebot *m.*; bateau *m.* à vapeur.
steep (*adj.*), raide.
steer (*verb*), diriger, conduire (une auto); gouverner (un navire).
step (*noun*), pas *m.* (**to take a step,** faire un pas); degré *m.*, marche *f.* (d'un escalier); (*verb*), faire un pas; marcher; **to step into,** monter dans; **to step back,** reculer.
stick (*verb*), coller; **the boy stuck a stamp on the letter,** le garçon a collé un timbre sur la lettre; (*noun*), bâton *m.*
still (*adj.*), tranquille; calme; (*adv.*), toujours (**he is still here,** il est toujours ici); encore (**still more,** encore plus); (*however*) cependant, pourtant, malgré cela.
sting (*verb*), piquer; (*noun*), piqûre *f.*
stocking (*noun*), bas *m.*
stomach (*noun*), estomac *m.*; (*belly*) ventre *m.*
stone (*noun*), pierre *f.*
stop (*noun*), arrêt *m.*; *halte *f.*; **full stop,** point *m.*; (*verb*), (s')arrêter; cesser; empêcher (**from,** de); (*stop up*) boucher.
store (*noun*), (*stock*) provision *f.*; (*shop*) magasin *m.*; (*verb*), mettre en réserve; approvisionner (**with,** de); (*of furniture, etc.*) emmagasiner, mettre en dépôt.
storey (*noun*), étage *m.*
storm (*noun*), orage *m.*; tempête *f.*
story (*noun*), histoire *f.*, récit *m.*, conte *m.*
stout (*adj.*), solide; fort; gros *m.*, grosse *f.*, corpulent.
stove (*noun*), (*for heating*) poêle *m.*; (*for cooking*) fourneau *m.*
straight (*adj.*), droit (**a straight line,** une ligne droite); **straight hair,** cheveux *m.pl.* raides; en ordre (**the room is straight,** la chambre est en ordre).
strange (*adj.*), étrange.
straw (*noun*), paille *f.*
strawberry (*noun*), fraise *f.*
stream (*noun*), ruisseau *m.*
street (*noun*), rue *f.*

strength (*noun*), force *f.*; vigueur *f.*; solidité *f.*
stretcher (*noun*), brancard *m.*; civière *f.*
strict (*adj.*), précis; exact; strict; sévère (**strict father,** père sévère).
strike (*noun*), (*in industry*) grève *f.*; **to go on strike,** se mettre en grève; (*verb*), frapper; (*of clock*) sonner; **to strike a match,** frotter une allumette.
string (*noun*), ficelle *f.*; (*musical*) corde *f.*; **string of beads,** collier *m.*
stripe (*noun*), raie *f.*, bande *f.*; (*military*) galon *m.*
stroke (*noun*), (*blow*) coup *m.*; trait *m.* (de plume); (*verb*), caresser.
stroll (*noun*), petite promenade *f.*; tour *m.*; **to go for a stroll,** faire un tour; (*verb*), flâner, déambuler.
strong (*adj.*), fort; solide.
structure (*noun*), structure *f.* (d'un pays); édifice *m.*, bâtiment *m.*
struggle (*noun*), lutte *f.*; combat *m.*; (*verb*), lutter.
stud (*noun*), (*on shirt collar*) bouton *m.*; (*on pedestrian crossing*) clou *m.*; (*on football boots*) crampon *m.*
student (*noun*), étudiant *m.*, étudiante *f.*; élève *m. & f.*
study (*noun*), étude *f.*; cabinet *m.* de travail; (*verb*), étudier; faire des études.
stumble (*verb*), trébucher; **to stumble over something,** buter contre quelque chose.
stupid (*adj.*), stupide, bête; (*foolish*) idiot.
subject (*noun*), sujet *m.*, thème *m.*; matière *f.*
submit (*verb*), soumettre (à); se soumettre (à); se résigner (à).
suburbs (*pl. noun*), banlieue *f.* (*N.B. French singular*).
succeed (*verb*), (*follow*) succéder à (quelqu'un, quelque chose); réussir (**to succeed in doing something,** réussir à faire quelque chose).
such (*adj.*), tel *m.*, telle *f.*; **such that,** tel que; **such a thing,** une telle chose; **in such a manner, to such a degree,** tellement.
suck (*verb*), sucer.
sudden (*adj.*), soudain; subit.
suddenly (*adv.*), tout à coup.
suffer (*verb*), souffrir.
sufficient (*adj.*), suffisant; **he has sufficient,** il en a assez.
sugar (*noun*), sucre *m.*; **sugar-basin,** sucrier *m.*
suggest (*verb*), suggérer, proposer; évoquer.
suit (*noun*), (*man's*) complet *m.*; (*woman's*) ensemble *m.*; (*verb*), convenir à, aller à (**this hat suits you,** ce chapeau vous va).
suitcase (*noun*), valise *f.*
sullen (*adj.*), maussade, morose.
sum (*noun*), somme *f.*, total *m.*; problème *m.* d'arithmétique.
summer (*noun*), été *m.*; **summer holidays,** grandes vacances *f. pl.*
summit (*noun*), sommet *m.*, faîte *m.*; **summit meeting,** conférence *f.* au sommet.
sun (*noun*), soleil *m.*; **in the sun,** au soleil.
Sunday (*noun*), dimanche *m.*
sunrise (*noun*), lever *m.* du soleil.
sunset (*noun*), coucher *m.* du soleil.
supervise (*verb*), surveiller; contrôler; superviser; diriger.
supper (*noun*), souper *m.*; **to have supper,** souper (*verb*).
supply (*noun*), approvisionnement *m.*; provision *f.*; vivres *m. pl.*; (*verb*), fournir, approvisionner, pourvoir (**with,** de).
support (*noun*), support *m.*; (*physical and moral*) soutien *m.*, appui *m.*; (*verb*), appuyer, soutenir, supporter; (*maintain*) entretenir.
sure (*adj.*), sûr; certain; convaincu.
surely (*adv.*), sûrement, bien sûr.
surgeon (*noun*), chirurgien *m.*
surprise (*noun*), surprise *f.*; étonnement *m.*; (*verb*), surprendre, étonner.
survive (*verb*), survivre (à); subsister.
suspend (*verb*), suspendre.
swallow (*noun*), (*bird*) hirondelle *f.*; (*verb*), avaler.
swan (*noun*), cygne *m.*

sweater (*noun*), chandail *m.*, sweater *m.*
sweep (*noun*), (*chimney-sweep*) ramoneur *m.*; (*verb*), balayer; ramoner (une cheminée).
sweet (*adj.*), doux *m.*, douce *f.*; sucré; (*of sound*) suave, mélodieux *m.*, -euse *f.*; (*noun*), bonbon *m.*
swift (*adj.*), rapide; prompt.
swim (*verb*), nager.
swimmer (*noun*), nageur *m.*, nageuse *f.*
swimming-pool (*noun*), piscine *f.*
swing (*noun*), (*device*) balançoire *f.*; (*act*) balancement *m.*; (*verb*), se balancer; (*of pendulum*) osciller.
syllable (*noun*), syllabe *f.*

T

table (*noun*), table *f.*; (*list*) tableau *m.*; **table-cloth,** nappe *f.*; **table-napkin,** serviette *f.*

tadpole (*noun*), têtard *m.*

tail (*noun*), queue *f.*; **heads or tails?** pile *f.* ou face *f.*?

tailor (*noun*), tailleur *m.*

take (*verb*), prendre, saisir; **to take something from someone,** enlever quelque chose à quelqu'un; **to take someone to a place,** conduire, mener, amener quelqu'un à un endroit; **to take something to a place,** porter, apporter quelque chose à un endroit; **to take away,** emmener (quelqu'un), emporter (quelque chose).

tale (*noun*), conte *m.*, récit *m.*; histoire *f.*; **to tell tales,** rapporter.

talk (*noun*), conversation *f.*; paroles *f. pl.*; (*verb*), parler, causer.

tall (*adj.*), (*of person*) grand; *haut; élevé.

tap (*noun*), (*for water*) robinet *m.*; (*blow*) tape *f.*; (*verb*), taper, frapper légèrement.

tart (*noun*), (*open*) tarte *f.*; (*covered*) tourte *f.*

task (*noun*), tâche *f.*; travail *m.*; **holiday task,** devoir *m.* de vacances.

taste (*noun*), goût *m.*; (*verb*), goûter (quelque chose); **to taste of,** avoir le goût de.

taxi (*noun*), taxi *m.*; **taxi-driver,** chauffeur *m.* de taxi; **taxi-rank,** station *f.* de taxi.

tea (*noun*), thé *m.*; **tea-caddy,** boîte *f.* à thé; **tea-pot,** théière *f.*

teach (*verb*), instruire, apprendre à (quelqu'un); enseigner (quelque chose); être professeur.

tear[1] (*noun*), larme *f.*; **to burst into tears,** fondre en larmes.

tear[2] (*noun*), déchirure *f.*; (*verb*), déchirer; **to tear off,** arracher (quelque chose).

tease (*verb*), taquiner.

telegram (*noun*), télégramme *m.*; dépêche *f.*

telegraph (*noun*), télégraphe *m.*; (*verb*), télégraphier.

telephone (*noun*), téléphone *m.*; (*verb*), téléphoner (à).

telescope (*noun*), télescope *m.*; longue-vue *f.* (*pl.* longues-vues); lunette *f.*

television, télévision *f.*; **television set,** poste *m.* de télévision; **on television,** à la télévision.

tell (*verb*), dire; raconter; faire connaître, énoncer; **to tell on someone,** dénoncer quelqu'un.

tempest (*noun*), tempête *f.*

ten (*adj. & noun*), dix *m.*; (**about**) **ten,** dizaine *f.*; **to count in tens,** compter par dizaines.

tent (*noun*), tente *f.*; **tent-peg,** piquet *m.* de tente.

tenth (*adj.*), dixième; **Charles the Tenth,** Charles Dix; **the tenth of June,** le dix juin.

terrible (*adj.*), terrible.

terrify (*verb*), terrifier; épouvanter.

texture (*noun*), (*of a fabric*) texture *f.*; (*of wood, skin*) grain *m.*

than (*conj.*), que (**he writes better than you,** il écrit mieux que vous); (*before numbers*) de (**less than five,** moins de cinq).

thank (*verb*), remercier (**for,** de); **thanks!** merci!; **no, thank you,** non, merci.

that (*adj.*), ce (cet) *m.*, cette *f.*; (*pl.*) **those,** ces; (*conj.*), que; (*pron.*), cela, ça; celui-là *m.*, celle-là *f.*, ceux-là *m. pl.*, celles-là *f. pl.*

thaw (*verb*), fondre, dégeler.

the (*definite article*), le *m.*, la *f.*, l'; les (*pl.*).

theatre (*noun*), théâtre *m.*

their (*adj.*), leur; leurs (*pl.*).

theirs (*pron.*), le leur *m.*, la leur *f.*; les leurs (*pl.*).

them (*pron.*), les (**I see them,** je les vois); **with them,** avec eux *m.*, avec elles *f.*; leur (**we told them the truth,** nous leur avons dit la vérité).

themselves (*pron.*), eux-mêmes *m.*, elles-mêmes *f.*
then (*adv.*), alors; ensuite, puis; (*conj.*), donc.
there (*adv.*), là, y, en ce lieu; **over there,** là-bas; **there is, there are,** voilà (**there she is!** la voilà!; **there they are!** les voilà!); il y a (**there are fairies in the garden,** il y a des fées dans le jardin).
therefore (*adv.*), donc, par conséquent; c'est pourquoi.
these (*pl. adj.*): *see* **this.**
they (*pron.*), ils *m. pl.*, elles *f. pl.*; (*stressed*) eux *m. pl.*, elles *f. pl.* (**it is they,** ce sont eux, ce sont elles); **they who . . .,** ceux *m. pl.* qui . . ., celles *f. pl.* qui . . .; (*impers.*), on (**they say that . . .,** on dit que . . .).
thick (*adj.*), épais *m.*, -sse *f.*; dense.
thief (*noun*), voleur *m.*, voleuse *f.*
thimble (*noun*), dé *m.* (à coudre).
thin (*adj.*), mince, maigre; (*of soup*) clair; **to get thin,** maigrir.
thing (*noun*), chose *f.*; objet *m.*; article *m.*
think (*verb*), penser (**what are you thinking about?** à quoi penses-tu?; **what do you think of my dress?** que penses-tu de ma robe?); réfléchir; songer; (*to believe*) croire, supposer.
third (*adj.*), troisième; (*noun*), tiers *m.*; **Henry the Third,** Henri Trois; **the third of September,** le trois septembre.
thirst (*noun*), soif *f.*
thirsty (*adj.*): **to be thirsty,** avoir soif.
thirteen (*adj. & noun*), treize *m.*
thirteenth (*adj.*), treizième.
thirty (*adj. & noun*), trente *m.*
this (*adj.*), ce (cet) *m.*, cette *f.*; (*pl.*) **these,** ces; (*pron.*), celui-ci *m.*, celle-ci *f.*; ceux-ci *m. pl.*, celles-ci *f. pl.* (**Here are two cars. This one is red, but that one is yellow,** Voici deux voitures. Celle-ci est rouge mais celle-là est jaune).
those (*pl. adj.*): *see* **that.**
though (*conj.*), quoique; bien que; (*adv.*), pourtant; (*however*) tout de même.
thousand (*noun & adj.*), mille *m.*; (*in dates*) mil; **(about) a thousand,** millier *m.*
thread (*noun*), fil *m.*; (*of screw*) pas *m.*; (*verb*), enfiler.
three (*adj. & noun*), trois *m.*; **three-legged,** à trois pieds.
through (*prep.*), à travers; par.
throw (*verb*), jeter, lancer; projeter; pousser.
thumb (*noun*), pouce *m.*
thunder (*noun*), tonnerre *m.*
Thursday (*noun*), jeudi *m.*
thus (*adv.*), ainsi, de cette façon.
ticket (*noun*), billet *m.* (de chemin de fer, de théâtre); ticket *m.* (d'autobus, de métro).
tidy (*adj.*), propre; net *m.*, nette *f.*; ordonné; (*of exercise book, room*) bien tenu; (*of person*) soigneux *m.*, -euse *f.*; (*verb*), ranger (une chambre); mettre en ordre.
tie (*noun*), cravate *f.*; (*verb*), lier, nouer; attacher; **to tie a knot,** faire un nœud.
tighten (*verb*), serrer; tendre (**to tighten a violin string,** tendre une corde de violon).
time (*noun*), temps *m.*; période *f.*; époque *f.*; durée *f.*; fois *f.* (**three times,** trois fois); heure *f.* (**what is the time?** quelle heure est-il?).
tin (*noun*), (*metal*) étain *m.*; (*container*) boîte *f.*
tip (*verb*), faire pencher; verser (**into,** dans); effleurer; **to tip over,** renverser; **to tip someone,** donner un pourboire à quelqu'un.
tire (*verb*), (se) fatiguer, (se) lasser.
tired (*adj.*), fatigué.
to (*prep.*), à (**to go to Paris,** aller à Paris; **to school,** à l'école); en (**to go to France,** aller en France); **a book to read,** un livre à lire; (*in order to*) pour (**we eat to live,** nous mangeons pour vivre); **ten minutes to six,** six heures moins dix.
tobacco (*noun*), tabac *m.*
tobacconist's shop (*noun*), bureau *m.* de tabac.
toboggan (*noun*), toboggan *m.*; (*verb*), faire du toboggan.

today (*adv.*), aujourd'hui.
toe (*noun*), orteil *m.*
together (*adv.*), ensemble; **all together,** tous ensemble.
toil (*noun*), labeur *m.*; peine *f.*; (*verb*), peiner, travailler dur.
toilet (*noun*), toilette *f.*; (*W.C.*) toilettes *f. pl.*, cabinets *m. pl.*
tomato (*noun*), tomate *f.*
tomorrow (*adv.*), demain.
tongue (*noun*), langue *f.*; **tongue-twister,** phrase *f.* à décrocher la mâchoire.
tonight (*adv.*), cette nuit, ce soir.
too (*adv.*), trop (**too far,** trop loin; **too much money,** trop d'argent; **too many friends,** trop d'amis); (*also*) aussi, également.
tool (*noun*), outil *m.*; **tool-box,** coffre *m.* à outils, boîte *f.* à outils.
tooth (*noun*), dent *f.*; **tooth-brush,** brosse *f.* à dents; **toothpaste,** pâte *f.* dentifrice.
top (*noun*), (*in general*) haut *m.*; (*of head, mountain*) sommet *m.*; (*of box*) couvercle *m.*; (*of stockings, boots*) revers *m.*; (*of page*) tête *f.*; (*of bus*) impériale *f.*; **spinning-top,** toupie *f.*
tortoise (*noun*), tortue *f.*; **tortoise-shell,** écaille *f.*
totter (*verb*), chanceler; (*of drunkard*) tituber; (*of building*) branler.
touch (*verb*), toucher.
towards (*prep.*), vers; envers.
towel (*noun*), serviette *f.* de toilette; essuie-mains *m.*
tower (*noun*), tour *f.*
town (*noun*), ville *f.*; **town-hall,** mairie *f.*, hôtel *m.* de ville.
toy (*noun*), jouet *m.*
track (*noun*), (*of animal, car*) trace *f.*; (*of person*) piste *f.*; (*railway*) voie *f.*; (*verb*), traquer (quelqu'un); suivre (une bête) à la piste.
tractor (*noun*), tracteur *m.*
trade (*noun*), commerce *m.*; emploi *m.*; métier *m.*; **trade-union,** syndicat *m.* (ouvrier).
tradesman (*noun*), marchand *m.*, commerçant *m.*
traffic (*noun*), circulation *f.*
train (*noun*), (*railway*) train *m.*; (*of dress*) traîne *f.*
translate (*verb*), traduire.
transport (*noun*), transport *m.*; (*verb*), transporter.
travel (*verb*), voyager, faire des voyages *m. pl.*
traveller (*noun*), voyageur *m.*, voyageuse *f.*; **commercial traveller,** voyageur de commerce, représentant *m.*
tree (*noun*), arbre *m.*
tribunal (*noun*), tribunal *m.*
trim (*adj.*), (*of person*) soigné; bien tenu; (*verb*), (*cut*) couper, tailler; (*decorate*) orner, garnir.
trimming (*noun*), garniture *f.*
trip (*verb*), trébucher; faire un faux pas; **to trip along,** aller d'un pas léger; (*noun*), excursion *f.*; voyage *m.* d'agrément.
trolley (*noun*), (*four-wheeled*) chariot *m.*; (*two-wheeled*) diable *m.*; **dinner trolley,** table *f.* roulante.
trot (*verb*), trotter; aller au trot.
trousers (*pl. noun*), pantalon *m.* (*N.B. French singular*).
truck (*noun*), camion *m.*; wagon-tombereau *m.*; (*railway*) wagon *m.*; **luggage truck,** chariot *m.* à bagages.
true (*adj.*), vrai.
truly (*adv.*), vraiment.
trumpet (*noun*), trompette *f.*
trunk (*noun*), (*of body, tree*) tronc *m.*; (*luggage*) malle *f.*; trompe *f.* d'éléphant; **trunk-call,** communication *f.* interurbaine.
trust (*noun*), confiance *f.* (**in,** en); (*verb*), se fier (à).
truth (*noun*), vérité *f.*
try (*verb*), (*attempt*) essayer; (*put to the test*) éprouver.
tube (*noun*), tube *m.* (de pâte dentifrice, etc.); (*pipe*) tuyau *m.*; **inner-tube,** chambre *f.* à air; (*underground railway*) le Métro.
Tuesday (*noun*), mardi *m.*; **Shrove Tuesday,** mardi gras.
tulip (*noun*), tulipe *f.*

tumble (*verb*), tomber; culbuter; bouleverser; dégringoler.

turkey (*noun*), dindon *m.*; (*as food*) dinde *f.*

turn (*verb*), tourner, faire tourner; changer, transformer; (*become*) devenir; **to turn over,** (*of car*) capoter; **to turn over the soil,** retourner le sol; (*noun*), tour *m.*; (*of wheel, etc.*) révolution *f.*

turtle (*noun*), tortue *f.* de mer; **turtle-soup,** potage *m.* à la tortue.

twelfth (*adj.*), douzième; **the twelfth of May,** le douze mai.

twelve (*adj. & noun*), douze *m.*

twenty (*adj. & noun*), vingt *m.*; **twenty-one,** vingt et un.

twice (*adv.*), deux fois.

twin (*adj. & noun*), jumeau *m.*, jumelle *f.*; **twin beds,** lits *m. pl.* jumeaux.

twist (*verb*), tordre; se tordre, s'enrouler.

two (*adj. & noun*), deux *m.*; **in twos,** deux par deux.

typewriter (*noun*), machine *f.* à écrire.

typist (*noun*), dactylo(graphe) *f.*

tyre (*noun*), pneu *m.*

U

ugly (*adj.*), (*of person*) laid; (*unpleasant*) vilain.

umbrella (*noun*), parapluie *m.*; (*for beach*) parasol *m.*

uncle (*noun*), oncle *m.*

under (*prep.*), sous, au-dessous de; **under repair,** en réparation; (*adv.*), dessous, au-dessous; **under there,** là-dessous.

underclothes (*pl. noun*), sous-vêtements *m. pl.*

underground (railway) (*noun*), métro (-politain) *m.*

underneath (*adv.*), là-dessous.

understand (*verb*), comprendre, entendre; (*know about*) s'entendre à; **to understand something,** se rendre compte de quelque chose.

undo (*verb*), défaire; (*untie*) dénouer; (*unbutton*) déboutonner.

undress (*verb*), déshabiller (quelqu'un); se déshabiller.

uneven (*adj.*), inégal; (*of ground*) accidenté.

unfortunately (*adv.*), malheureusement.

unhappy (*adj.*), malheureux *m.*, -euse *f.*

universe (*noun*), univers *m.*

university (*noun*), université *f.*

unless (*conj.*), à moins que.

unload (*verb*), décharger.

unlock (*verb*), ouvrir (une porte).

unlucky (*adj.*), malheureux *m.*, -euse *f.*; infortuné.

unpleasant (*adj.*), désagréable; déplaisant; (*nasty*) vilain.

until (*prep.*), jusqu'à (**until six o'clock,** jusqu'à six heures); **not until,** pas avant (**not until six o'clock,** pas avant six heures); (*conj.*), jusqu'à ce que; **not until,** pas avant que.

up (*adv.*), en haut; (*standing*) debout; levé (**up at six,** levé à six heures); **up there,** là-haut.

upset (*verb*), renverser (une bouteille, etc.); bouleverser (quelqu'un); déranger (les plans de quelqu'un).

upstairs (*adv.*), en haut (de l'escalier).

upwards (*adv.*), vers le haut; en haut (**to look upwards,** regarder en haut).

urchin (*noun*), gamin *m.*, gamine *f.*; gosse *m.* & *f.*

urgent (*adj.*), pressant, urgent.

us (*pron.*), nous.

use (*noun*), usage *m.*, emploi *m.*; **to make use of something,** faire usage de quelque chose; **for the use of schools,** à l'usage des écoles; **directions for use,** mode d'emploi; (*verb*), se servir de, employer; user de; **to be used to doing something,** être habitué à faire quelque chose.

useful (*adj.*), utile.

useless (*adj.*), inutile.

usual (*adj.*), habituel *m.*, -elle *f.*; **as usual,** comme d'habitude.

utensil (*noun*), ustensile *m.*; instrument *m.*; (*tool*) outil *m.*

V

vacant (*adj.*), vacant, vide; inoccupé, libre.
vacate (*verb*), vider.
vacation (*noun*), vacances *f. pl.*
vaccinate (*verb*), vacciner.
valid (*adj.*), (*of documents*) valide; (*of ticket, excuse, etc.*) valable; **valid argument,** argument *m.* solide.
valley (*noun*), vallée *f.*; (*small*) vallon *m.*
valuable (*adj.*), précieux *m.*, -euse *f.*
van (*noun*), camion *m.*; **guard's van,** fourgon *m.* à bagages.
vanish (*verb*), disparaître, s'évanouir.
vase (*noun*), vase *m.*
veal (*noun*), veau *m.*
vegetable (*noun*), légume *m.*; **vegetable garden,** potager *m.*
vehicle (*noun*), véhicule *m.*; voiture *f.*
vein (*noun*), veine *f.*
ventilate (*verb*), aérer, ventiler.
ventilator (*noun*), ventilateur *m.*; (*on car*) déflecteur *m.*
venture (*noun*), entreprise *f.*; (*verb*), **to venture to do something,** oser faire quelque chose; **to venture a guess, an opinion,** hasarder une conjecture, une opinion; **to venture out,** se risquer à sortir.
very (*adj.*), même (**the very day,** le jour même); seul (**the very thought,** la seule pensée); juste (**this very moment,** juste à ce moment); (*adv.*), très, bien, fort.
victory (*noun*), victoire *f.*
view (*noun*), vue *f.*; perspective *f.*; (*verb*), regarder, voir, envisager, examiner.
vigil (*noun*), veille *f.*; **to keep vigil,** veiller.
village (*noun*), village *m.*
vine (*noun*), vigne *f.*; **vine-grower,** viticulteur *m.*
vinegar (*noun*), vinaigre *m.*
vineyard (*noun*), clos *m.* de vigne; vignoble *m.*
violent (*adj.*), violent; fort.
violet (*adj.*), violet *m.*, -ette *f.*; (*noun*), (*flower*) violette *f.*; (*colour*) violet *m.*
violin (*noun*), violon *m.*
visit (*noun*), visite *f.*; (*verb*), faire des visites; être en visite; rendre visite à (quelqu'un).
voice (*noun*), voix *f.*; **in a loud voice,** à haute voix; **in a low voice,** à voix basse.
vowel (*noun*), voyelle *f.*
voyage (*noun*), voyage *m.* sur mer; (*verb*), voyager sur mer.

W

wages (*pl. noun*), (*for workmen*) paie *f.*; (*for domestic workers*) gages *m. pl.*; salaire *m.*
wag(g)on (*noun*), charrette *f.*; chariot *m.*; (*railway*) wagon *m.*
waist (*noun*), taille *f.*; **waist measurement,** tour *m.* de taille.
wait (*verb*), attendre; **to keep someone waiting,** faire attendre quelqu'un; **to wait for someone,** attendre quelqu'un.
waiter (*noun*), garçon *m.*; **head-waiter,** maître *m.* d'hôtel.
wake (*noun*), (*of ship*) sillage *m.*; (*verb*), s'éveiller, se réveiller; (*to be awake*) être éveillé; réveiller (quelqu'un).
walk (*verb*), marcher; aller à pied; (*to go for a walk*) se promener; (*noun*), marche *f.* (**it is half an hour's walk from here,** c'est à une demi-heure de marche d'ici); (*for pleasure*) promenade *f.*
wall (*noun*), mur *m.*; (*of castles, town*) muraille *f.*
wallet (*noun*), portefeuille *m.*
want (*verb*), vouloir; (*to wish*) désirer; (*to need*) avoir besoin de; (*to lack something*) manquer de.
war (*noun*), guerre *f.*
wardrobe (*noun*), armoire *f.*, garde-robe *f.*
warm (*adj.*), chaud; **to be warm,** avoir chaud; **it is warm,** (*of weather*) il fait chaud; (*verb*), chauffer.
warmth (*noun*), chaleur *f.*
warn (*verb*), prévenir, avertir (**of,** de); **to warn someone against something,** mettre quelqu'un en garde contre quelque chose.
wash (*verb*), (se) laver; **to wash up,** laver la vaisselle, faire la vaisselle; **wash-basin,** lavabo *m.*; cuvette *f.* de lavabo.
washing (*noun*), lessive *f.*; **to do the washing,** faire la lessive.
waste (*noun*), ordures *f. pl.*; (*verb*), gaspiller; **to waste one's time,** perdre son temps.
watch (*noun*), (*at night*) veille *f.*; (*time-piece*) montre *f.*; garde *f.*, surveillance *f.*; (*verb*), observer, regarder attentivement; **to watch over,** garder, surveiller; **to watch for someone,** guetter quelqu'un.
water (*noun*), eau *f.*; **water-colour painting,** aquarelle *f.*; **water-pipe,** conduite *f.* d'eau; **hot water bottle,** bouillotte *f.*; (*verb*), arroser; irriguer; faire boire (des bêtes).
wave (*noun*), (*of sea*) vague *f.*; (*of hair*) ondulation *f.*; (*verb*), (*of flag*) flotter; (*of hair*) onduler; faire signe de la main; agiter (un mouchoir, etc.).
way (*noun*), chemin *m.*; voie *f.*; route *f.*; façon *f.* (de faire quelque chose); **in this way,** de cette façon (**The man takes a taxi. In this way he will arrive home more quickly,** L'homme prend un taxi. De cette façon il arrivera chez lui plus vite); **way in,** entrée *f.*; **way out,** sortie *f.*
W.C. (*noun*), cabinets *m. pl.*
we (*pron.*), nous.
weak (*adj.*), faible, sans vigueur, sans force.
weapon (*noun*), arme *f.*
wear (*verb*), porter; **to wear something out,** user quelque chose.
weary (*adj.*), fatigué, lassé; (*verb*), fatiguer, lasser; (*bore*) ennuyer.
weather (*noun*), temps *m.*
web (*noun*): **spider's web,** toile *f.* d'araignée.
Wednesday (*noun*), mercredi *m.*
week (*noun*), semaine *f.*
weekend (*noun*), weekend *m.*
weekly (*adv.*), toutes les semaines.
weep (*verb*), pleurer.
weigh (*verb*), peser.
weight (*noun*), poids *m.*
welcome (*noun*), bienvenue *f.*; accueil *m.*; (*verb*), souhaiter la bienvenue à, faire bon accueil à; (*adj.*), bienvenu.
well (*noun*), puits *m.*; (*adv.*), bien; **as well,**

aussi; eh bien (**well, what did you say?** eh bien, qu'avez-vous dit?); (*exclamation of surprise*) ça alors!

west (*noun*), ouest *m.*

wet (*adj.*), mouillé; **wet through,** mouillé jusqu'aux os; (*damp*) humide; (*noun*), humidité *f.*

what (*adj.*), (*interrogative & exclamatory*) quel *m.*, quelle *f.* (**at what time?** à quelle heure? **what a surprise!** quelle surprise!; (*pron.*), (*relative*) ce qui, ce que; (*interrogative*) que (**what are you doing?** que faites-vous?); quoi (**what are you thinking of?** à quoi pensez-vous?); qu'est-ce que (**what do you want?** qu'est-ce que vous voulez?); qu'est-ce qui (**what has happened?** qu'est-ce qui est arrivé?); **what** (**did you say**)? comment?

wheat (*noun*), froment *m.*; blé *m.*

wheel (*noun*), roue *f.*; **steering wheel,** (*of car*) volant *m.*; (*verb*), (*of birds*) tournoyer; rouler, pousser (une bicyclette).

wheelbarrow (*noun*), brouette *f.*

when (*adv.*), quand; (*conj.*), quand, lorsque; **the day when I was ill,** le jour où j'étais malade; **one day when I was ill,** un jour que j'étais malade.

where (*adv.*), où.

which (*adj.*), (*interrogative*) quel *m.*, quelle *f.*; (*pron.*), (*interrogative*) lequel *m.*, laquelle *f.*, lesquels *m. pl.*, lesquelles *f. pl.* (**of all these hats which do you like best?** de tous ces chapeaux lequel préférez-vous?); (*relative*) qui, que (**the room which is to let,** la chambre qui est à louer; **the room which he prefers,** la chambre qu'il préfère); ce qui, ce que (**she says that I am lazy, which is not true,** elle dit que je suis paresseux, ce qui n'est pas vrai); quoi (**with which,** avec quoi; **after which,** après quoi).

while, whilst (*conj.*), tandis que, pendant que.

whisper (*noun*), chuchotement *m.*; (*verb*), chuchoter, parler bas.

whistle (*noun*), sifflement *m.*; (*instrument*) sifflet *m.*; (*verb*), siffler.

who (*pron.*), (*interrogative*) qui, qui est-ce qui (**who told you that?** qui (est-ce qui) vous a dit cela?); (*relative*) qui (**my friend who came yesterday,** mon ami qui est venu hier).

whole (*adj.*), entier *m.*, -ière *f.*; complet *m.*, -ète *f.*; **the whole time,** tout le temps.

whom (*pron.*), (*interrogative*) qui, qui est-ce que (**whom are you looking at?** qui est-ce que vous regardez?); (*relative*) que (**the man whom you saw,** l'homme que vous avez vu).

whose (*pron.*), de qui (**whose daughter are you?** de qui êtes-vous la fille?); (*ownership*) à qui (**whose gloves are these?** à qui sont ces gants?); (*relative*) dont (**the pupil whose work I showed you,** l'élève dont je vous ai montré le travail).

why (*adv.*), pourquoi; **why not?** pourquoi pas? (*interj.*) (*expressing surprise*) tiens!

wide (*adj.*), large; vaste.

width (*noun*), largeur *f.*

wife (*noun*), femme *f.*; épouse *f.*

wild (*adj.*), sauvage.

win (*noun*), victoire *f.*; (*verb*), gagner; **to win the prize,** remporter le prix; atteindre (une place).

wind (*noun*), vent *m.*; (*breath*) souffle *m.*; **to go like the wind,** aller comme le vent.

wind (*verb*), tourner, faire tourner; (*into a ball*) enrouler.

windmill (*noun*), moulin *m.* à vent.

window (*noun*), fenêtre *f.*; **French window,** porte-fenêtre *f.*; **display-window,** étalage *m.*; **shop-window,** vitrine *f.*; **window-blind,** store *m.*; **window-pane,** vitre *f.*

wine (*noun*), vin *m.*; **wine-grower,** viticulteur *m.*

wing (*noun*), aile *f.*

winter (*noun*), hiver *m.*; (*verb*), passer l'hiver (**at,** à).

wipe (*verb*), essuyer; **to wipe one's nose,** se moucher.

wire (*noun*), fil *m.* métallique, fil de fer; **barbed wire,** fil de fer barbelé.
wireless (*noun*), radio *f.*; T.S.F. *f.*; **wireless set,** poste *m.* de T.S.F.
wise (*adj.*), sage, sagace.
wish (*noun*), désir *m.*; souhait *m.*; (*verb*), **to wish for something,** désirer, vouloir, souhaiter quelque chose; **to wish to do something,** désirer, vouloir faire quelque chose.
witch (*noun*), sorcière *f.*
with (*prep.*), avec (**to cut with a knife,** couper avec un couteau; **I play with my children,** je joue avec mes enfants); chez (**she lives with us,** elle habite chez nous); à (**a man with a red beard,** un homme à la barbe rousse); (**he was a man with a good appetite,** c'était un homme de bon appétit).
within (*adv.*), à l'intérieur, (en) dedans, là-dedans; (*prep.*), à l'intérieur de, en dedans de; dans; **within half an hour,** en moins d'une demi-heure; **situated within ten miles of Paris,** situé à moins de dix milles de Paris.
without (*prep.*), sans (**without his brother,** sans son frére).
wolf (*noun*), loup *m.*
woman (*noun*), femme *f.*
wonder (*verb*), se demander; s'étonner.
wonderful (*adj.*), merveilleux *m.*, -euse *f.*
wood (*noun*), bois *m.* (**pine wood,** bois de pins); forêt *f.*; (*material*) bois *m.*
wool (*noun*), laine *f.*; **ball of wool,** pelote *f.* de laine.
word (*noun*), mot *m.*; (*spoken*) parole *f.*; **to give someone one's word,** donner sa parole à quelqu'un.
work (*noun*), travail *m.*; ouvrage *m.*; (*job*) emploi *m.* (**to be out of work,** être sans emploi); **works** (*pl.*), usine *f.*; fabrique *f.*; (*verb*), travailler; (*to have an effect*) agir, opérer; (*of machine*) fonctionner, aller, marcher.
worker, workman (*noun*), ouvrier *m.*
workshop (*noun*), atelier *m.*
world (*noun*), monde *m.*
worm (*noun*), ver *m.*
worn (*adj.*), usé.
worry (*noun*), souci *m.*, tracas *m.*, ennuis *m. pl.*; (*verb*), (*bother*) tracasser (**that worries him,** ça le tracasse); importuner; (*harass*) harceler; se tourmenter, se tracasser (**he worries too much,** il se tracasse trop).
worth (*noun*), valeur *f.*; **to be worth,** valoir; **is it worth it?** cela (en) vaut-il la peine?
worthless (*adj.*), sans valeur.
wound (*noun*), blessure *f.*; plaie *f.*; (*verb*), blesser.
wrap (*verb*), envelopper; **to wrap (oneself) up,** s'envelopper; **to wrap something around something,** enrouler quelque chose autour de quelque chose.
write (*verb*), écrire; **to write down,** noter; (*be a writer*) être écrivain.
writing (*noun*), écriture *f.*; **writing-paper,** papier *m.* à lettres.
wrong (*adj.*), mauvais; faux *m.*, fausse *f.*; (*of idea*) erroné; **to be wrong,** avoir tort, se tromper.

X

X-ray photograph (*noun*), radiogramme *m.*

xylophone (*noun*), xylophone *m.*

Y

yacht (*noun*), yacht *m.*; (*verb*), faire du yachting.

year (*noun*), an *m.* (*used especially when counting*) (**he is ten years old,** il a dix ans; **I stayed three years in Paris,** j'ai passé trois ans à Paris); année *f.* (**happy New Year!** bonne année!; **from year to year,** d'année en année; **second-year student,** étudiant de seconde année; **school year,** année scolaire).

yellow (*adj. & noun*), jaune *m.*

yes (*adv.*), oui; (*in reply to question put negatively*) si.

yesterday (*adv.*), hier; **the day before yesterday,** avant-hier.

you (*pron.*), vous; (*familiar*) tu; (*object*) vous; te, toi; on (**when you are young you have fewer worries,** quand on est jeune on a moins de soucis).

young (*adj.*), jeune; **young people, young men,** jeunes gens (*always pl.*).

your (*adj.*), votre (*sing.*), vos (*pl.*); (*familiar*) ton, *m.*, ta *f.*, tes *pl.*

yours (*possessive pron.*), le tien, la tienne; le vôtre, la vôtre.

youth (*noun*), jeunesse *f.*, adolescence *f.*; jeune homme *m.*, adolescent *m.*

yourself (*pron.*), vous-même; (*familiar*) toi-même; **yourselves,** vous-mêmes.

Z

zebra (*noun*), zèbre *m.*; **zebra crossing,** passage *m.* clouté.

zero (*noun*), zéro *m.*

zigzag (*noun*), zigzag *m.*; (*verb*), zigzaguer.

zoo (*noun*), zoo *m.*